Mrs.
Goodfellow

Mrs. Goodfellow

THE STORY OF AMERICA'S FIRST COOKING SCHOOL

BECKY LIBOUREL DIAMOND

WESTHOLME
Yardley

Frontispiece: An illustration facing the title page of *The Useful and the Beautiful: or, Domestic and Moral Duties Necessary to Social Happiness*, 1850.

Westholme Publishing, LLC
904 Edgewood Road
Yardley, Pennsylvania 19067
Visit our Web site at www.westholmepublishing.com

First Printing May 2012
10 9 8 7 6 5 4 3 2 1

ISBN: 978-1-59416-157-5

Also available as an eBook.

Printed in the United States of America.

For Joe, Cate, and Patrick,
with love and appreciation

CONTENTS

Preface   ix

ONE

Who Was Mrs. Goodfellow?

I

TWO

Ingredients

41

THREE

Dining Out

63

FOUR

Mrs. Goodfellow's Cooking School

83

FIVE

Directions for Cookery

116

SIX

Lemon Meringue Pie

151

SEVEN

Modern Cooking Schools

177

Epilogue: The End of the Day 207

Recipes 211

Notes 235

Bibliography 253

Index 271

Acknowledgments 281

Preface

America's first cooking school instructor, and arguably the mother of American cookery, is considered by most food historians to be Mrs. Elizabeth Goodfellow. She and her culinary influence have been described as extraordinary by several experts, and her best-known creation—the lemon meringue pie—is considered an American classic. Yet, as these historians have also lamented, she is an elusive and neglected figure.[1]

Mrs. Goodfellow appears to have been a savvy business-woman, running her cooking school out of her Philadelphia pastry shop during the first half on the nineteenth century. For several decades in the early to mid-1800s, her luxurious confections and cookery classes were sought out by the most prominent families in and around Philadelphia. Her philosophy stipulated using only pure, wholesome ingredients—a concept she passed along to the numerous students who had the benefit of her training. Documented by these women in manuscript cookbooks, Mrs. Goodfellow's recipes and methods steadily trickled into mainstream cookery and were adapted by cooks around the country. This helped pave the way for cooking authorities ever since, from her own student Eliza Leslie to Fannie Farmer, Julia Child, and James Beard, right up to today's celebrity chefs.

Although food historians often recognize the essential part Mrs. Goodfellow played, numerous details of her life and background have been lost or muddled over the years, causing her to be largely forgotten. I first read about her in a cooking magazine, where an article about modern-day recreational cooking schools stated that "cooking skills in the U.S. were first taught in an organized way around 1820 at Mrs. Goodfellow's Cooking School in Philadelphia." Was this intriguing claim true? If so, how did cooking schools evolve from this model to what they are today?

As I started researching the history of cooking schools, I discovered that while there may have been a handful of other small cooking schools in America before Mrs. Goodfellow's, it was her school that had the greatest impact on American food and cooking due to its longevity, impeccable reputation, and widespread acclaim. This fact was confirmed by food history experts such as William Woys Weaver, Jan Longone, and Janet Theophano, as well as by my own sifting through numerous historical texts, papers, and documents. In addition, the many Philadelphia area nineteenth-century manuscript cookbooks that contained Goodfellow recipes provide concrete evidence of her extensive influence. One from the Morris Family Papers collection at the Independence National Historical Park Library in Philadelphia was particularly exciting as it contained a direct quotation from Mrs. Goodfellow about making pastry, surely transcribed from one of her classes.

Based on the many sources I have consulted, I have done my best guess at re-creating a day in the life of Mrs. Goodfellow, circa 1815. Beginning with her awakening at 4 A.M. to start baking, the following chapters take a peek inside her cooking school. They depict her daily routine and show how tightly she needed to schedule her day in order to fulfill her tasks as pastry cook and cooking school teacher, as well as reconstruct the experience of being a student in one of her classes.

Mrs. Goodfellow was described by those who knew her as a no-nonsense, practical cook and teacher with a focus on using only the finest quality and freshest ingredients in her recipes. These same values align with present-day cooks' renewed interest in many concepts from the past such as artisan baking and using fresh, locally produced foods, making her achievements all the more relevant today.

ONE

Who Was
Mrs. Goodfellow?

Philadelphia, 64 Dock Street
Wednesday, September 20, 1815
4 a.m.

It was still dark in her room when Eliza began to wake, and she took a moment to allow her eyes to adjust to the dusky dimness before slowly rising out of bed. Though it was only September, the air in her bedroom was cool and slightly damp, chilling her feet a bit when they touched the wooden floorboards. Lighting a small candle she kept by her bedside, she quickly dressed, putting on stays, stockings, shoes, petticoats, and finally her plain dark gray linen skirt and bodice. Draping a white neckerchief around her shoulders, she tucked it into the neckline of her bodice, and then pinned on her starched linen work apron and tied her hair up under her cap.

So began the routine of an early nineteenth-century woman about to perform her usual daily tasks. Although many of these duties were common for that time in our nation's history, this woman, Elizabeth Goodfellow, was different in that she left a rather remarkable impression behind—one not known to many people.

Ready to begin the day's baking, she carefully grasped the candle to light her way as she headed down the two flights of narrow stairs to the basement kitchen. She greeted her servant Mary, who was putting on her cloak to fetch several buckets of water from the outdoor water pump. The fire Mary had already lit in the large fireplace and its separate brick oven chamber was blazing nicely.

While Mary went to retrieve the water, another servant, Hannah, opened the windows a bit and then busied herself with sweeping and dusting the kitchen, taking special care to thoroughly sweep any ashes off the hearth. She checked the scales that hung from a small beam affixed to the end of the kitchen dresser to make sure the chains were functioning properly and that all the weights were in their box, since they would soon be needed for weighing cooking ingredients. She then wiped the kitchen work table, dresser, chairs, cooling racks, and shelves with a soft cotton cloth.

After making sure all the work surfaces were clean, she began to prepare the baking ingredients that would be needed later that day. First she took a hard molded cone of sugar from the small storage closet and pinched off some pieces with iron sugar nippers, a kitchen tool resembling a pair of pliers. She placed the sugar bits in a large mortar and pounded them with a pestle into a fine powder, which she scooped up into a wooden box and closed the lid. She also grated some fresh nutmeg and ground some blades of mace into a fine powder with a spice grinder and placed them in small bowls. Last, she retrieved some jars of dried basil and marjoram and mixed a little of each with some of the powdered mace, peppercorns, and salt and tied the mixture up with a piece of cheesecloth.

Mary returned from her last trip to the pump and carefully poured the water from the buckets into two heavy iron pots and hung them on the fireplace crane. When they were secure, she swung them around toward the fire so they would be ready for boiling and stewing later that morning. She then fetched a basket of artichokes from the larder. Pulling out a dozen, she stripped off the coarse outer leaves and cut off the stalks close to the bottom of each. After washing the artichokes thoroughly to remove any dirt and debris, she gently placed them in a basin of cold water to sit for a couple of hours.

After saying good morning to Hannah and checking on her progress, Eliza headed over to the fireplace. The oven door was ajar, and she peeked in, pushing the burning wood farther back towards the center with a long stick, stirring it up a bit. She next walked over to the large table in the center of the room and began to assemble the ingredients she needed to begin making up a batch of puff pastry or "paste": flour, butter, and cold water. She also got out her rolling pin, her large marble pasteboard, and a sharp knife.

Scooping flour out of the huge barrel into a bowl, she walked over to the scales and carefully weighed one pound and two ounces and then sifted it through a sieve into a large deep dish. She placed about one quarter of the sifted flour on a corner of the pasteboard to use for rolling and sprinkling.

Next she washed a pound of fresh butter, kneading it in cool water to release some of the salt. Squeezing it hard with her hands, she first shaped it into a round ball, and then divided it into four equal parts. She placed one lump in the dish with the flour, and the other three she positioned next to the pasteboard. Using a sharp knife, she cut the butter into very small pieces while mixing it with the flour in the dish. Once it was well mixed, she slowly added a little of the cold water, continuing to stir until it formed a lump. She then scattered some of the flour she had set aside on the middle of the pasteboard. Making sure she did not touch the dough with her hands (as the warmth would soften it too much), she carefully flipped the mound out of the pan with the knife, laying it on top of the board.

As she had perfected over her many years of baking experience, she picked up the rolling pin, rubbed it with flour, and sprinkled a little on the lump of paste. With a deft hand, she rolled out the dough in quick, even strokes, pressing on the rolling pin very lightly. She then took another piece of butter, and dabbed bits at equal distances all over the sheet of paste with her knife. Sprinkling some more flour on top, she folded up the dough, and then rolled it out a second time, after again dusting the surface with flour.

After it was rolled out, she did the same process all over again two more times: sticking butter all over it in little bits, coating surfaces with flour, folding up the paste, and rolling it out, always making sure she was pressing with a light touch. The final time she rolled the dough out into a large round sheet, and then cut off the sides to form a square, laying the strips of dough on top. She folded it up with the edge trimmings inside and, making little notches on the surface with the knife, she placed it in a covered dish and set it on a cool larder shelf away from the heat of the oven. This large batch of puff paste would serve as the base for an apple pudding, two lemon puddings, and several small square cheesecakes.

After that was done she mixed the dough for an order of jumbles (ring-shaped butter cookies) and then walked over to a small bench near the fireplace where she had placed several tins of "Spanish Bunns" she had prepared the night before. She noticed the soft yeasty dough had risen nicely; its surface was foamy with light airy bubbles which puffed over the top edges.

Since it was a market day, Mary would work on baking the jumbles and some delicate little "Queen cakes" after Eliza went to shop for some eggs and a few other supplies. These and the cheesecakes required a hot oven, so they would have to go in before the puddings, which baked best at a more moderate temperature. Eliza also had orders for a batch of kisses (meringue cookies) and some fine custards, but these needed to be made later in the day when the oven was cooler.

Eliza's pastry shop was a specialized, high-end business. She was supplying fancy, sugary creations of all kinds—cakes, puddings, desserts, pastries, and so on—not the plain "sustenance" foods like pies or buckwheat cakes sold by some of her contemporaries. In addition to selling items in her shop, she also did a brisk catering business—taking orders and sending out food to private dinner parties.

While Eliza was busy preparing the puff paste and other items, Mary had mixed up the cheesecake filling, which involved grating day-old sponge cake into some cottage cheese that she had made very smooth by pressing through a small strainer. She then creamed butter and sugar together with a paddle-shaped hickory spoon in a separate deep earthen dish, eventually adding some brandy and wine, and then a little grated nutmeg and rosewater. The two mixtures were then combined.

Eliza retrieved the puff pastry from the larder, and unfolding a sheet, she rolled it out again, but with a firmer hand this time. She cut the pastry into rounds which she placed in the bottoms of small square tin patty pans, leaving half-circles of paste hanging over each side. She then gently stirred the rind and juice of one lemon into the cheesecake filling and spooned it into the pans on top of the pastry, scattering some currants on top. Last she cut long slits in the overhanging curves of pastry and flipped them over, laying them on the top of the cheesecakes. She then walked over to check on the oven.

Black soot from the smoldering wood had already burned off. Mary had raked the coals over the bottom of the oven and, after letting them rest for a minute, she swept it out clean and wiped the inside surface with a damp rag tied to the end of a long stick in order to generate a moist heat. Eliza stuck her hand inside the oven and after holding it in there for about twenty seconds, determined it was the necessary temperature.

Carrying the cheesecakes over from the table, she placed the pans in the oven, pushing them toward the back with her long-handled wooden peel (a shovel-like tool designed to safely move bread and pastries in and out of a bake oven). She asked Mary to check on them once or twice to make sure they were not burning on top, and to remove them when done. She then wiped her hands on her apron and carefully unpinned it so she could get ready to go to the market.

As a pastry cook, Eliza had to arrange her schedule according to the heat of the oven. The huge brick oven burned hottest when first fired up, and then cooled off as the day went on. If she were baking bread, this would go in first; on the day just described it would be the puff paste items, then cakes and cookies, next puddings and buns, and last, custards and meringues. In planning her day, she also needed to make sure she filled any orders by the requested delivery time as well as had fresh baked goods to sell in her shop.

For Eliza, however, there was an additional factor to consider—lesson preparation. Known more formally as Mrs. Elizabeth Goodfellow, she was also the instructor of what is considered by most food historians to be America's first cooking school, which she opened in Philadelphia in the early 1800s and continued to run for thirty years or more.

*M*rs. *Elizabeth Goodfellow* focused on teaching mostly upper-class young ladies how to make rich dishes and luscious desserts worthy of the fanciest dinner parties, making their mothers proud and dazzling any potential male suitors. A highly underrated cooking authority, her goods and services were eagerly sought after by Philadelphia's elite during the first half of the nineteenth century. As recently as 1994, Patrick Dunne and Charles L. Mackie wrote in *Historic Preservation* magazine that she was "an extraordinary, neglected figure in culinary history and should be credited as the mother of American cookery."[1] Her culinary style and techniques were considered paramount at that time, not only in Philadelphia, but around the country as well. It is no wonder mothers wanted their daughters to attend her school.

Mrs. Goodfellow was born in 1768 as Elizabeth Baker, the daughter of William and Ann Baker, most likely in Maryland.[2] She was married (and widowed) three times. So little is known about her that it is a mystery how she spent her life before opening the shop and cooking school, including how and where she received her culinary training. And as far as what she looked like, there is only one identified photograph in existence, taken at the very end of her life when she was about eighty.

It is probable that Mrs. Goodfellow was from a British background, since many families with the "Baker" surname immigrated to America from England starting in the late 1600s. In addition, her recipes and pastry-making bear striking similarities to British cooks of the day, including

Elizabeth Raffald, Maria Eliza Ketelby Rundell, and Hannah Glasse. In fact, it appears that cookbooks written by Rundell and Glasse were used as instruction manuals in her school.[3]

Her first husband had the last name Pearson, but his first name and other personal information are unknown. We also do not know when and where they were married. They had a daughter, Sarah, born on March 4, 1800. By 1801 they were living in Philadelphia, where she is first mentioned in a city directory as Eliza Pearson, pastry cook.[4] She is listed as Elizabeth Pearson in 1802 and 1803, with the shop location of 64 Dock Street. Her husband must have died in 1803 or 1804, since the 1804 Philadelphia directory lists her as Elizabeth Pearson, widow.[5]

This husband may have been a pastry cook as well. In the book *Literary Landmarks of Philadelphia*, Mrs. Goodfellow is described as "the widow of a pastry cook, and herself a pastry cook, succeeded her husband in a shop at 64 Dock Street, somewhere between Second Street and Walnut,"[6] although there are no instances of a male pastry cook with the last name Pearson in any of the early 1800s Philadelphia directories.

Eliza then wed Robert Coane sometime in 1803 or early 1804, and their son, also named Robert Coane, was born October 1, 1804. Not much is known about this husband either, other than that he came to the United States from Ireland by 1796 and was naturalized on August 2, 1805.[7] According to one of his descendants, Abigail Coane Leibell, he was thought to be Protestant and from Higginstown, outside Ballyshannon, county Donegal.[8]

Coane quite possibly may have found employment in the U.S. Army upon his arrival. There is a record of a Private Robert Coane who received payment of $26.53 for his work as a soldier and servant to Brigadier General Wilkinson from June 12 through December 31, 1797. It

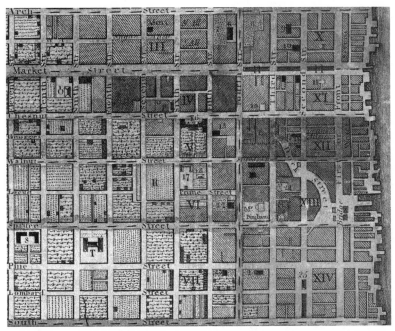

Detail from a map of Philadelphia published in 1802. Mrs. Goodfellow was list-ed in a directory at the time under her first husband's name, Pearson, operat-ing a pastry shop at 64 Dock Street, the conspicuous curved street a block from the Delaware River wharfs. At this time, Philadelphia was one of the largest English-speaking cities in the world. Nonetheless, note the amount of open space dedicated to agriculture abutting the city's dwellings (marked with crosshatching). Key public buildings, such as the State House (number 16) and Market Street sheds (number 11) are solid. The future Washington Square where Mrs. Goodfellow would relocate her business in 1835 is a block marked R along Sixth and Walnut Streets. (*David Rumsey Map Collection*)

appears that this may have actually been some sort of pun-ishment, although no specifics are given and he did get paid for his service.[9] No other instances of Coane having any further affiliation with the U.S. military could be found.

The *Philadelphia Directory* for 1805 lists Eliza twice—as both Eliza Cone, pastry cook, 68 Dock Street and Elizabeth Pearson, widow, 64 Dock Street. We can assume

they are referring to the same person. ("Coane" was sometimes written phonetically as "Cone," a common practice
for the time.) Also, the listing for the shop location changes
back and forth between 64 Dock Street and 68 Dock Street
until about 1828.[10] Philadelphia directories were customar-
ily published a year after the data was collected, which
could explain why her name is listed both ways.

It is likely Robert Coane died sometime in 1807 or
1808, as Elizabeth is still listed as Eliza Cone, pastry cook,
68 Dock Street in 1808. According to Coane descendant
Kathy Cundith, the family Bible says he was "lost at sea."[11]
Perhaps he was a sailor or fisherman, or turned to one of
these occupations later in life in order to make ends meet.
In any case, he must have been deceased by at least 1808
because later that year on October 16 Eliza wed her third
husband, watch and clockmaker William Goodfellow, at
Old Swedes Church in Philadelphia.[12]

William Goodfellow was born in 1749 or 1750 in
Scotland to John and Margret Goodfellow and arrived in
the United States around 1790.[13] He first appears in
Philadelphia directories in 1793 as Wm. Goodfellow,
watchmaker, 24 Chestnut Street.[14] In 1796 he married
Sarah Wood of Philadelphia, also at Old Swedes Church.[15]
She died in November 1805 at the age of forty-eight.[16]

By the time he married Eliza in 1808, he was in his late
fifties and she was around forty. In 1809, they are both listed with their businesses at 64 Dock Street—she as a pastry
cook and he as a clockmaker.[17] Eliza appeared to stay at this
location until at least 1825. She had no children with
William, and he died July 1, 1818. Although this was the
longest of her three marriages, it still lasted only ten years.

Like many other Philadelphia artisans from this time,
William Goodfellow was an involved and respected mem-
ber of the Philadelphia community. In 1799 he joined the
St. Andrew's Society of Philadelphia and signed the charter

of 1808. According to its charter, the St. Andrew's Society was created for the "sole purpose" of providing "relief [for] distressed Scottish immigrants" throughout the city.[18]

He was also a member of the Universal Society, a small deist debate club established in Philadelphia in 1790. This group met weekly for instruction, conference, and debate upon moral and philosophical subjects.[19] They covered a wide range of topics, from the appropriateness of polygamy, capital punishment, and the central tenets of Christianity, to questions about physics and meteorology. One issue raised by Goodfellow was whether belief in an afterlife was conducive to human happiness.[20]

Members of the Universal Society were able to keep out of the public eye by expressing their deism in the semiprivate realm of a debate club, where their unconventional ideas and conversation would only be heard by and shared with people who willingly joined. Therefore, this group was able to discuss their provocative religious opinions without attracting community ire.[21] It is unknown whether Elizabeth shared these thoughts and opinions.

William's obituary from the July 4, 1818, *United States Gazette* characterizes him as follows:

> Departed this life, on Wednesday morning, Mr. William Goodfellow, late a watchmaker in this city, and for twenty eight years a respectable citizen of the American Republick. Inheriting all those undeviating principles of rectitude, which characterize a Scottish gentleman, he could not be swayed from their immutable laws by the mercenary advantages of profit or gain. His energy was strong and vigorous, enriched with "Learning's Lore," his conversation was pleasing and instructive. His mind was reflective and discriminative, and solution, with few exceptions, was the result of his investigation.[22]

William had chosen a lucrative profession, as watches were an essential fixture in Philadelphia from its early days onward. By the time he became a resident they were even more vital due to the presence of the affluent merchant and mariner class. In fact, in Philadelphia watches were symbols of economic prosperity and dependability of character more than in any other city in the United States.[23]

However, it appears that William might not have been as prosperous as some of the other watchmakers in the city, as he did not leave a will for Eliza. According to the administration that was filed, she estimated that the total of his estate to be worth not more than $200 at the time of his death. In fact, she had to settle debts of $400 for him, payable to the Commonwealth of Pennsylvania.[24] He is listed sporadically in city directories in the years leading up to his death, so perhaps he was ill toward the end of his life.

Eliza Goodfellow continued her business at the Dock Street location for a number of years after William's passing. Situated with a view of the Delaware River and its many wharfs, Dock Street was within easy reach of the numerous daily auctions of newly arrived goods which were held right on the docks and in stores nearby. The wide range of items included foodstuffs such as English mustard, fresh nutmegs and cloves, green coffee, imperial tea, muscovado sugar, lemons, figs, and lime juice.[25] In addition, her shop was an easy walk from the twice-weekly markets on High Street (later Market Street) featuring locally grown produce, fresh meats, and high-quality dairy products. Many of these ingredients would have been incorporated into her recipes.

The docks were a major point of commerce from Philadelphia's earliest days. Quaker business connections in England and the West Indies helped many Philadelphians maintain a comfortable livelihood and created a profitable marketplace based on mercantile trade. The lush farms bor-

The signature of Eliza Goodfellow on an 1818 document to confirm that her husband William Goodfellow died intestate. This is among the few known examples of her autograph. (*Register of Wills, Philadelphia*)

dering the city produced an abundance of wheat, flour, and grain. A portion of these goods were then shipped to the West Indies to trade for sugar and molasses; another percentage was sold for profit to buy imported merchandise from England.[26] The London market paid top prices for Pennsylvania wheat, which produced harder flour than British wheat and yielded more loaves of bread per barrel.[27]

Philadelphia became the greatest of the colonial seaports, and Quaker shipping operations there and in Wilmington, Delaware, could obtain luxury foods not available elsewhere in the United States such as fresh pineapples from the Caribbean, Seville oranges, and winter grapes from the Canary Islands.[28] This rapid growth enabled Philadelphia to quickly become the third most important commercial city in the British Empire, behind only London and Liverpool. This was a direct result of Quaker business savvy combined with its port location and nearby rich farmland.[29]

Even though New York's population had surpassed Philadelphia's by 1810, Philadelphia was considered more metropolitan, leading all the other U.S. cities commercially and in its openness to new ideas and free thinking.[30] Philadelphia was, after all, founded on the acceptance of diversity. Both citizens in the city and those living on surrounding farms were able to retain their own traditions while simultaneously influencing each other. Food was one

Two of the famous views of Philadelphia drawn by Thomas Birch and sons at the turn of the nineteenth century. At the top, the neoclassical Library and Surgeons Hall stands among modest shops along Fifth Street. At the bottom, a view looking east along High (Market) Street from Ninth Street. In the distance are the Market Street stalls. (*Library of Congress*)

way they could maintain a sense of identity with their individual cultures while forging New World customs and styles.[31]

An established and cosmopolitan city, Philadelphia had good hotels, theaters, restaurants, circuses, bookstores, a fine library, museums of natural history, science, and art, and groups of talented and interesting people. And as new cities were founded in the U.S. middle and far west, their planners laid them out in the same grid pattern of streets William Penn had used to design Philadelphia in the 1680s.[32]

A writer describing the city in 1805 said the following: "The streets of Philadelphia are paved with pebblestones, and bordered with ample footways, raised one foot above the carriageway, for the ease and safety of passengers. They are kept cleaner than those of any city in Europe, excepting the towns of Holland. . . . London is the only capital in the world that is better lighted at night. Many of the New Streets have been latterly planted with Poplars."[33]

Due to the city's thriving interest in scholarship and fine arts, Philadelphia was referred to as the "Athens of America" between 1790 to 1840, although the term was being used to describe the city before those dates.[34] Visitors both foreign and domestic continued to praise the city's beauty and individuality. French botanist André Michaux described it as "the most extensive, handsomest and most populous city in the United States."[35]

However, by the 1840s, the passion in Philadelphia that had generated the comparison "Athens of America" tapered off, as New York began to dominate Philadelphia as well as other U.S. cities, both culturally and economically.[36] This was a result of several factors. First, when the federal capital moved to Washington in 1800, Philadelphia lost its political power. Then the War of 1812 strained the city's trade and shipbuilding, and it never regained its leading position. Additionally, New York's harbor was considered easier to navigate and its port was closer to the ocean than Philadelphia's. When New York replaced its seasonal spring and fall sailings by launching the Black Ball Line of regular ships in 1817, a new business model was created.[37]

Although Philadelphia remained a major seaport, by 1824 its foreign commerce had declined to third or fourth place in the United States. However, this was not as much of a blow as it might sound. The removal of the capital to Washington forced Philadelphians to focus even more on their industries and drum up new sources of revenues. Philadelphia had always had important commercial interests, excelling in this area over other U.S. cities.[38] Houses and shops continued to multiply along the Delaware and back toward the center of the city.

The part of Dock Street between the Delaware River and Second Street had existed as a business district since the founding of the city. In the eighteenth century boats frequently discharged flour at a bakery located at the southwest corner of Dock Creek and Second Street, and ferried goods up the creek to the High Street markets.[39]

Originally two branches of Dock Creek flowed into a nearby tidal basin, but this mosquito-ridden marshy spot was paved over by the time Mrs. Goodfellow lived there as the vicinity's population boomed, thus becoming the wide, curved avenue known as Dock Street. The hub of maritime activity near the docks enticed skilled workers to be closer to the action in order to sell their goods and services. As a result, Mrs. Goodfellow's neighbors in the Dock Ward district were tanners, curriers, bookbinders, cabinet and furniture makers, ship captains, and ship makers, in addition to some well-to-do merchants, whose daughters would have been likely student candidates for her cooking school.[40]

It was a lively and crowded area, supporting residents from a variety of cultures, religions, and occupations. The common thread tying Philadelphians together was a strong desire for success, which they realized was indeed possible, as they watched many of their industrious fellow residents work their way into the city's upper levels of society.[41] It was not uncommon for more than one family to share a home in order to make this dream happen. Rents were expensive, and splitting the cost would have helped to make ends meet. Space was at such a premium that many folks often used the lower level of these narrow buildings for their businesses, with their respective families using the upper floors as their living quarters.

Many artisans and merchants worked by themselves. Some craftsmen hired themselves out as journeymen (free to work for anyone, being paid by the day); others made and sold their goods out of these rented homes, which also doubled as their places of business. A few merchants had partners or enlisted family members to help. They all performed their jobs within very limited geographical boundaries.[42]

It is very probable that Mrs. Goodfellow and her family were in this category, at the very least sharing the 64 Dock Street location with other enterprises. Philadelphia newspaper announcements from the early 1800s advertise several other businesses at this address during the same time Mrs. Goodfellow is listed in city directories. For example, in 1803 artist James Cox ran a "Drawing and Painting Academy" for young ladies and gentlemen at 64 Dock,[43] and between 1810 and 1820 goods such as fresh fruits, Malaga wine, Muscatel white grapes, sun raisins, and "genuine gum Arabic"[44] were sold by merchant William Read from this location.[45] Read also provided real estate services, offering homes for sale in both the city as well as a fifty-three-acre "country seat near the Falls of Schuylkill."[46] In addition, an unnamed navy agent advertised space for freight on a route to Portsmouth, New Hampshire, in 1819.[47]

So although space might have been tight for Goodfellow and her family, the selling of these other products and services in the same spot would have surely given her business more exposure and likely increased her clientele. It is easy to imagine that a gentleman coming to purchase a cask of wine might have also bought some of her pastries to bring home. After rave reviews from his family, perhaps they then used her catering services for their next party, and signed up their daughter for cooking school lessons. Word among their friends would have spread quickly, increasing Goodfellow's customer base and increasing student attendance.

And how convenient for Mrs. Goodfellow to have some of the merchandise she needed to produce her confections right on the premises; William Read may have cut her a price break on the imported goods he was selling or bartered with her to obtain her baked goods. Additionally, having a drawing and painting school in tandem with a cooking school would have been a stroke of pure genius, as many of the same girls could have had instruction in both cooking and art at the same location. Perhaps Cox and Goodfellow even worked out special deals for young ladies—cooking lessons in the morning and drawing and painting in the afternoon. Any of these scenarios could have been possible business arrangements—we simply don't know.

Mrs. Goodfellow likely appreciated all the help she could get. Her life must have been rather difficult and stressful, with her first two husbands dying within five years, leaving her with two young children to support and a business to run. Her three marriages spanned a total of only fifteen to twenty years of her eighty-three-year life.

So, she had to learn to be self-sufficient and provide for her family, transitioning in and out of marriage while coping with the successive deaths of her husbands. It was not uncommon for women to be widowed during the colonial and federal eras; many men were killed fighting in the Revolution or War of 1812, those working in the maritime trade were often lost at sea and there were numerous casualties from yellow fever and other diseases. By staying in the city where it was easier to get work, many women became heads of households. Indeed, like Goodfellow, Philadelphia resident Betsy Ross also survived her third husband and ran a successful business.[48]

Once widowed, a woman's economic situation determined who else shared her residence, including the hired help she could afford. Her fellow inhabitants were especially dependent on the type of work she could perform in her home.[49] In Goodfellow's case, it is likely she had family or servants helping her with the pastry making and running the shop. It is not known who was living under her roof during 1800–1810 when she was twice widowed, but at the time of the 1810 census, the household she shared with husband William Goodfellow totaled eleven members. In addition to William, Eliza, and her two children, there were seven other members, all females ranging in age from children to adults.[50]

At least some of these women and girls probably assisted Mrs. Goodfellow not only in the shop, but also with performing all the duties required to maintain her home. The list of tasks between both must have been endless: cooking, cleaning, running errands, stoking the fire, fetching water, sewing and mending, as well as taking pastry orders, working in the shop as storekeeper, and bookkeeping, just to name a few.

At least she would have had a steady stream of labor to choose from. In nineteenth-century America, many girls worked as servants before they married, and most adults of all social classes had household help at some point. The assistance came from a variety of sources: their own children, relatives and the children of relatives, neighbors, servants, or slaves. Servants were either "hired" (paid wages) or "boarded" (living and working under the same roof as family members).[51]

In Goodfellow's case, it appears that she maintained a full household during the time she ran her business, as shown by census records from other years. For instance, the 1820 census shows ten individuals living under her roof at the Dock Street residence, which would have included herself and her two children. Widowed for the third time at this point, she still has seven people outside her family living under her roof, including three males in addition to her son Robert. Two were in the sixteen-to-twenty-five age range,[52] so perhaps they were pastry chefs or apprentices. Whether these people were family, servants, or boarders, any of these scenarios would have been extremely useful, even necessary to her in order to keep things running smoothly.

When nineteenth-century advancements led the Dock Street area to become increasingly commercial, private residences and shops were pushed out in favor of large warehouses and boardinghouses.[53] Likely one of these casualties, Elizabeth relocated her shop to 134 South Second Street in 1828. By 1835 she had moved to the more picturesque 91 South Sixth Street (just off Washington Square), and was there until 1845 when the location changed slightly to 71 South Sixth, probably a consequence of a shift in street numbers, not a true location change.[54]

Eliza Goodfellow,

Respectfully informs her friends and former customers, that she has taken her Son, into the business, and having considerably enlarged the Establishment they are now prepared to furnish in any quantity, Ice Cream, Jelly, Blanche Mange, and Fancy Cakes of every description.

ALSO, Candy Baskets, Pyramids, Confectionary, Fruit &c. &c.

☞ *N. B. As it is our determination to Manufacture all our goods of the best materials, we hope to merit a continuance of Public favour.*

E. GOODFELLOW, & SON.

No. 91, South Sixth Street,

ONE DOOR ABOVE SPRUCE.

Phila. Jan. 1837.

The January 1837 notice that Mrs. Goodfellow had taken her son Robert Coane into the business at its fashionable South Sixth Street location where she had relocated in 1835. (*Atwater Kent Museum*)

Beginning in 1830, her son Robert Coane's occupation was listed as a cabinetmaker, first at 4 Laurel Street and then later at Sixth Street above Spruce.[55] However, in January 1837 he went into the confectionery business with his mother at the 91 South Sixth Street location. The shop was expanded and renamed E. Goodfellow, & Son. A receipt from the shop dated September 1837 has on the reverse an announcement confirming that "Eliza Goodfellow has taken her son into the business, and having considerably enlarged the establishment they are now prepared to furnish in any quantity, ice cream, jelly, blanche mange, and fancy cakes of every description. Also, candy baskets, pyramids, confectionary and fruit."[56]

We can assume that as she was getting into her seventies she must have recruited him to help out, or perhaps he offered to do so. Did they both need the money? Did she stop teaching at this point, or did they expand the shop so that she could concentrate more on the cooking school? This is unlikely due to her advanced age. Perhaps her business was prospering and the timing was such that a partnership seemed a good business move.

It is not clear whether the types of confectionery mentioned in the announcement are new offerings with this shop expansion, or more of an increase in the quantity available. Also, it seems kind of unusual for Robert to switch careers so suddenly, but his mother could have been training him to make pastry for years, prepping him for a time when they might go into business together. Or he could have been more of a pure business partner, taking care of the administrative tasks and employing other pastry chefs to help.

According to the 1850 U.S. census, two other confectioners are listed as living with the Coanes in Dock Ward, City of Philadelphia—Robert Moffit, age twenty, and Parker Smith, age twenty-four, so it is almost certain they were working for Goodfellow and Coane. In addition, five young women ranging in age from fifteen to twenty-six are living at this residence, two who listed Ireland as their place of birth, and one England. Their occupations are not given, but it can be assumed they were servants. Robert Coane is recorded as a confectioner, but not Elizabeth, although she is logged as living in the same location as her son and his family.[57] In her eighties at this point and just one year before her death in January 1851, she surely had finally "retired."

After her death, the shop remained Goodfellow & Coane's Confectionary, Pastry and Fancy Cake Bakery until at least 1856, which is the last directory listing. By

1854 Robert had moved his residence to Green Street above Tenth.[58]

Robert went on to become an established figure in Philadelphia society. *The Encyclopedia of Pennsylvania Biography* cites him as a businessman in Philadelphia and a director of the Tradesmen's National Bank. He was also prominent in community affairs as a Republican, as the city's representative on the directorate of the Wills Eye Hospital, and as commissioner for the relief of families of volunteers during the Civil War. For his war work he was highly complimented by Major Alexander Henry of Philadelphia.[59]

He married Mary McLeod Stinger in 1831 and they had eight children.[60] Mary died in 1844, and he later wed Mary Margarette. At the time of the 1850 census, he had seven children (one child, Mary, had died in 1839), the oldest being a son, also named Robert Coane.[61] One daughter was named Elizabeth Goodfellow Coane, after her grandmother. She entered the Moravian Seminary in Bethlehem, Pennsylvania, in 1853 and later married William W. Allen.[62] Robert Sr. died on February 1, 1877, and it does not appear that any of his children ever picked up the confectionery business.

Mrs. Goodfellow's daughter from her first marriage, Sarah, had married Michel Bouvier (the great-great-grandfather of Jacqueline Bouvier Kennedy Onassis) in 1822. Having arrived from France in 1815 after serving in Napoleon's army, Michel made his way to Philadelphia and set up shop as a carpenter and cabinetmaker. Through hard work and perseverance he established friendships and working relationships with local Frenchmen Joseph Bonaparte (Napoleon's brother and the former king of Spain) and businessman Stephen Girard.[63] Michel and Sarah's marriage was short-lived. They had a son, Eustache, in 1824. Two years later Sarah gave birth to their second

child, Therese, and then died shortly after at the age of
twenty-six. Michel later remarried Louise Vernou, with
whom he had ten children, including a son, John, from
whom Jacqueline Kennedy Onassis is descended.

Eustache was the oldest of the Bouvier clan but unfortunately did not live up to his father's expectations. He was an
unambitious philanderer type who never married and died
at the age of forty-two. Their daughter, Therese, however,
married Jonathan Patterson, Jr., the son of a prosperous
merchant and part of a distinguished Philadelphia family.
They had seven children, including Mary Patterson Stuart,
Michel's first granddaughter, who was 101 and still very
active and alert at the time John F. Kennedy was elected
president.[64]

Mrs. Goodfellow was well connected to Philadelphia
society, which undoubtedly helped her business thrive.
Even before Michel had begun work for Stephen Girard,
Mrs. Goodfellow was selling him baked goods. (Perhaps it
was actually Girard who introduced young Sarah and
Michel at some point.) In any case, on October 28, 1817,
Girard paid Goodfellow $13.25 for making cakes for the
wedding of his niece Henriette and General Lallemand.[65]

Additional existing receipts from her shop show that
other distinguished patrons included the wives of well-
respected Philadelphia lawyer Edward Shippen Burd and
successful merchant and landowner Daniel W. Coxe, a
descendant of one of the oldest families in Philadelphia.[66]

Mrs. Goodfellow also donated nineteenth-century "care
packages for the troops," supplying cakes for soldiers during the War of 1812, much to their delight. While at Camp
du Pont near Wilmington, Delaware, William Wood
Thackara wrote in a November 27, 1814, diary entry, "Benj.

Mitchell (brother of the conveyancer) of our compy took charge of a large pound cake, made by Mrs. Goodfellow for Captn. T.F. Pleasants, with his name handsomely cypherd in coloured sugar on the top, and with some of his cronies on the way down, demolished it."[67]

As a large number of Mrs. Goodfellow's customers were from prominent Quaker families in and around Philadelphia, and many women from these families attended her school, it has been commonly thought that Mrs. Goodfellow was also of a Quaker background (and was likely born into a Quaker family in Maryland). Several factors point to the fact that she may have resigned her membership or been "disowned" at some point. Neither of her first two husbands (Pearson or Coane) could be found in any Quaker records, and in addition, the fact that Robert Coane may have served in the

Successful merchant and banker Stephen Girard was a French-born naturalized American citizen who made Philadelphia his home. During the War of 1812, he saved his adopted country from financial collapse. He was the wealthiest person in America at the time of his death in 1831. Having no children, Girard ended up leaving much of his vast fortune to the care and education of orphans. Girard had a keen interest in food and dining and his esteem for Mrs. Goodfellow is shown by trusting her to the pastries served at some of his most important dinners. (*Library of Congress*)

U.S. military (which is contradictory to Quaker pacifist views) makes it very unlikely he was a member of the Religious Society of Friends. It was common practice for any Quaker who married a non-Quaker to be disowned for disunity or at the very least disciplined. So perhaps her first husband (Pearson) was a Quaker, and then Eliza was disowned when she married Robert Coane, but was able to retain her Quaker network of business contacts and acquaintances. Disownment did not mean shunning, and in many cases, disowned Quakers continued to be very much a part of the larger Quaker social community.[68]

Another indication that Eliza was no longer a practicing Quaker was her marriage to her third husband, William Goodfellow, in 1808; they were wed in Old Swedes' Church, not during a Quaker meeting, as per Quaker custom. In addition, when he died, William was buried in Philadelphia's Free Quakers Cemetery.[69] More a social than a religious society, the Free Quakers included many former Friends who had been disowned or had resigned their membership at the time of the Revolution.[70] Eliza's children also married non-Quakers and her son Robert was actually a pewholder at the Sixth Presbyterian Church in Philadelphia from 1836 to 1841 and possibly other years.[71]

Regardless of whether or not Mrs. Goodfellow was a Quaker, at the very least it can be said that Quakers influenced cookery in Philadelphia and the surrounding region, through both the foods they ate as well as the way they prepared them. Some historians have claimed the Quakers produced a distinct type of cookery, while others disagree. It is clear, however, that the Friends favored quality ingredients. Even though they were inclined toward simplicity, the mercantile aristocracy in Philadelphia was very well-off indeed. While their clothes, homes, and carriages were plain, they were always the best money could buy.[72] In Philadelphia, Mrs. Goodfellow would have had access to the tropical foods, imported European delicacies, and most important, the sugar necessary to create her confectionery.

The strict Quaker codes of conduct and peaceful contemplation did not deny good eating and drinking, and the Friends partook of the Pennsylvania bounty. Quaker tables groaned under the weight of tempting foods from garden and dairy as well as poultry, beef, and mutton.[73] They viewed luxury as a sign of God's grace, and the culinary riches available in the region created an environment of prosperity and excellence for Pennsylvania foods.[74]

Quakers were known for their substantial springhouses which provided high-quality dairy products such as Philadelphia cream cheese, which rose to fame in the nineteenth century. The fresh milk and cream they produced were also used to make Philadelphia ice cream, considered a rich indulgence at this time.[75] Quaker Elizabeth Ellicott Lea's 1845 cookbook, *Domestic Cookery,* included four recipes for authentic Philadelphia ice cream, all of which called for using real cream, not milk.[76]

Likewise, Mrs. Goodfellow was well-known as a proponent of pure, whole foods. Most of her recipes called for just a few simple ingredients, but with a frugal, resourceful eye she would turn them into rich, inviting dishes and sumptuous desserts. Nothing was wasted and everything was presented in the most artistic way.

This sense of thrift was an important component for the Quakers, especially since large numbers of Friends were served at Monthly, Quarterly, and Yearly Meetings, where they assembled to worship and discuss church business. "Quarterly Meeting Pie," a popular dessert served at Quarterly Meeting dinners, was actually a baked potato pudding.[77]

In the *Colonial Receipt Book: Celebrated Old Receipts Used a Century Ago by Mrs. Goodfellow's Cooking School,* a version of this dish attributed to Mrs. Goodfellow is referred to as "White Potato Pie." The potatoes are grated instead of mashed, then mixed with butter, sugar, eggs, brandy, and flavorings. Although this recipe made only one pie, another potato pudding recipe in the book uses two pounds of potatoes to make four pies, which would have been useful in feeding a crowd. The recipe calls for the potatoes to be boiled well and sifted through a colander before being mixed with the other ingredients to make the custardy pies.[78]

WHITE POTATO PIE
Contributed by Mrs. William Henry Kennedy,
Philadelphia, Pa
Mrs. Goodfellow's Recipe
1/2 pound of butter, 1/2 pound of sugar creamed together; add 1/2 pound of white potatoes boiled and grated, 4 eggs well-beaten, a gill of cream, a glass of wine, brandy and rose-water mixed. Flavor with cinnamon or nutmeg. Bake in puff paste.

POTATO PUDDING
Mrs. Thomas Painter, Sunbury, Pa.,
A Pupil Of Mrs. GoodFellow, Philadelphia, Pa.
Contributed by Mrs. Wm. P. I. Painter, Muncy, Pa.
Of butter and sugar each 24 of a pound beaten well together, 2 pounds of potatoes boiled well and sifted through a colander, then mix with the sugar and butter 8 eggs beaten light. Add 1 glass of brandy and 1 of wine, a little rose water, cinnamon and nutmeg. This will make four puddings to be baked in puff paste.

So how exactly did Mrs. Goodfellow obtain all this cooking knowledge, particularly the highly skilled art of pastry making? From circumstantial evidence it appears that her first husband had been a pastry chef. It is also possible that her father, a brother, or an uncle was a pastry chef or baker, and she was able to observe and learn from them. At a time when home and shop were under the same roof, female family members often helped with whatever trade was being performed. Others actually took over their husband's and father's trades when they died.[79]

Perhaps Goodfellow learned to cook through one or more of the Quaker women in her life when she was a girl in Maryland. In colonial America, young girls learned cookery, candle dipping, and sewing from their mothers and grandmothers.[80] And although Quakers viewed men and women as equals, more attention was paid to educating girls in housework and homemaking than in teaching them academic subjects. It was considered much more worthwhile for a young girl to know how to spin, knit, sew, and cook than to be able to recite Latin or literature.[81]

In addition to being taught household skills, however, Quaker girls were usually given some degree of schooling, as Quakers were particularly forward thinking about education and equality among the sexes. Therefore, Quaker girls and boys received at least a basic education, either from their parents, aunts, and uncles, or from neighborhood "dame schools" (private elementary schools usually taught by women in their homes).[82]

Among the Quakers in America, those in Philadelphia were especially progressive in terms of the learning they provided. Shortly after the city's founding, William Penn granted a charter to provide a public school, the foundation of which still survives in the William Penn Charter School and the Friends Select School: "all children, within the province, of the age of twelve years, shall be taught some useful trade or skill, to the end none may be idle, but the poor may work to live, and the rich, if they become poor, may not want."[83]

So, they saw the benefit of teaching a variety of subjects, both academic and occupational. By 1742, four different types of Quaker-founded schools were available to the general public: primary schools teaching reading, writing, and arithmetic fundamentals; a more advanced secondary school teaching English and mathematics; a vocational school which prepared students for business, surveying, and carpentry; and a Latin school for scholars planning to go on to college.[84]

The curriculum of these early schools reflected Penn's bias toward a religiously oriented and practical education, with emphasis on simplicity and the basic skills of reading, writing, and arithmetic. Penn's own university experience led him to believe that "much reading is an oppression of the mind and extinguishes the natural candle, which is the reason of so many senseless scholars in the world." Therefore, more support was given to moral and vocational education, and the Quakers in Philadelphia did not found a college until the mid-nineteenth century.[85]

Philadelphia was a thriving, prosperous city at the turn of the nineteenth century, and because its residents highly valued the learning of domestic arts by women, it provided the perfect environment for Mrs. Goodfellow's cooking school to succeed. It may not have been a chance occurrence that she set up her business in such a city where female education was fostered, particularly the focus on practical skills. With the supportive Quaker environment, her idea made sense. Additionally, the fact that the Quaker network was comprised of many merchants and tradesmen would have provided a ready clientele and access to a variety of ingredients.

We can dismiss one possible means Eliza Goodfellow could have learned the art of pastry making. If Mrs. Goodfellow had been a man, she could have been hired as an apprentice to learn the baking trade. In colonial America, a young man usually apprenticed between his fourteenth and sixteenth birthdays and was contractually bound to this service until the age of twenty-one. Apprentices lived with and worked for their masters, who taught them not only their trade but also the math skills necessary to run a business and basic reading and writing. Room, board, and clothing were provided, and often a

An early nineteenth-century bakeshop. Apprentices—who were strictly limited to males—would have learned the craft in a shop. Women, including the wife of a baker, could be employed as help, as in this illustration where a woman is preparing loaves of dough on a large table. The baker at left is sliding a loaf into the oven using a baker's peel while another man, right, is preparing a new batch of dough in a special trough. Note the sacks of flour, the hanging scale for measuring, the large sifter on the wall, and the loaves proofing on shelves. (*Bettman Archive*)

small cash payment and a set of tools were given at the end of the agreement.[86]

Although the shops in Philadelphia were undoubtedly male-dominated, at least a third of all retailers were female, and a large number of inns, taverns, and boardinghouses were managed by women. Quaker women were often partners with their husbands in some kind of profession. They were able to manage a home, children, and a job nearly a hundred years before the opportunity arose for most women.[87] In terms of trade professions, women could find work as bakers, braziers, distillers and winemakers, mantua makers, glovers, and tailors, to name a few.[88]

However, it was quite unusual for a woman to be a pastry cook at this point in time, which is another mystery surrounding Goodfellow's success. There were women in

Philadelphia who advertised themselves as pie cooks, and even those who sold buckwheat cakes, but they probably were not selling to upper-class customers like Goodfellow did. Real pastry cooks were in the high end of the market. Yet it is unclear where women fit into the larger world of this profession because the business of bakers and cooks in Philadelphia was organized—they were not quite guilds in the European sense but they had associations. Who belonged to them and who did not is an important issue that has not been determined. Male pastry cooks probably would have had no trouble getting in, but it is unknown (and unlikely) whether women were allowed to belong.[89]

What benefits would Goodfellow have gained as a member of one of these associations? She would have been able to establish agreements with the flour merchants, since apparently quite a bit of price fixing took place. It was also a way to obtain supplies, keep costs down, manage labor issues, and acquire an apprentice quickly if needed.[90]

Her Quaker connections may have helped get around this, or it could have been purely her impeccable reputation for producing such high-quality goods, or a combination of both. If she learned her pastry-making skills from a family member or close friend, she would have been more easily accepted, as the Quakers were willing to recognize women who were skilled at a trade.

Another possibility is that as a girl in Maryland, Goodfellow received on-the-job training like Elizabeth Whitaker Raffald, a native of Doncaster, Yorkshire, England. Raffald was born in 1733 and educated according to the standard for women at the time. At the age of fifteen she began working as a housekeeper for Sir Peter and Lady Elizabeth Warburton at Arley Hall, Cheshire, where she perfected her knowledge of cookery. She was with the Warburtons for six years, during which time she married their gardener, John Raffald.

After leaving this position, she became an acclaimed confectioner, caterer, author, hotelier, and supplier of goods and services in Manchester, England. In 1764 she opened the city's first confectionery, and soon thereafter launched a cooking school for young ladies, which she ran out of her shop. In 1769 she published *The Experienced English Housekeeper,* which covered a range of kitchen subjects from family meals to banquets. The book was dedicated to her former employer, Lady Warburton, and included eight hundred recipes which Raffald ensured were original, well-tested dishes. One whole chapter was devoted to the fancy desserts that were her specialty, including jellies, sweets, and other confections like those sold in her shop.[91]

The similarities between Raffald and Goodfellow are striking, from their talents as pastry chefs and fine cooks to their shrewd marketing of goods and services, including sharing their knowledge of pastry making by offering classes from their shop locations.

Unlike Raffald, Mrs. Goodfellow never published a cookbook. It is possible she had written down some of her recipes for her own use that are now lost, but nothing has ever been found. Fortunately, her recipes and cooking methods were well-preserved by her most famous pupil, Eliza Leslie. Leslie's father died when she was just seventeen, and to support her family, Leslie's mother Lydia opened a boardinghouse in Philadelphia in 1808. It has been surmised that Eliza started taking classes at Mrs. Goodfellow's cooking school in order to assist her mother with the meals at the boardinghouse. While there she took detailed notes of the lectures, and at her brother's urging, had the recipes published in a cookbook entitled *Seventy-five Receipts for Pastry, Cakes and Sweetmeats,* which became very successful.[92]

According to food historian William Woys Weaver, Eliza Leslie's published "notebook" is really the first hard evidence of the kind of information that was being taught in cooking schools at that time. These recipes show up in manuscript and printed cookbooks from all over the country, not necessarily because they were lifted from Eliza Leslie, but because girls like Leslie went to Goodfellow's school. They then took these recipes back to Kentucky, Charleston, South Carolina, or wherever they were from.[93]

Leslie became a successful author, writing several more cookbooks, many with recipes learned from Mrs. Goodfellow, as well as etiquette guides for young women. She became known as Miss Leslie and also published some literary works (which was her true desire), including juvenile stories, fiction, magazine articles, and editorial pieces.

While Leslie made a few mentions of Mrs. Goodfellow and her successful techniques in her books, she did not take advantage of Goodfellow's notoriety by attributing the recipes to the famed "Goodfellow School of Cooking," which would have provided a boon for its marketing. Perhaps Mrs. Goodfellow asked Leslie not to mention her in her books, or maybe Eliza felt she should take credit since she was doing all the work of compiling the receipts.

One can imagine Mrs. Goodfellow would not have had much time to write down recipes between keeping her shop and her cooking school running smoothly. Perhaps she just didn't have the desire to publish a book on her own. She was a businesswoman, after all, not a writer. She preferred to stay behind the scenes. Another factor could have played a part—it has been conjectured that the two women were actually related.[94]

However, one of Goodfellow's students did capitalize on her name and reputation, publishing a cookbook in 1853 (two years after her death) entitled *Cookery as It Should Be*, which the author claimed represented the finest receipts and procedures taught at the Goodfellow school of cookery.[95] A later edition published in 1865 was called *Mrs. Goodfellow's Cookery as It Should Be: A New Manual of the Dining Room and Kitchen*, with Mrs. Goodfellow herself actually listed as the author.

It has never been determined who the real author is, but according to Weaver, *Cookery As It Should Be* was definitely published by someone who was not Eliza Leslie and not Mrs. Goodfellow, but was probably a graduate of Mrs. Goodfellow's cooking school, likely hailing from the southern United States. He feels the book takes advantage of the Goodfellow name and products, and it was published after she died so she was not around to sue.[96]

COOKERY AS IT SHOULD BE;

A NEW MANUAL

OF THE DINING ROOM AND KITCHEN,

FOR PERSONS IN MODERATE CIRCUMSTANCES.

CONTAINING

ORIGINAL RECIPTS ON EVERY BRANCH OF COOKERY;
DOMESTIC BEVERAGES; FOOD FOR INVALIDS;
PICKLING, &c., &c.

TOGETHER WITH

BILLS OF FARE FOR EVERY DAY IN THE YEAR;
RULES FOR CARVING, &c.

BY

A PRACTICAL HOUSEKEEPER,
AND PUPIL OF MRS. GOODFELLOW.

THIRD EDITION, REVISED AND ENLARGED, WITH ILLUSTRATIONS.

WILLIS P. HAZARD, 190 CHESTNUT STREET,
PHILADELPHIA.
1856.

The title page of *Cookery As It Should Be* by an anonymous author who claimed to have learned the techniques and recipes while attending Mrs. Goodfellow's school. (*Author*)

Eliza Leslie mentions this book with a negative tone, pointing out that a number of the recipes were not in the style of Mrs. Goodfellow. For example, some call for newfangled leavenings that began to be used as rising agents in the nineteenth century, such as pearlash (potassium carbonate, refined potash obtained from wood ashes), saleratus (an early form of baking soda), and baking soda. But Mrs. Goodfellow was so concerned about using only fresh ingredients that she would have nothing to do with any of these "chemicals," as she thought they imparted an artificial taste to baked goods. She continued to use yeast and beaten eggs to make her products light and airy even when these other baking aids were available and being used by her contemporaries.

To leaven cakes using eggs as the rising agent, air must be beaten into the eggs to produce a mass of air bubbles called a foam. The expansion of the air bubbles during the baking lightens the cake—a "mechanical" leavening as opposed to the chemical leavening of baking powder.[97] Of course, in the nineteenth century this was a long and tedious process as the beating was done by hand using several eggs. Timing as well as the equipment used were important; if the eggs were not beaten correctly (especially the yolks), the cake could end up heavy, tough, and streaky with an "eggy" taste.

Eliza Leslie wrote in her book *The Lady's Receipt-Book: A Useful Companion for Large or Small Families*, "In making cakes it is of the utmost importance that the eggs should be properly and sufficiently beaten; otherwise the cakes will most certainly be deficient in the peculiar lightness characterizing those that are made by good confectioners. Cakes cannot be crisp and light without a due proportion of the articles that are to make them so; and even then, the ingredients must be thoroughly stirred or beaten; and of course thoroughly baked afterwards."

Her specific, step-by-step instructions continue, reflecting the notes copiously and carefully taken while she was a student under Goodfellow's tutelage:

> Persons who do not know the right way, complain much of the fatigue of beating eggs, and therefore leave off too soon. There will be no fatigue, if they are beaten with the proper stroke, and with wooden rods, and in a shallow, flat-bottomed earthen pan. The coldness of a tin pan retards the lightness of the eggs. For the same reason do not use a metal egg-

beater. In beating them do not move your elbow, but keep it close to your side. Move only your hand at the wrist, and let the stroke be quick, short, and horizontal; putting the egg-beater always down to the bottom of the pan, which should therefore be shallow. Do not leave off as soon as you have got the eggs into a foam; they are then only beginning to be light. But persist till after the foaming has ceased, and the bubbles have all disappeared. Continue till the surface is smooth as a mirror, and the beaten egg as thick as a rich boiled custard; for till then it will not be really light. It is seldom necessary to beat the whites and yolks separately, if they are afterwards to be put together. The article will be quite as light, when cooked, if the whites and yolks are beaten together, and there will then be no danger of their going in streaks when baked. The justly-celebrated Mrs. Goodfellow, of Philadelphia, always taught her pupils to beat the whites and yolks together, even for sponge-cake; and lighter than hers no sponge-cake could possibly be.[98]

Mrs. Goodfellow also knew the benefit flavorings could bring to her products. The use of these flavorings and spices would have helped overcome any eggy taste that dared assert itself. Lemon was especially useful for this purpose. Indeed, the Queen Cake recipe from Eliza Leslie's *Directions for Cookery* advises stirring in twelve drops essence of lemon after beating ten eggs very light and mixing with the flour,[99] and her sponge cake instructions require beating twelve eggs with lemon "for a long time" before folding in the flour.[100] This idea continued even into the twentieth century, with a 1932 issue of *American Cookery Magazine* recommending adding the juice of half a lemon to the eggs after beating moderately, and then allowing the mixture to stand until it thickens before using in the cake in order to eliminate any overpowering egg flavor.[101]

In addition to incorporating lemons in her recipes, Mrs. Goodfellow also used rosewater and orange flavoring, and took advantage of spices such as nutmeg, allspice, cloves, ginger, and cinnamon. These spices would be freshly grated or pounded fine for greatest impact—packing more of a punch than the powdery and often stale-tasting bottled versions lining the shelves of grocery stores today.

Wines and spirits can also add flavor, as well as helping baked goods rise. Many of her recipes call for brandy, which cleverly reacts with the gluten and causes a chemical reaction with the other ingredients to create a subtle new taste.[102] Another reason brandy was used was to keep cakes from growing moldy, and this preservative was one more way to effectively mask the taste of too much egg.[103]

Goodfellow also advocated the use of New World ingredients, helping pave the way for the establishment of an "American" cuisine. Amelia Simmons is considered the first American woman to promote home-grown foods such as corn, pumpkins, and cranberries in her 1796 book *American Cookery*. Many of Simmons's recipes were copies of those printed in *The Frugal Housewife* by British cookbook author Susannah Carter, but others substituted American products for those that were typically British—such as making pudding with cornmeal instead of oats. Thus began the melding of English culinary traditions with New World foods, creating an "American" style.[104]

Continuing the trend, Mrs. Goodfellow incorporated these and other foods native to the United States in her recipes. Her Indian Pound Cake recipe, which utilizes Indian meal (known today as cornmeal), was one of her signature dishes and appears frequently in nineteenth-century Philadelphia manuscript cookbooks.[105]

INDIAN POUND CAKE

Eight eggs; the weight of 8 in sugar-the weight of 6 in
Indian meal sifted, 1/2 lb of butter, one nutmeg grated or
one teaspoonful of cinnamon, stir the butter and sugar to
a cream, then put the meal and eggs alternately into the
butter and sugar, grate in the nutmeg and stir all well;
butter a tin pan put in the mixture and bake in a moderate oven.

(*Source: Bellah, Manuscript Recipe Book, 40, Independence
National Historic Park Library*)

References to Goodfellow and her products in nineteenth-
century texts provide additional insight into her character.
An 1851 article about the Paris Hippodrome mentions that
when horse riders from the Philadelphia circus were sent to
Paris to perform their tricks, their remarkable skills were
likened to an art form. The author then continues,
"Another branch or school of Philadelphia Art might succeed here—Mrs. Goodfellow's pastry-cooking, whose
cocoanut pudding, for example, is equal to the best inspiration of suicidal and immortal Vatel."[106] This zealous comparison to the famous seventeenth-century French chef
shows just how highly she and her products were regarded.

Other literature highlighted the culinary prowess that
society required of young women, with comparisons to
Goodfellow being the gold standard. A short story by jour-
nalist Timothy Shay Arthur in 1871 was written twenty
years after her death, showing that comparisons to
Goodfellow continued even into the late nineteenth century. In the sketch, a young bride has difficulties producing
appetizing food, much to the dismay of her new husband
(and mother-in-law). Determined to please them both, the
bride buys a cookbook which she studies intensely. Soon
she is serving fragrant tea, hot biscuits, and cream toast

which pass inspection with flying colors. In the author's words, "Even Mrs. Goodfellow herself could not have surpassed them."[107]

Although much mystery surrounds Mrs. Goodfellow and her private life, it is known that she was highly respected in and around Philadelphia for her fine cakes and baked goods as well as her cookery school. The foundation for her success in all these domains? The choicest ingredients.

TWO

Ingredients

Philadelphia, 64 Dock Street
Wednesday, September 20, 1815
5:45 a.m.

Eliza Goodfellow quickly pulled on her soft gray cloak and tied its hood snugly under her chin. She handed her eleven-year-old son Robert a small basket, and then grabbing one herself, shut the heavy wooden door behind them and set out to do the day's marketing. She could have sent Mary in her place, but she was choosy about her ingredients and liked to make her own selections as often as possible.

Just a little light was beginning to show as the sun was slowly making its rise on the horizon. A few seagulls squawked overhead, and she looked up briefly to see them circling the wharf area where dozens of tall ships lined the harbor. Tied to the masts were colorful flags from nations around the world, waving in the breeze. Sailors shouted to each other in the distance as they unloaded crates of imported goods in addition to the day's local fish and produce.

The sights and sounds fascinated Robert, and he paused for a moment to survey the scene. He longed to linger, but Eliza was on a tight schedule and she firmly grasped his hand to urge him along. Plenty of other people were also heading toward the markets, as the merchants were allowed to begin selling their wares at 6 A.M., signaled by the chiming of the Town Bell. By arriving early, these first shoppers knew they could choose from the crispest, most brightly colored fruits and vegetables and the freshest eggs, meats, and cheeses.

The odors of the Dock Street area were not kind to its residents—the fishy harbor tang mixed with a slightly malty scent from several nearby breweries and the musty, foul-scented tanneries—and Robert crinkled his nose in disgust. But to Eliza, who was used to spending her days indoors dashing between her busy shop and basement kitchen, the outside air felt slightly cool and crisp, a sure sign of autumn's imminent approach, and she savored the experience. It was likely to be the only fresh air she would be exposed to all day.

She welcomed the fall season as it provided not only a bounty of produce from local Pennsylvania and New Jersey farms, but also refreshing relief from the stifling heat and humidity that often engulfed the city in the summer. Her shoes made light clicking noises on the stone footpaths as she and Robert briskly headed down Dock Street toward the High Street marketplace, passing rows of identical red brick houses, ranging in height from two to four stories. The walkways were lined with rows of buttonwood, poplar, and willow trees, which were both pretty and practical, shading the paths from the sun when it was hot.

In typical Philadelphia style, the narrow, rust-colored brick buildings were accented with large windows topped with keystone lintels and flanked by heavy wooden shutters, painted black, white, or green. The floors at the very top featured attic dormer windows that marked the garret rooms where children or servants usually slept, which were uncomfortably hot and stuffy spots during the summer months. Many shopkeepers used the upper floors as living quarters and the lower levels as places of business. Those shops lacking signs advertising their trade were distinguished from residences by their showy multi-paned bulk windows or drop-leaf shutters on the ground floor which displayed their products.

As Eliza and Robert hurried along, they noticed some businesses had already extended the lower half of their shutters, allowing air to circulate within, while also providing open-air product placement, and Robert caught a pleasant whiff of freshly baked bread as they passed a baker's shop. These were the early versions of modern retail stores, allowing residents to window shop. The open shutters' upper half also helped cut the glare from the sun as it rose higher in the sky and shielded goods from rain during inclement weather.

As Dock Street curved into Second Street, they walked past the City Tavern, a popular meeting place for Philadelphia notables, including merchants, politicians, and businessmen. A large cloth awning protected its front steps from sun and rain. Later in the day, a steady clientele of men would be streaming in and out as they all hoped to catch the latest news. Like many of the other buildings, angled wooden planks marked the bulkhead entrance doors to the underground cellar, which stood open as workers unloaded casks of wine and goods, causing Eliza and Robert to steer clear of the bustling activity.

Next door, the white marble-faced Bank of Pennsylvania[1] building seemed to glow in contrast to the ruddy brick structures surrounding it. Built in the Greek Revival archi-

City Tavern, left, and the Bank of Pennsylvania, the first Greek Revival building in the United States. Shown in a 1799 Birch's view, both buildings were
centers of business during the early republic. This was a familiar scene to
those walking to the markets a few blocks to the north. (*Library of Congress*)

tectural style that became popular at the turn of the nineteenth century, it looked like an ancient temple, with six
Ionic-style columns gracing both the front and back of the
building, supporting large porticos. At the top sat a circu-
lar dome with a rounded roof that housed a huge lantern;
the banking room was located in a rotunda directly underneath.

As they approached the High Street area, home to many
of the wealthier merchant population, the buildings
became even more ornate. Some of the wooden front doors
were topped by a pitched roof overhang and a bit of fancy
scrollwork and adorned with polished silver knockers and
handles. Many of the white marble steps leading to these
entrances were bordered by decorative wrought iron rail-
ings. In front of a few houses, women were scrubbing steps,
doors, and windows, as per the daily Philadelphia custom
of keeping these front entrances immaculately clean.

Robert liked to spot the hitching posts, which were often more elaborate in this part of the city, with fluted iron shafts topped with a swan shape or a horse's head instead of the common plain round or square wooden posts.

The gable roofs of the market houses soon came into view, and Robert strained to get a better look, tugging at his mother's hand. Supported by sturdy brick columns, they were open on both sides and lined the middle of High Street for about six blocks to form a central covered building. As they approached the entrance, the stalls were already buzzing with activity. The lanterns suspended from the high arched roof overhead gave off a cozy light. The sellers had already spread clean white cloths over the counters and then stacked and prepared items for sale, each seeking to create the most appealing display. Shelves between the columns were filled with a variety of local and imported goods, including breads, flour, spices, coffee, and tea. Cuts of meat, small game, and fowl hung from racks on iron hooks. Along the curbs, farmers had parked their canvas-covered wagons containing an abundance of garden-fresh produce and dairy items.

Eliza's first stop was the Jersey Market shed between Second and Front streets where she was hoping to purchase some freshly picked apples. They arrived at her favorite fruiterer's stall and she surveyed the colorful, artfully arranged produce. The apples she was seeking were neatly piled into baskets in front, surrounded by displays of pears, plums, a few melons, and some late-season blackberries and raspberries. Just then the bells began ringing to announce that selling could begin. A crowd had already formed, but she was a well-known customer and therefore one of the first served. She carefully chose some Newtown Pippins, making sure their skins were smooth and unblemished. After paying the fruiterer, she lined the bottom of her son's basket with the rosy, sweet-smelling fruit and they proceed-

The terminus of the Jersey Market at Front Street photographed in 1859, the year it was torn down. Built in 1822 to improve the market, it housed a clock and bell to signal the beginning and closing of business. Mrs. Goodfellow purchased fresh vegetables, fruits, spices, dairy products, and meats at this location for the duration of her school and shop. (*Free Library of Philadelphia*)

ed through the covered stalls to the wagon that sold her favorite dairy items.

Newly laid eggs, tubs of butter, and crocks of soft cheese were attractively displayed, brought into town that morning from a cool springhouse. Anna, the Pennsylvania German woman selling the goods, smiled and nodded her head in greeting as she filled orders, while her daughter Polly shyly offered small cubes of creamy pale yellow cheese as samples to customers. Anna knew Eliza would want some of her fine butter, eggs, and cream and so quickly and expertly began to package them up. First she filled the shiny butter kettle Eliza had brought along and then carefully protected the several eggs Eliza required for the day's baking by gently layering them in some straw and nestling them in her basket. Next she took Eliza's crock, poured in some rich cream, and tightly sealed the lid. As Eliza reached in her pocket for a few coins, Anna held up a finger to wait a minute, and quickly reached around to grab a small cherry

The stalls of the High Street Market in the early nineteenth century. (from *America's Most Historic Highway*)

tartlet for Robert to nibble. She placed it in his hand, flashing a wide smile. He grinned back and murmured a shy "thank you." Anna was also selling peach butter, sauerkraut, sausage, and a variety of freshly baked cakes, doughnuts, and pies, and gestured in their direction to see if Eliza was interested. She smiled back, but shook her head no. She was in a rush to get to her final stop, the butcher, so she paid for her purchases and hurried on.

Although the market was a busy place, it was all very organized and orderly. Some folks were short on time, like Eliza, but nobody pushed or jostled, and many finely dressed women strolled slowly about, browsing while servants followed behind them, toting market baskets. Eliza and Robert continued through the covered marketplace, pausing at the open alley between the stalls to see a few horses tied to hitching posts, twitching their tails to shoo away some late-summer flies. These side alleys were roped off on market days to prevent horse and carriage traffic from entering the covered sheds. Through the alley they could see some street vendors strolling about with their carts and wheelbarrows getting ready to peddle their wares: waffles, fresh fruit, cakes, bread, and muffins.

When they reached the butcher Eliza preferred, fresh cuts of beef, pork, mutton, veal, and dressed poultry hung from the hooks of his stall. It was the poultry she wanted, as she was planning to teach the students in her cooking school how to make chicken fricassee later that day. As with the other merchants, she was well acquainted with the butcher, and he made sure she was able to purchase three fine birds already dressed, which he assured would be delivered to her Dock Street shop later that morning.

She had brought Robert to help carry everything. With her shopping list complete, they headed home to prepare for her students' arrival and the day's cooking lessons.

Now, almost two hundred years later, this type of shopping is coming back into fashion. While farmers' markets in America never entirely went away, the convenience of supermarket shopping took over in the twentieth century. However, buying fresh and local (and now organic) foods is more and more popular as consumers seek to reduce their carbon footprint, food miles, and pesticide use, as well as support local farmers and preserve heirloom foods and traditions.

Taste is of course another huge benefit in using fresh, quality ingredients and was Mrs. Goodfellow's main objective, although she didn't have much of a choice in how she obtained her food. Living in a city, she could not easily grow her own produce or make her own butter and cheese. She had to shop at the local markets and was limited to what was sold there and what was imported from other locations.

However, luckily for her, nineteenth-century Philadelphia was a treasure trove of foodstuffs. In addition to the locally produced fruits, vegetables, dairy products, and meats, an abundance of exotic foods such as bananas, pineapples, and coconuts worked their way up the east coast of North America from the Caribbean, and citrus fruits such as lemons and oranges, as well as the Madeira wine favored by Thomas Jefferson, were shipped from Lisbon, Portugal.

Until the mid-1800s, Philadelphia's commercial success was very much determined by its port location along the Delaware River. The time right after the Revolutionary War was a particularly prosperous period for the city as it served as the temporary capital of the United States from 1790 to 1800, becoming a hub of political and trade activity for the new nation. A precursor to today's busy train stations and airports, Philadelphia's waterfront was the site of constant motion, bringing both people and merchandise to and from the city.[2] This was highly beneficial to Mrs. Goodfellow and her business.

The large variety and quantity of foods available in Philadelphia allowed her to be extremely selective regarding the quality of the food she bought and used. This alternative was not available to many people in the early 1800s, and it definitely worked out to Mrs. Goodfellow's advantage. She felt very strongly that in order to turn out the best tasting and most visually appealing products, only the finest quality food items must be used in making them. She likewise would have wanted her students to learn using the best possible ingredients, and it is likely she developed marketplace connections to obtain the groceries needed to teach the lessons in her school.

Even before Philadelphia was laid out or settled, William Penn had the notion to create a wide main thoroughfare where markets could be held on regular days of the week under certain restrictions and rules, similar to the high-street shopping areas so popular in England. Prior to this, no town or city in the American colonies had a similar convenience for its residents. Because of the markets, people began to refer to the area as Market Street, and the name was officially changed from High Street to Market Street in the 1850s.[3]

The markets quickly became a favorite meeting place and focal point for Philadelphia town life. Since the market sheds were under cover, shoppers could browse freely in all kinds of weather, lingering to chat with friends and neighbors. It was a place to gossip and share news, and surely many ladies looked forward to their marketing as a result.

Along the sides of these sheds were heavy counters with padlocked cabinets underneath where the merchants could store amenities such as stools, baskets, measures, and wooden trays. Children enjoyed running along the counters when they were empty, jumping across the frequent breaks.[4]

Ladies and gentlemen, followed by their servants, would often sample goods before making a purchase. Taking a coin, they would skim a pat of butter at each stall until they found one that met their standards for taste and freshness. Operating under strict regulations, the markets were monitored by inspectors who seized items thought to be unwholesome and fined the respective sellers. For example, if a pound of butter looked small, they would weigh it; and if found to be underweight, it would be taken away and given to Pennsylvania Hospital to be used there. In addition, no smoking, vehicles, or animals were allowed in the market houses or stalls.[5]

Since Wednesdays and Saturdays were traditionally market days, traffic from the surrounding farms to Philadelphia would become heavy on Tuesdays and Fridays with Conestoga wagons carrying produce for the next day's market. Farm families would pile into the wagons with the goods, bringing blankets and food to camp overnight. These wagons were considered the freight cars of Pennsylvania—huge and heavy with monstrous wheels sometimes a foot wide. Shaped something like a boat, they were painted a bright red and blue and covered with white cloth tops. Then in these evenings prior to market day the bells of Christ Church (also referred to as the "butter bells") were rung to remind residents the following morning would be their chance to shop.[6]

Market rules prohibited these farmers from selling any goods on their way into Philadelphia, and the hucksters and peddlers who bought their wares and then resold them outside the market area had to wait until the market was open for at least two hours before trolling the city with their handcarts.

Although attending these vast markets may have been commonplace for Philadelphians, to those from out of town, it was a wonder to behold. Visitors would eagerly rise early with city residents to view the variety of items for sale beginning at 6 A.M., from newly picked flowers to fresh produce, dairy, and meats, as well as baked goods from the Pennsylvania German farm kitchens.[7]

One visitor in 1818 thought that the Philadelphia markets probably offered for sale the largest amount of fruits and vegetables in the world. The market began on the banks of the Delaware River and continued for a mile along High Street toward the city center. In addition to the produce brought in on wagons from surrounding farms, goods were also transported via river boats and ships from faraway locations. Light carts carried fish from New York and Burlington, New Jersey, which were packed in ice during the summer.[8]

Steam ferry boats were first used to cross the river in about 1810, allowing vehicles and passengers to travel

The Fish Market at Market and Front streets in 1850. (from *America's Most Historic Highway*)

between Camden, New Jersey, and Philadelphia.[9] Later in the century produce from western Pennsylvania was shipped by canal through the mountains to a mule-drawn railway which ran down High Street north of the market houses, all the way to Dock Street. The goods were then taken to warehouses near the Delaware River where the produce was shipped or distributed.[10]

The Fish Market was located right near the wharf area on the river. Fish, eel, and shellfish (oysters, clams, and lobsters) were sold here. Behind this, going toward the center of the city was the Jersey Market, which was filled with New Jersey produce, including herbs, vegetables, peaches, apples, plums, strawberries, and grapes. Beef, pork, and other farm-raised meats were sold in the meat section inside the market house. In addition, hunters brought game and wild fowl from the forest to sell; it was not unusual for wild turkeys to weigh twenty-five pounds or more, but these quickly became scarce as the area developed.[11]

On a visit to Philadelphia in the late 1820s, Frances Trollope of London remarked,

I was particularly requested to visit the market of Philadelphia, at the hour when it presented the busiest scene; I did so, and thought few cities had anything to show better worth looking at. The neatness, freshness, and entire absence of everything disagreeable to sight or smell, must be witnessed to be believed. The stalls were spread with snow-white napkins; flowers and fruit, if not quite of Paris or London perfection, yet bright, fresh, and fragrant; with excellent vegetables in the greatest variety and abundance, were all so delightfully exhibited, that objects less pleasing were overlooked and forgotten. In short, for the first time in my life, I thought a market a beautiful object.[12]

Although the market was a busy place, with people milling about in all directions, it was unusually calm. Both the buyers and sellers were quiet and polite as they went about their business; folks did not argue with each other. Friendly conversation and genial laughter were the typical noises. One visitor said it was like "a market of brothers."[13]

New York, Boston, Baltimore, and later Washington, D.C., had similar food markets, but Philadelphia's were continually referred to as the best in the country, and indeed often the world. The variety of foods for sale as well as the cleanliness of the stalls received the highest praise.[14] A visitor to the New York City markets in 1825 quipped that the "neatness and order fell below that of the Philadelphia market."[15]

And in 1802 when comparing Philadelphia's markets to those in Baltimore, Philadelphia merchant Thomas P. Cope wrote in his diary, "It does one good to walk thro' the Jersey Market and observe the spruce appearance of the blooming Quaker girls who came there to sell the various products of their industry. The nicely rigged, bucksome lass from Chester County with her butter wrapped in cloths as white as the driven snow and stored in a vessel as carefully scoured as if to serve at a wedding is a sight which, however grateful, you would in Baltimore look in vain." Cope also noted the contrast of the "decent appearance" of the butchers housed in the spacious, well-constructed Philadelphia Market House to the disgusting process in Baltimore by which "joints of veal and mutton were thrown in jumbled confusion and without much regard to cleanliness" on top of a dirty cloth strewn on the pavement.[16]

Indeed, the Philadelphia butchers must have been impressive to those lucky enough to experience the marketplace, as these gentlemen and their wares consistently got positive reviews from nineteenth-century observers. In 1826, Mrs. Anne Royall could have been describing the meat counter at a modern-day gourmet grocery: "Nothing can exceed the whiteness of the benches and stalls; the meat, which consists of every sort, is exquisitely neat, cut with the greatest care, smooth, as disposed upon tables, on cloths as white as the whitest cambric. The butchers wear a white linen frock, which might vie with a lady's wedding dress."[17]

Another visitor in 1820, James Flint, appreciated the cleanliness and civility of the market vendors: "If a speck is to be seen on the white apron of the butcher, it may be inferred that it came there on the same morning," he wrote. He described how girls arrived to the market on horseback or driving light wagons to sell their produce or dairy products. "Many of these females, I am told, are the daughters of farmers who are in good circumstances," he remarked. "Here are none of the lazzaroni hucksters of fruit and sweet-meats, that form such a deplorable spectacle in the finest cities of Britain."[18]

But even Philadelphia's market was limited by the seasons. Produce would have obviously been more bountiful in warmer months, but the summer heat would also cause meats and dairy products to go bad more quickly. While visiting Philadelphia in 1807, British citizen Charles Janson observed that because of climate differences, U.S. residents had fashioned seasons for the "articles of life" which were barely perceived in London.[19] Another Englishman, Isaac Weld, was amazed how Eastern U.S. summers could taint meat in just a day, poultry was usually killed only four hours before it was needed, and milk often spoiled in just one or two hours.[20]

However, in true Quaker fashion, the thrifty Philadelphians devised a way to enjoy the morning's milk that had turned to curd by the evening. They called it "bonny clabber," and served it with honey, sugar, or molasses. Some likened it to custard, and the ladies were particularly fond of it.[21]

In the 1820s and 1830s, improvements in ice harvesting made the ice business more profitable and large companies were formed in northern U.S. cities. Shipments of ice to southern locales also increased, but because of transportation costs ice shipments and icehouses were more common in the North.[22]

Thomas Moore patented the first domestic icebox in 1803, which enabled city residents to keep perishables such as meat, dairy products, and fruit cold and fresh. Iceboxes were usually one wooden box inside another, with an insulating material in between. A tin container at the top held the ice and the lower one kept the food. Blocks of ice were sold in baskets, and would only last about a day, even inside the insulated icebox.[23] A drip pan on the bottom caught the melting water. This was emptied when full and new ice was added.[24]

Although iceboxes throughout the nineteenth century were simple and inefficient, the ability to have ice at home year-round greatly changed American eating and drinking habits. Larger amounts of perishable foods could be purchased at a time, and ice cream and other cold desserts were more easily crafted.[25]

By 1840 Eliza Leslie described refrigerators as "conveniences no family should be without." She even suggested that households should have two—one for dairy products and one for meats.[26] Although prices for these luxury appliances could range from twenty to two hundred dollars, they soon became a fixture in American homes.

It is not known when Mrs. Goodfellow first utilized an icebox in her shop and school. She surely would have purchased one by the time she moved her business to Washington Square in the 1840s, as it was advertised as a fancy cake bakery and ice cream saloon. Refrigeration would have also made her teaching much easier, giving her the ability to keep some perishable items on hand.

Regardless of when Mrs. Goodfellow gained access to home refrigeration, her primary and most alluring ingredient did not need to be kept cold. The key factor in her success was sugar.

Initially considered a precious spice, sugar was kept under lock and key like saffron, cinnamon, and cumin.[27] The art of manufacturing confections and sweet preparations was mainly limited to the apothecaries and physicians of Europe as a way to disguise their medicines.[28]

By the late 1600s, demand for sugar was so strong that it began to be seen as a type of food, rather than a spice, medicine, or flavor enhancer,[29] and the making of confectionery for pure enjoyment purposes developed into a separate and distinct business.[30] As a result, sugar cane became the most significant tropical export during the seventeenth and eighteenth centuries, supporting the early colonial empires of the Dutch, French, and English.[31]

Britons especially developed a sweet tooth, and the nation would go to great lengths to obtain sugar for its citizens. While initially monopolizing the sugar industry, exporting twice as much as it consumed, Britain eventually began importing and consuming more and more sugar, and exporting very little.

By the 1700s sugar was a symbol of economic power and luxury, not only for Europeans, but also for colonial Americans.[32] The British Quakers and Germans who settled Philadelphia were both heavy sugar users and pastry bakers, and brought their sweet-making expertise with them, as did the French once they arrived. They opened pastry shops, also known as "confectioners," in America starting in the eighteenth century. The sweets they sold were very much luxury items,[33] such as preserved and candied fruit, syrups and fine sugar work, as well as small pastries and cakes. Some were made by the confectioners themselves, and some were imported from the West Indies or London.[34]

Confectioners often had a "confectionery line" of items (candies, sweetmeats, etc.), in addition to a general assortment of cakes and biscuits, ice creams, cordials, jellies, custards, and tarts. But it appears there were confectioners who were pure candy makers (they did not use flour in their shop), and others who also made pastry (like Mrs. Goodfellow). This reflects the degree of specialization in both professions.[35]

A skilled confectioner could make a good deal of money because the public was willing to pay considerable sums for the beautifully handcrafted indulgences they produced. It was not easy to make them at home due to the artistic talents and equipment required, which helped to ensure demand.[36]

Fruiterers also often sold extravagant imported sweets such as Bordeaux prunes, almonds, lemons and limes, raisins, currants, cordials, and licorice. In fact, one of the earliest references to confectioners in Philadelphia was in 1765; a man named Abraham Smith ran a fruit business and sold a few simple candies.[37]

In June of that same year, German immigrant John William Millers placed an advertisement in the *Pennsylvania Gazette* announcing a huge display of sugar work he had sculpted. Millers claimed to have worked for the royal Prussian family, and the sculpture was a depiction of a grand temple housing the king of Prussia and goddess Pallas, as well as Prussian guards and a procession of carriages pulled by exotic animals such as lions, elephants, and camels. Millers hoped to bring patrons to his shop by showing his incredible artistry. Indeed, Philadelphians came in droves to view this sugar work, at first paying eighteen pence apiece to see it. Millers offered refunds for those who felt the sculpture was not as mentioned, and lowered the fee to six pence in October when the number of visitors began to drop. For sale to the public he offered finer confections for gentlemen's tables, weddings, or other entertainments, which he claimed were reasonably priced.[38]

It is not known whether this large-scale advertising enhanced Millers's business or not. However, it does show that as a variety of cultures continued to populate Philadelphia and began to create a new American cuisine, the love of sugar remained a constant.

Still a rather expensive commodity in Goodfellow's time, white sugar and its products were usually reserved for the well-to-do. As acknowledged by Philadelphia pastry chef Robert Bennett, these "baked goods and confectionery played a special role in Philadelphia's culinary history. Due to the high cost of ingredients such as sugar, chocolate,

Confectionery—A term that has come to represent a vast number of edibles or compounds that have sugar as a base or principal ingredient.

Pastry—When first introduced, pastries referred to both sweet and savory dishes that featured a "paste" of heavy dough made from flour, fat, and liquid. Today the term encompasses a wide variety of baked or fried sweet foods, and a paste is not necessarily a main ingredient.

Sweetmeats—Commonly used from medieval times through the end of the nineteenth century, it simply means a sweet food, which was often put on the table at the end of a meal. Wet sweetmeats were eaten with a spoon and included jellies, creams, floating islands, and preserved fruits in heavy syrups. Dry varieties included nuts, fruit peels, glacéed fruit, sugared comfits and flowers, chocolates, and small cakes.

Sugar work—Large ornamental structures, sometimes edible, sometimes purely artistic, constructed from sugar paste, almond paste, and royal icing.

nuts, citrus, and spices, sweet dishes were greatly prized. Indeed, only wealthy Philadelphians could afford to prepare or purchase these items with regularity. Research, however, shows that shops around the city sold expensive, imported ingredients from Europe, the Caribbean, and neighboring colonies, and confectioners selling prepared goods maintained a steady patronage."[39]

This access to foreign imports is apparent in looking at the goods sold by another early Philadelphia confectioner, Elizabeth Hannah Willing. A bill from Mrs. Willing's shop dated December 8, 1774, lists a variety of products containing exotic ingredients, including preserved ginger, pickled mangoes, and guava jelly.[40]

Sebastian Henrion was one of the best known and innovative of Philadelphia's confectioners. He sold imported chocolate and bonbons, as well as nuts, syrups, and fruits both fresh and candied.[41] He joined forces with A. J. Chauveau in 1844 and together they became world famous for their cream caramels, which they shipped to New York and Caracas, as well as to London, Paris, and Vienna.[42] They were also the first to manufacture gumdrops, jujube paste, and marshmallows in America, and in 1845 imported the first revolving steam pan for large-scale candy production in the United States.[43]

Finding accurate statistics regarding the number of sugary items sold is difficult because many confectioners and pastry chefs combined their sweets offerings with other products and services, and there was much crossover with occupational terminology. However, all the figures show that the use of sugar in America continued to rise at a steady pace throughout the eighteenth and nineteenth centuries.[44]

By the beginning of the 1800s, large-scale sugar production had become possible by the unfortunate spread of slave labor in the Caribbean, and by the 1820s Americans were well acquainted with sugar, although it was still considered a luxury item for most. Then sugar processing improvements, combined with the development of beet sugar, increased the supply and lowered costs.[45]

Sugar use in America really accelerated at this point, as more and more people were able to afford it. This development, in addition to better refrigeration, probably played a part in Goodfellow's shop expansion in the late 1830s. Her clientele would have increased, and she would have been able to keep dairy products fresher longer and make larger and more cost-efficient quantities of ice cream and other treats, such as blancmange, that had to be kept cool.

Philadelphians were among the first Americans to serve frozen desserts, and "Philadelphia ice cream" became the standard of excellence. Its list of ingredients was simple, but all had to be the finest quality: pure cream, ripe fruit, and sugar—no thickening substances were added. Again, Philadelphia's Quaker influence was coming into play. The city's residents adamantly claimed that their "Philadelphia-style" ice cream (made without eggs) was tastier than New York's recipe, or even the French method which used a custardy base of beaten eggs.[46]

Ice cream was advertised in Philadelphia newspapers as early as 1784, and ice cream houses cropped up soon after.[47] While the ice cream served in Goodfellow's shop may not have been considered one of her signatures, it is important to note that she did begin advertising it after her expansion in the 1830s, probably to keep up with the competition.

The members of Philadelphia high society who craved all these sweet treats kept Goodfellow busy and provided an outlet for her products and services. When these wealthy families gave parties or banquets, guests expected to see complicated and fanciful desserts such as charlottes, creams, meringues, jellies, blancmanges, tarts, syllabubs, soufflés, and special ice creams.[48] Some of the specialties sold by Goodfellow included lemon pudding, Queen cake, cheesecakes, citron cake, jumbles, kisses, macaroons, and apple pie.[49]

Society ladies would go to great lengths to arrange luscious and eye-catching dessert tables, trying to outdo each other in creating unique and artistic spreads that would be discussed by their guests afterward. This feat was of such importance that these women's status as hostesses was often at stake each time they held a social event. It was a popular trend for a table brimming with sweetmeats to be hidden or covered, and then revealed with a grand gesture as the high point of the festivities, usually around 11 P.M.[50] In addition to the desserts, rich sideboard dishes and regional specialties such as terrapin soup and oysters were also popular.

As Quaker Martha J. Garrett writes in her *Memories of Philadelphia in the Nineteenth Century,*

> Simple tea parties—by which we understood going out to supper in a friend's home—were common among us. For such occasions the table was loaded with good things, all put on at once, and set with taste and harmony. A silver cake basket might occupy the centre of the table, and pretty dishes of clear preserves the middle of one side. The lady of the house sat behind the tea service, placed on a large tray. At the other end of the table was the principal dish, which might be oysters, while plates of hot rolls, muffins, or "Sally Lunn," and olives and sliced tongue, appeared in symmetrical arrangement. Ice cream, lemonade or apples and nuts might be brought into the parlor about nine o'clock.[51]

The women hosting these social events needed to learn how to put together appropriate menus and then either make these items on their own or be able to instruct their cooks how to do so. As Louise Conway Belden notes in her book *The Festive Tradition,* "A hostess could rise to heights of excellence or sink to mediocrity in the opinions of guests who judged her efforts not alone on the quantity and quality of the dessert but on its novelty, beauty and wit."[52] It was a rite of passage for young ladies to be able to make at least some fine cakes and confectionaries; in fact, it was often a way to attract a husband. Goodfellow's school had found its niche.

THREE

Dining Out

$\mathcal{A}s$ with many other culinary advancements, the evolution of the food service industry, particularly restaurants, can be traced back to the French.[1] Although the idea of taverns and inns as places to eat and drink had been around for years, the French popularized the concept of restaurant dining. The main advantage of a restaurant was that it offered diners a choice rather than the limited selection available in taverns and boardinghouses. As noted by the French gastronome Antoine Brillat-Savarin, this concept allowed people to eat when they wanted, what they wanted and how much they wanted, knowing the cost in advance.[2] Early nineteenth-century Philadelphia was the perfect setting for this development.

Although British influence in the colonies had prejudiced Americans against French cookery, affluent Americans, particularly in Philadelphia, began to develop an appreciation for it, perceiving traditional English cookery to be less sophisticated. As a result, the city's significant French presence and awareness helped cultivate the idea of fine dining, as well as increase interest in French pastry-making and confectionery skills. The French alliance of 1778 added to this popularity, and the first four U.S. presidents enjoyed Parisian cuisine. Thomas Jefferson even brought a French chef to the White House.[3]

Many French came to the United States after the French Revolution and settled in Philadelphia, bringing their culinary expertise and pastry-making skills with them. The part of the city around Third and Fourth and Walnut streets near the Delaware River actually became a kind of French Quarter, and until the 1820s about one quarter of Philadelphians were of French descent.[4]

Additionally, others fled the French colony of Haiti during the slave rebellion there in the 1790s and relocated to Philadelphia. Some were upper-class mixed-race people with advanced culinary training who knew their services would be in demand in Philadelphia owing to the existing French influence and the city's role as the U.S. capital.[5] Here, they set up catering and pastry-making operations. Through their business presence and the wide renown they achieved, many new dishes were added to Philadelphia menus, including chicken croquettes and desserts such as meringue glace.[6]

West Indian immigrant Peter Augustin ran one of the most successful of these operations, making Philadelphia catering famous throughout the young country. His business was known to provide the best and most elegant food service at the city's social gatherings.[7] He had actually ended up in Washington, D.C., around 1815 after becoming the private chef to the Spanish ambassador. However once Augustin's wife became pregnant, she wanted to leave, since she didn't want to have her baby anywhere slavery was legal (which it still was in Washington at the time). He also turned down a job in a fancy Baltimore hotel because slavery was also legal in Maryland. And so they came to Philadelphia and established a culinary empire. The Augustins became fabulously rich catering private dinners and established restaurants later on.[8]

As interest in more innovative and sophisticated dishes increased, housewives began to feel the need to familiarize themselves with French culinary techniques in order to stay fashionable.[9] This may have helped increase attendance at Goodfellow's school. It is not known what training or experience she had with French cuisine, but recipes appear in cook-

Nightlife in Philadelphia—an Oyster Barrow in front of the Chestnut Street Theater, painted in 1813 and attributed to John Lewis Krimmel. Oysters were a quick and inexpensive food sold on the streets and in oyster houses throughout the city. (*Courtesy Metropolitan Museum of Art*)

books from this era, including one published by her student Eliza Leslie in 1832 entitled *Domestic French Cookery*.

It was around this time (the early nineteenth century) that the words "restaurant," "menu," and "café," as well as "à la" dishes came into use in Philadelphia and other U.S. cities.[10] Café Français in Philadelphia was one of the country's first "French" restaurants.[11] However, it was still mainly the wealthy that had a chance to enjoy a true restaurant experience, which was at first also reserved for men; women were not usually included. It was not until the twentieth century that the idea of "eating out" at a dining establishment became available and affordable to the general public.

A meal could be had in colonial America as early as the seventeenth century at a tavern, inn, or boardinghouse, but the cooking there was usually simple; supplying alcoholic beverages was often their primary business. Ordinaries were taverns similar to an eating-house, a cross between a restaurant and a boardinghouse. Oyster houses and coffee-houses also appeared in many coastal American cities in the eighteenth century. Oysters were abundant and inexpensive at the time and were often sold in these places on an all-you-can-eat basis for just a few cents. Coffee-houses were found near city financial districts and marketplaces and offered spirits as well as coffee, serving as sort of a business-man's tavern.[12]

In rural locations, taverns and inns were located on main thoroughfares and were sometimes simply log cabins or farmhouses. They served not only as rest stops for people traveling, but also as popular gathering places for the local residents. By 1840, there were about sixty taverns between Lancaster, Pennsylvania, and Philadelphia. Here travelers could expect a hot meal and a place to sleep.[13] Meals were offered at set times and quickly eaten; those who arrived after the dining hour were out of luck. Sleeping arrange-ments were crude—it was not unusual for people to share a room or even a bed.[14]

In towns and cities, taverns were traditionally central meeting places where individuals could conduct business, such as buying and selling ship's cargo, organizing new companies, and posting notices. They were also important socially as sites where news was shared, fraternal societies met, political discussions held, and dances and live music staged.[15]

Many Quakers were not keen on these activities beyond providing food and shelter, since taverns back in England were often viewed as corrupt places of ill repute, spawning public drunkenness and political deception.[16] However, the

The Yellow Springs, or Chester Springs "Watering Place" was described by its proprietor in this 1845 advertisement as being thirty-two miles from Philadelphia and of having "secured the services of the best cooks, Confectioners and Servants, by which efforts he hopes to render his Establishment both agreeable and stylish." (*Library of Congress*)

oldest inn or tavern in Philadelphia, the Blue Anchor, was ironically owned by a Quaker, George Guest. It was on this sandy beach along the Delaware that William Penn first stopped and "broke bread" upon his arrival in what was to become Pennsylvania. This house was the southwestern one in a row of houses on Front Street, which was known as Budd's Long Row and formed what is now the northwest corner of Front and Dock streets. The Blue Anchor was subsequently renamed the "Boatman and Call."[17]

The original tavern was viewed as Philadelphia's first place of business, "the proper key of the city," at the time. All boats made their landings here, and a public ferry carried people over Dock Creek to Society Hill, before the causeway and bridge over Front Street were built. Residents could also ride to Windmill Island, where there was a windmill for grinding their grain, or travel over to New

Jersey. As John Fanning Watson noted in his *Annals of Philadelphia and Pennsylvania*, "It was, in short, the busy mart for a few years of almost all the business the little town required."[18]

From this important Dock Street location, eating and drinking places multiplied throughout the city. A 1799 Philadelphia city directory lists 248 taverns, plus 42 combination taverns/boardinghouses.[19] Many were right along the wharves lining the Delaware River, conveniently located for all the ships coming in and out of Philadelphia's port. Sea captains could barter their goods, particularly perishables which had to be quickly sold before they spoiled due to the lack of refrigeration. Cargo was often auctioned on the docks to the local tavern owners and caterers.[20] Mrs. Goodfellow probably made some purchases in this manner, as her first shop and school would have been just a short walk away on Dock Street.

Although the city had quite a large number of these establishments for its size, this was not due only to the residents' drinking habits. It is more a direct result of the stream of immigrants coming into Philadelphia during the first half of the eighteenth century, as well as the large numbers of newcomers who made the city their home during and after the Revolution. In addition, the fact that Philadelphia was a port city meant that ships brought a steady flow of sailors and travelers to the area. All these people needed food and lodging, and many innkeepers and boardinghouse owners profited from the demand.[21]

There were more than two hundred boardinghouses in Philadelphia at the turn of the nineteenth century. Like the taverns, over half were clustered along the Delaware River, often side by side within a block of the waterfront. For example, Short Elbow Alley had four pairs of boardinghouses on both sides of the street as well as three taverns. Four boardinghouses were on Arch Street between Front

Street and the river, and the same size block of Spruce Street featured six boardinghouses and a tavern.[22]

Many boardinghouses were run by widows who needed an income after their husbands passed away. It appears that food service was not a top priority. In the early nineteenth century most boardinghouse-keepers offered three meals daily: breakfast, dinner, and tea. These were rushed affairs, served family style at set times. Food was quickly devoured, so latecomers would have ended up with cold scraps, if anything was left.[23]

Eliza Leslie's mother Lydia may have at least tried to improve the caliber of the dishes she served by enrolling young Eliza at Mrs. Goodfellow's. Perhaps other boardinghouse owners picked up on this idea, also sending daughters or employees to Mrs. Goodfellow for instruction. Goodfellow's original shop on Dock Street, and then the one on South Sixth Street, were both close to inns and boardinghouses, conveniently located for any women working at them to take classes.

An offshoot of the tavern model that developed in Philadelphia as a result of the large British influence was the idea of eating and drinking establishments as meeting places and information hubs for an elite upper-class clientele, mainly the city's merchants and other influential leaders.

Claiming to be the oldest social organization speaking the English language, "The Colony in Schuylkill" or "Schuylkill Fishing Company" was founded as a men's fishing club in 1732 by a few of the original Philadelphia settlers, many of whom immigrated with Penn to the New World. Their first meeting house, which they called "the castle," was built on the west side of the Schuylkill River when the area was still a wilderness. In 1781 the group was renamed the "State in Schuylkill" and for generations they fished in the city's streams, then cooked and ate what they caught themselves, each one serving the other.[24]

Also referred to as the "Fish House Club," members have always prepared their own food, and in the beginning devoted much time to hunting and fishing, enjoying the time spent outdoors and sticking to simple cooking techniques. For example, club rules stipulate that "high seasoning" should not be used when grilling steaks. Although city development, pollution, and overfishing have caused the club to move its location several times over the years, the citizens (as club members are called) still gather along the Schuylkill to feast on barbecued pork, grilled steaks, planked shad, and perch "thrown" in skillets, all prepared by club members and served with the group's famous Fish House Punch, a potent rum-based brew.[25]

Many members of the Fish House Club have also belonged to the Philadelphia Club, a private gentleman's club which claims to be the oldest metropolitan men's club in the United States. A group of men began meeting in a coffee-house at Fifth and Minor streets around 1830 to play cards. Joined by friends, they organized the Adelphia Club in 1834; the name soon became the Philadelphia Club. Since 1850 the club has occupied the Thomas Butler Mansion at 1301 Walnut Street and is known as the city's most exclusive club, its membership limited largely to old Philadelphia families. Prior to the 1950s, ladies were only admitted three times, for balls in 1851 and 1869, and a centenary tea in 1934 at which Mrs. John Markoe, the belle of the ball of 1869, poured tea for the distinguished veterans. Beginning in 1953, women have been allowed in as dinner guests, although they are still excluded from membership. Today members dine on Old Philadelphia-style lunches of chicken salad, fried oysters, and ham-and-veal pie.[26]

The London Coffee House was established in 1754 by newspaper publisher William Bradford and had a prime location—Front and High streets, overlooking the Delaware and next to the market stalls. Although coffee, tea, lemonade, and beer were served, its patrons preferred wine and liquor. Basically an upper-class tavern, the London Coffee House was the first stop for many ship captains and travelers; messages were exchanged and auctions posted and held. Merchants gathered at noon to read newspapers, discuss prices, and schedule goods for shipping.[27]

However, as the city grew, the import merchants did not need to be so close to the marketplace, and they began to separate into groups. When the City Tavern opened on Second Street in Philadelphia in December 1773, it soon became the fashionable spot for the merchant class, exceeding the old London Coffee House in popularity. A five-story building with kitchens, a bar room, two coffee rooms, and three dining rooms, it also boasted the "second largest ballroom in the New World," five lodging rooms, and servants' quarters. The tavern became the premier entertainment spot for wealthy Philadelphians, featuring a continuous succession of banquets and balls.[28]

Wild game, fresh fish, seasonal fruits and vegetables, and local wines were enjoyed by men of all social classes at the City Tavern. Sample dishes would have included hearty fare such as chicken or pork cooked with Madeira wine, turkey stew with fried oysters, ham-and-veal pie, and West Indies pepper pot soup; as well as desserts such as pastries, puddings, and fruit pies and cobblers.[29]

In addition to its reputation for food, the tavern had many interesting uses throughout the late eighteenth century. In the fall of 1774 it became the unofficial meeting place of the delegates before and after sessions of the first Continental Congress, which was assembled at nearby Carpenters' Hall. It was used by both Continental and

British armies to house prisoners of war, and military courts-martial were held there. Washington used the location as his headquarters briefly in 1777, and the tavern hosted a banquet in his honor in 1789 as he passed through Philadelphia on his way to New York for his presidential inauguration.[30]

Also in 1789 the City Tavern's two front rooms were rented and turned into the Merchant's Coffee House and Place of Exchange. A portico was added, and its former smaller rooms opened into one big entrance room.[31] The tavern was damaged by fire in 1834 but never properly repaired, and therefore was torn down twenty years later. One newspaper claimed it had been "immolated on the altar of improvement." Today, a reconstruction of the tavern on the original site at Second and Walnut streets serves typical eighteenth-century dishes.[32]

Hotels also became places for the elite to meet and dine, in addition to providing accommodations for well-to-do travelers. Elizabeth and Daniel Rubicam owned the Washington Hotel at 20 South Sixth Street in Philadelphia, which became well-known for providing superb food and first-rate lodging.

Mrs. Rubicam was best known for her green turtle and terrapin soups. Green turtle soup was prepared using huge sea turtles that were caught in the Caribbean and shipped north. It was highly esteemed, and as a result these turtles soon became scarce and very expensive. Terrapins were smaller turtles found more locally in the Chesapeake, New Jersey's Egg Harbor, and the Delaware Bay and became a substitute for green turtle.[33]

A list of articles sold in the Philadelphia markets in 1818 refers to them as "tarapins," or bay tortoises. The price was from $1 to $2 per dozen. Prior to this they had been eaten by slaves in Delaware, Maryland, and Virginia; the slave-owners eventually realized what a delicacy they had been

An 1840s watercolor of James M. Sanderson's Franklin House Hotel on Chestnut Street. (*Library of Congress*)

missing.[34] Food connoisseurs in Britain also quickly picked up on this fact, and Londoner Frank Schloesser praises them in *The Greedy Book*: "One of the most valuable products of the United States (gastronomically speaking), the terrapin must be eaten to be believed. It must also be specially imported. It is a species of turtle—but even more so—and quite exquisite in its subtlety."[35]

The Rubicams capitalized on this discovery, gaining status as the first caterers in Philadelphia who presented terrapin as a gourmet dish. When Mrs. Rubicam took over managing the business after the death of her husband, a large portion of the fame she achieved as a cook was due to the way she dressed terrapin. In 1869, *The Universal Recipe Book* by H. W. Harper refers to terrapin as "a favorite dish for suppers and parties, and, when well cooked, they are certainly very delicious. Many persons in Philadelphia have made themselves famous from cooking this article alone.

Mrs. Rubicam, during her lifetime, always stood first in that way."[36]

Mrs. Rubicam's version of terrapin soup was considered so delectable that it became a standard item for caterers not only in Philadelphia, but in New York and Baltimore as well. James M. Sanderson, a fellow Philadelphian who was chef and owner of Franklin House Hotel, went so far as to describe Mrs. Rubicam as the creator of terrapin cookery in his cookbook. Eliza Leslie also published Mrs. Rubicam's terrapin recipe in her 1837 book *Directions for Cookery*, but did not cite her as the source.[37]

TERRAPINS

Have ready a pot of boiling water. When it is boiling very hard put in the terrapins, and let them remain in it till quite dead. Then take them out, pull off the outer skin and the toe-nails, wash the terrapins in warm water and boil them again, allowing a tea-spoonful of salt to each terrapin. When the flesh becomes quite tender so that you can pinch it off, take them out of the shell, remove the sand-bag, and the gall, which you must be careful not to break, as it will make the terrapin so bitter as to be uneatable. Cut up all the other parts of the inside with the meat, and season it to your taste with black and cayenne pepper, and salt. Put all into a stew-pan with the juice or liquor that it has given out in cutting up, but not any water. To every two terrapins allow a quarter of a pound of butter divided into pieces and rolled in flour, two glasses of Madeira, and the yolks of two eggs. The eggs must be beaten, and not stirred in till a moment before it goes to table. Keep it closely-covered. Stew it gently till everything is tender, and serve it up hot in a deep dish.

Terrapins, after being boiled by the cook, may be brought to table plain, with all the condiments separate, that the company may dress them according to taste.

For this purpose heaters or chafing dishes must be provided for each plate.[38]

Mrs. Rubicam may have actually been a competitor to Mrs. Goodfellow, as it is thought that she also provided cooking instruction to wealthy ladies. According to food historian William Woys Weaver, it stands to reason that if she created terrapin cookery in the early 1800s, she must have taught other people how to do it because there was a trick to cooking these turtles without making the whole soup bitter.[39] The Rubicams' hotel was not far from Goodfellow's second shop location, so perhaps they even worked together rather than competed in order to maximize their profit. It is also possible that Mrs. Rubicam taught the recipe to Mrs. Goodfellow who then incorporated it into her classes, which would explain how the recipe was known to Eliza Leslie.

A reference is made to the teaching skills of these two ladies in a 1914 historical perspective about the old Patterson Mansion in Philadelphia. A member of Philadelphia's wealthy merchant class and a veteran of the War of 1812, General Robert Patterson was well-known throughout the city during his lifetime. He had married Sarah Engle of Germantown in 1817. In the article Sarah Patterson is described as "an intellectual woman and gifted musician, whose love of society and gracious charm of manner rendered her a perfect fit helpmeet for her distinguished husband. . . . Mrs. Patterson was a wonderful housekeeper, having been taught the art by both Mrs. Rubicam and Mrs. Goodfellow."[40]

Rubicam recipes for dishes other than terrapin can be found in nineteenth-century manuscript cookbooks. One owned by Ellen Markoe Emlen includes chickens curried and Rubicam Pudding.[41]

RUBICAM PUDDING
14 eggs
1 qt cream or rich milk, quite fresh
1 vanilla bean

1/2 lb sifted white sugar
1/4 lb of bloom raisins, stoned and cut in half
2 wine glasses of brandy
A wee pinch of salt
1/2 a nutmeg grated
This pudding is always eaten quite cold.
If this pudding is cooked too long it will become watery
and not eatable, it must be watched.

Another famous Philadelphia hotel that had a restaurant was the Mansion House Hotel, launched in 1807 by William Renshaw out of the Bingham mansion on Third Street. It had become fashionable in the early part of the nineteenth century to open an inn or tavern in a house of historical significance, particularly the residences of Philadelphia's founding fathers or places frequented by Revolutionary War heroes. The Mansion House's former owners, Mr. and Mrs. William Bingham, were of the Philadelphia elite merchant class, epitomizing social prestige, wealth, and luxury. Their house was considered one of the most elegant in Philadelphia, if not all of America. Renshaw soon left this location in 1812 to open the "New Mansion House Hotel" on Market Street, but returned two years later and stayed there until it was destroyed by fire in 1823.[42]

The hotel was later rebuilt and reopened by Chester Bailey, and eventually put under the proprietorship of Joseph Head. Originally a member of Philadelphia's upper-class society, Head had the unfortunate experience of losing most of his money. He then decided to use his knowledge of fine dining to open a "Private Gentlemen's Restaurant and ClubHouse" at the corner of Columbia Avenue (now Seventh Street) and Walnut, in what had first been the McClellan, and then later the Randall family mansion. He established himself there and then took over the larger Mansion House until it was badly damaged by fire in 1847, when the hotel was closed.[43]

Head was serious and enthusiastic about gastronomy, even making his way over to France to learn French culinary techniques and using this knowledge to open a French cooking school at the Mansion House Hotel in the late 1830s. However, unlike Mrs. Goodfellow, Head was probably teaching other men to be professional cooks.[44]

Even confectionery shops became places to go out to get something to eat, especially ice cream, a Philadelphia favorite. Many of these shops would provide a pleasant garden setting and fireworks to enhance the experience of enjoying the sweet, creamy treat. In the 1790s Frenchman Peter Bossee (sometimes referred to as Bossu) opened Bossee's Gardens, which included music and fireworks, and by 1800 began advertising Bossee's Ice Cream House which offered ice cream, syrups, French cordials, cakes, claret, and jellies.[45]

The most popular of these open-air ice cream eateries was Vauxhall Gardens, a perfectly manicured botanical garden named after the famous London attraction, featuring rare trees and decorative accents such as Chinese bridges and a pagoda. Ice cream was prepared in the Italian manner—molded into fruit shapes including pineapples, strawberries, and lemons, as well as orange-flavored goldfish. Fireworks were part of the festivities, and in 1825 Vauxhall even presented a dramatic re-creation of Mt. Vesuvius erupting.[46]

Other ice cream eateries were ice cream parlors and dining saloons. The main difference between the two was that ice cream parlors had carpeting and the saloons had bare floors (the type of shop Mrs. Goodfellow opened with her son in 1837). Both were popular with prosperous middle-class customers who enjoyed the elaborate interior (which often featured fancy tables, gilded picture frames, and shiny mirrors) as much as the treats served there. Both places usually featured a candy counter on one side, and a soda fountain which sold ice cream on the opposite. Or the ice cream may have been served in the back section of the building, with a small bakery on one side of the front and the candy and soda fountain on the other. Many owners would temporarily convert their ice cream parlors to oyster bars during the winter months, serving oysters, sandwiches, cake, and coffee.[47]

In 1859 Jos. Garland and Bros. advertised their "New confectionary and ice cream saloon" located at 926 Chestnut Street. Hailed as a "ladies and gents dining saloon," it featured "foreign and domestic confections, including ice creams, jellies, water ices, and fruits, as well as plain and fancy assorted cakes, fine pastries, &c." The establishment was also available to rent for large or small supper parties, and they would cater elsewhere as well, offering free delivery of their goods to private parties and weddings.[48] One can imagine it to be a popular social place for young men courting their ladies.

Parkinson's and Isaac Newton's were well-known Philadelphia spots for providing exquisite frozen treats and other confections. At Parkinson's, ice cream was served in long-necked champagne glasses, with vanilla and lemon being the most popular flavors. One patron wrote, "In the summer season, immense quantities of the finest ice cream are sold in Philadelphia. Indeed the city vaunts itself on producing the best ice cream in the world; and strangers generally give the preference to that which is sold at such establishments as Parkinson's and Isaac Newton's over any which is to be found in our other great cities."[49]

The Parkinson family name became synonymous with fine ice creams and confections throughout the United States in the mid-1800s. This culinary dynasty can be traced back to George Parkinson, who bought the Pennsylvania Arms tavern in 1818. His wife Eleanor opened a confectionery shop next door, and it became so well-known and lucrative that they joined forces, eventually including their son James in the business. Mother and son published the cookbook *The Complete Confectioner* in 1844, and in addition to selling sweets, they also ran a restaurant at 180 Chestnut Street. Philadelphia society continually marveled at James's culinary skills and innovative techniques, including for example, his invention of champagne frappe à la glace in 1850.[50]

In addition to the French-style pastries and sweets that had become fashionable in Philadelphia, those made according to Italian technique became popular as well. A confectioner and distiller named Lawrence Astolfi announced in an 1817 newspaper that he had just returned from Italy where he received training in sugar work and pastry-making in order to bring this knowledge back to Philadelphia. The advertisement also declares that he brought back with him some highly skilled confectioners, many of whom had been employed in the Courts of Naples and Rome, as well as other principal Italian cities. In addition to the pastry and desserts for sale to private families and public companies, his shop at 136 Market Street also featured a coffee room in the "European style," which sold delicate cordials and a variety of elegantly molded ice creams.[51] Another ad in 1818 mentions a shop run by a Mr. Charrier, which sold all kinds of fresh pastry in addition to "Coffee and Chocolate, served up in the Italian style."[52]

And in a nineteenth-century version of today's fast food, Philadelphia businessmen were known to pick up "little dainties" at an eating house or pastry shop to take the edge off of their late-afternoon hunger when dining later in the day was fashionable.[53] An example of some of these offerings appeared in an 1817 issue of *Poulson's Daily Advertiser* which announced for sale "Pepper Pot and Pastry: Made and sold in Cherry Street, No. 136, between Seventh and Eighth streets, on the south side—where also may be had, pickle pipers and other little niceties, from 11 in the morning until 10 in the evening."[54] A Philadelphia tradition, "pepper pot" was soup flavored with a bouquet garni of locally available herbs including sweet marjoram, thyme, parsley, a carrot, a leek, and a sharp red pepper.[55] And "pickle pipers" can be assumed to mean "pickled peppers."

Street vendors were another popular source of a small bite to eat. Pepper pot soup was commonly sold this way, especially in and around the High Street markets. Vendors with pushcarts holding a big vat of the spicy soup would peddle it door-to-door; others would sell it from their market stalls.[56] Waffles were also sold by street vendors who baked them over charcoal burners affixed to their horse-drawn carts.[57] Pastries such as cherry tartlets and small "Dutch cakes," which were oblong-shaped and iced, were piled on trays and sold by hawkers to children for six cents.[58]

While all these dining opportunities provided another outlet for the wealthy to make food purchases, possibly taking business away from Goodfellow's shop and catering service, they also showed the world that Philadelphia was a place where excellent and unique cooking could be enjoyed. These folks and places were essentially trend-setters, creating not only foods distinctive to the Philadelphia region, but also helping to develop an American style. Mrs. Goodfellow was right in the thick of all this—she knew where her business would thrive.

Mrs. Goodfellow's school set her apart from other pastry chefs and confectioners in Philadelphia. Word of mouth is the best form of advertising, especially in those days of limited press coverage, and she used her two businesses in tandem to market her goods and services. Women may have initially patronized her shop to purchase some cakes and other dainties for a tea they were hosting, and then learned she was giving instruction in how to make them. They could have then enrolled their daughters or even signed up for classes themselves. The news would spread to others within their social circle, ensuring Mrs. Goodfellow a constant supply of customers and students. She probably would have done well in New York, Boston, or Baltimore at the turn of the nineteenth century, but not as successfully as in Philadelphia, the wealthiest city and food capital of the United States.

Sunday Morning in front of the Arch Street Meeting House, Philadelphia. This watercolor from 1813, attributed to John Lewis Krimmel, shows the dress of a well-to-do Quaker family on their way to or from meeting. The daughters are representative of those who would have attended Mrs. Goodfellow's Cooking School. (*Courtesy Metropolitan Museum of Art*)

FOUR

Mrs. Goodfellow's Cooking School

Philadelphia, 64 Dock Street
Wednesday, September 20, 1815
9 a.m.

Mrs. Goodfellow was in her pastry shop boxing up an order of jumbles when Hannah hurried in from the kitchen, wrapped in her cloak and toting a market basket. She was on her way to Sim's Wharf to purchase some lemons. Mrs. Goodfellow had read in *Poulson's Daily Advertiser* the previous day that seventy boxes from Lisbon would be auctioned there beginning at 9 A.M. Mrs. Goodfellow took a few coins from the cash box and handed them to Hannah, who put them in the plain cotton pocket tied around her neck and headed out the door.

As Hannah started out on her errand, she saw a small group of women and girls approaching the shop. She turned around quickly to alert Mrs. Goodfellow that some of her students were arriving, and then continued toward the wharfs. Mrs. Goodfellow wiped her hands on her apron and walked around from behind the display counter to welcome the group of shy young ladies. Some were accompanied by their mothers or servants who carried baskets filled with groceries they had purchased on the way.

Like Mrs. Goodfellow, several of the women and their daughters wore plain gray linen dresses typical of the Quaker fashion, with white caps to cover their heads. The servants also dressed in plain grays and browns, but their clothing was homespun. Other ladies, however, were wearing gowns or skirts that were brighter shades of blues and yellows, and some even had frills around their necks, as some Friends had begun to break away from the traditional unadorned Quaker dress. The non-Quaker women were also dressed more colorfully because they were not bound to these customs.

As the ladies exchanged greetings, a few more girls came to the door, giggling and nibbling on waffles they had purchased from street vendors as they passed through the markets. Once they were all inside, Mrs. Goodfellow quickly counted heads and determined all ten girls were present and class could begin. They would be making white fricassee chicken, boiled artichokes, and lemon pudding, all of which would be suitable for a company dinner. When done, they would get to sample the dishes as part of their lesson.

The mothers and servants said their goodbyes and headed on their way. Mrs. Goodfellow called for Mary to come into the shop to take over in her absence and then ushered the girls down the cellar stairs to the kitchen. They hung up their capes and carefully unfolded the freshly starched white aprons and caps each had brought with her.

As they pinned the caps on each other and tied their hair up under the caps, they surveyed the kitchen that would serve as their classroom. Although it was in a basement, the floors and ceiling were made of grooved yellow pine boards and the walls were whitewashed plaster, which made the room seem brighter and more spacious. Some light was coming through the small cellar windows, which had been secured with wire netting on the outside to prevent rats from trying to sneak in.

Rich cooking smells permeated the close space. The cheesecakes Mrs. Goodfellow had prepared earlier were cooling on one of the large wall racks. On another rested little tins of heart- and diamond-shaped Queen cakes, waiting to be prettily decorated later with fluffy sweet meringue icing, colorful nonpareils, and fine sugar sand. The "Spanish Bunns" were baking in the oven, giving off a spicy, yeasty aroma. Mary had placed the artichokes in one of the iron pots hanging over the fire where they were now boiling gently, releasing a fresh, grassy smell.

On one end of the wooden work table Mrs. Goodfellow had set out crocks of fresh butter and cream, and some small bowls of flour, herbs, and spices to make the chicken. At the other end sat earthenware dishes of butter and eggs, the box of powdered white sugar Hannah had prepared, and separate demijohns of white wine, brandy, and rosewater for the lemon pudding. The butcher's apprentice had already delivered the three chickens, which Mrs. Goodfellow had put in a large clay basin of cool water which rested on a side table along the wall.

Some of the girls tittered together and didn't seem overly eager to learn, but Mrs. Goodfellow ignored them and started immediately with the lesson. Gathering the girls around her, she boldly asked them all if they hoped to marry well someday. Most of the girls were taken aback. They blushed and looked down at their feet and nodded or whispered, "yes, Ma'am." A few of the bolder ones blurted out, "yes," or "certainly, Ma'am."

Mrs. Goodfellow then explained the importance of being able to plan and put together a fine table, whether for a simple family supper or a fancy dinner party with guests. She stressed that cooking skills are required not only to attract a worthy husband, but also to keep him satisfied and interested after the marriage. Some of the girls blushed even more, as it was rumored that not only was Mrs. Goodfellow a talented pastry maker, but she also had a knack for providing matchmaking services for her students.

She knew very well these girls would need to understand how to cook and present a variety of rich and wholesome dishes in order to select first-rate cooks for their households. And the ability to create eye-catching pastries and luscious desserts was a must to entertain and impress their society contemporaries.

"Cutting corners is not at all desirable in the cooking process," Mrs. Goodfellow emphasized to the girls. "Careless and hasty methods will not be tolerated. We must select the finest ingredients in order to produce the tastiest and most nutritious meals." She guaranteed that by purchasing fresh, high-quality products and making sure that nothing of value was wasted or thrown away, a wife would feed her family very well indeed.

She gestured for the girls to follow her over to the work table. As it was the first session, Mrs. Goodfellow began with the basics, starting with the need for a clean kitchen, from hands and aprons to the work table and utensils. In addition, she told them they must always pull their hair up under a cap to prevent strands from ending up in the food.

It is important to set out all necessary items before beginning a recipe, she instructed, waving her arm over the work table as an example. "This eliminates the need to stop in the middle and search for an ingredient or utensil. The items you see here on this table are what we need to make

Mrs. Goodfellow would have taught cooking in the first decades of her school at an open hearth. Temperature control was achieved by moving the pots suspended on cranes and chains in and out and up and down in relation to the fire. A baking oven is to the left of the hearth. (*Library of Congress*)

the two dishes." Thus, she was already preaching the now-familiar concept of *mise en place*.

Making eye contact with each girl in turn, Mrs. Goodfellow stressed that skill in baking is the result of practice and experience, but much depends on the state of the fire, the size of the items to be baked, and the thickness of the pans or dishes. This holds true for both cakes and puddings, she noted.

She also suggested that the girls bring a little blank book to take notes and write down the recipes, which she noticed a few had already done. She explained that because this was their first lesson, she would do most of the work herself, instructing as she went along, with minimal help from the students. As the classes progressed, she would gradually have them take part in the preparatory work and actual cooking and baking so that by the last lesson she would step back and let them do everything themselves.

Leading the girls over to the immense fireplace, she explained they would be cooking the chicken in a pot of boiling water over the open fire. Both of the heavy cast-iron pots Mary had filled earlier were hanging on the fireplace crane and now boiling gently—one was empty and the other held the artichokes. Mrs. Goodfellow demonstrated the wrought-iron crane's swinging motion in and out of the open fire, as well as its adjustable trammels which raised and lowered the pots or kettles suspended from it. She took the lid off the pot that contained the artichokes and carefully pulled one out with a pair of long iron tongs, placing it in a shallow dish. She showed the girls how Mary had removed the coarse outer leaves and cut off the stalks close to the bottom. Since the artichokes had to soak for a couple of hours before boiling, she explained, there wouldn't have been time for the whole process during the lesson. She then placed the artichoke back into the cooking water, and after resetting the crane at the desired height, swung the heavy cauldron over the fire to resume boiling.

Next she beckoned them all to gather around the large central work table. She wrapped one of the chickens in a clean towel and brought it over to the table, laying it down in a wooden chopping bowl with the breast up and the neck to the left. She explained that care must be taken to chop the chicken pieces evenly without splintering the bones, which gives the finished dish not only an unappealing look, but is a potential choking hazard. With a small sharp knife she made an incision in the thin skin between the inside of the legs and the body. She then proceeded to cut the chicken into pieces with a large cleaver, showing the students how the bones easily separate at the joint when the tendon and gristly portion connecting them have been severed.

Once the chicken was in pieces, she removed the skin and placed them into another basin filled with fresh, cool water.

She continued this process for all three birds, and then carried the basin over to the fireplace where the pot filled with water was boiling nicely. Swinging it toward her, she gently added the chicken pieces to the pot and called out to Hannah, who had just come back with the basket of lemons. Hannah placed the lemons on the table and walked over to the fireplace. Mrs. Goodfellow asked her to keep an eye on the pot to make sure the water was kept at a gentle simmer and to occasionally stir the chicken with a long spoon so that the meat would cook evenly.

Mrs. Goodfellow then led the girls back over to the work table to start on the lemon pudding. First she carefully picked through the basket of lemons, and choosing a large one with a smooth, thin rind, she wiped it with a soft cloth. She then grated the outer part of the rind onto a plate, explaining to the girls that it is essential to remove only the yellow part of the skin, as the white is very bitter. She then cut the lemon in half and squeezed the juice onto the plate that contained the grated rind. After carefully removing all the seeds with a small dessert spoon, she mixed the rind and juice together.

Next she walked over to the kitchen dresser and used the scales to measure half a pound of powdered sugar. While measuring the sugar, she told the students that scales should hang in a convenient place. If they are stored in the scale-box, the chains can become twisted and unlinked each time they are taken out. The weights, however (of which there should be a set ranging from two pounds to a quarter of an ounce), should be kept in the box, so that none get lost.

After placing the sugar in a deep earthen pan, she weighed half a pound of fresh butter and then washed it in some cold water, carefully squeezing and pressing out water with her hands. She explained this removed any excess buttermilk and salt. She then mixed the butter with the sugar using a knife. Once the butter was in small pieces, she took a long, round hickory paddle and creamed the butter and sugar together, her arm a dizzying blur. As she vigorously stirred, she explained that if a recipe calls for butter and sugar to be mixed together, this should always be done before the eggs are beaten. If the eggs are beaten before the other ingredients are ready, they fall quickly, she warned.

She kept up this brisk pace until she was satisfied with the consistency of the butter and sugar, which took quite a long time and required a strong arm. Instructing the girls to gather closer, she tilted the dish a bit, letting them get a good look at the smooth, silken mixture. It was a lovely pale yellow color and stood up in the pan like thick cream.

Next she took an egg and broke it into a saucer. Once she determined it was fine, she tipped the egg into a broad clay pan and then repeated the process with five more eggs. She explained that every egg needs to be tested for freshness in this way before adding to the pan so that one bad egg does not spoil the whole recipe. When all six eggs were in the pan, she then beat them with a hickory egg beater until they were glossy and thick, like a boiled custard. As her arm tirelessly swirled the wooden whisk, she explained that eggs should always be beaten in a shallow earthen pan like the one she was using, and butter and sugar in a deep one. Pans made of tin are not suitable, as the coldness of the metal prevents the mixtures from becoming light, she added.

She then stirred the eggs gradually into the butter and sugar mixture. Once they were well combined, she poured some white wine and then some brandy into a wine glass, and added it to the pan a little at a time, alternating with two dessert spoonfuls of rosewater. Finally, she gradually blended in the lemon juice and rind, and then stirred the pudding thoroughly, making sure all the ingredients were well incorporated.

Mrs. Goodfellow then walked over to the larder to retrieve the plate of puff paste she had made earlier. She brought it to the work table, and then turned to get her pastry board, rolling pin, and some flour. She told the girls that although she would fully demonstrate how to make puff paste from beginning to end in a later lesson, she always covered the fundamentals of pastry making in the first session. She felt this skill was of utmost importance and therefore repeated its guidelines throughout her classes, encouraging the students to take detailed notes.

As she sprinkled some flour on the board and rolling pin and then carefully unfolded one sheet of paste, she explained that it was essential to use only small amounts of flour to sprinkle and roll with, as too much flour will make the pastry tough when baked. Placing the sheet on the board, she picked up her rolling pin and rolled out the dough with short, quick strokes, demonstrating how it was important to always roll away, not toward yourself. As it was the second rolling, she told them she was also using a firmer touch with the rolling pin than when she had first made up the paste that morning. A lighter hand in the beginning produces a lighter paste, she advised. Then, cutting the large sheet in half, she folded up each piece and rolled them out again into two separate circles, pressing down so that the paste was thinner in the middle and thicker toward the edges.

Picking up a soup plate, she explained to the girls that the paste had to be just large enough to cover the bottom, sides, and edges. Taking a little piece of linen cloth, she rubbed some butter on the inside of this dish and another of the same size and then gently lay the rounds of pastry in each, making it neat and even around the broad edge of each plate. She then trimmed off the extra dough and notched the edges around the rims with a sharp knife. Giving the pudding mixture one last stir, she spooned some into one dish, and then the other, making sure it was divided equally between the two.

She then asked the girls to follow her over to the fireplace to test the heat of the bake-oven. She showed them how to hold their hand in the front of the oven, and to start counting; if they were able to count to twenty, the heat was about right for the puddings.

The girls took turns tentatively reaching their small pale hands toward the brick opening, turning their faces away from the intense heat. They all made it to a count of twenty and nodded their heads that it seemed the correct temperature. Mrs. Goodfellow agreed, and went back to the table to get the puddings. She put one inside the oven and pushed it back further with the peel. She then went back for the second pudding and pushed that one into the oven as well.

Wiping her hands on her apron, she told the girls it was time to check on the chicken, so they all turned toward the fire where Hannah was busy stirring the bubbling pot with a long iron spoon. As Mrs. Goodfellow adjusted the crane, lowering the pot so they could see inside, they all caught a whiff of the savory, peppery smell. Taking the spoon from Hannah for a moment, Mrs. Goodfellow stirred the pieces around a bit, scooping up a few with the spoon so she could have a better look. She told them that although the chicken was coming along nicely, it needed a bit more cooking time. So she placed the pot back over the fire, but raised it a bit higher than before so the heat was less direct. She told Hannah she no longer needed to watch the pot and asked her to please start preparing the necessary items for the dinner table. She then peeked into the other pot where the artichokes were simmering. Lifting one out, she gently pulled on one of its outer leaves with a fork. Since it was not yet detaching easily, she determined they also needed a little more time in the pot, so she replaced the lid and then walked back over to the work table, gesturing for the girls to follow.

Gathering the girls around her, she finished up her pastry-making discussion, stressing the significance of keeping everything involved with the process as cool as possible, from the ingredients to the equipment and even the environment where the pastry is made. It is difficult to make puff paste in the summer, unless in a cellar or very cool room, and on a marble surface, she told them. If ice is available, it should be placed under the butter as it sits on the paste board and also in the water used to mix with the paste. Even the warmth of the hands can injure the paste, she explained, so it is best to use a knife to transfer it. After the paste is mixed it should be set in a cool place until it is time for the last rolling.

She also told them that while it is fine to use lard for a regular pastry (pie) crust, or a combination of lard and butter, puff paste needs to be made entirely out of butter, as the result is much more flavorful and it helps the dough rise into delicate paper-thin sheets when baked.

Although many of the cooking basics and concepts Mrs. Goodfellow preached have been integrated into contemporary cooking instruction, her cooking school and classes were quite different from those we know today. Goodfellow's students were not attending to get a culinary degree so they could become a restaurant chef or food critic. Lessons did not take place in a classroom setting, but rather in the kitchen in her pastry shop.

Not much is known about Mrs. Goodfellow's teaching style or how the classes were structured. Eliza Leslie's books probably give the most insight, and her commentary in addition to other brief descriptions depict Mrs. Goodfellow as being no-nonsense, yet fair and kind. There is also the feeling that she was passionate about her work, and this enthusiasm was passed on to at least some of her students.

Those attending the lectures were all women—mostly the daughters and wives of upper-class society in Philadelphia as well as other American locations as far away as Charleston, South Carolina. (There is a possibility that servants and boardinghouse workers were also sent to Mrs. Goodfellow's by their employers from time to time in order to enhance their cooking abilities.) These society women needed to learn how to create extravagant dinners and desserts for a variety of entertaining situations. Although men were indeed pastry chefs, cooks, and caterers at this time, they learned their craft through apprenticeships.

This model was based upon what had been happening in England in terms of cooking education, where confectioners and pastry chefs had been teaching classes and writing books about their talents since the eighteenth century, thus giving them a second income source. An enterprising gentleman named Edward Kidder is considered to be proprietor of perhaps the most well-known of England's early cookery schools, which he operated out of several London locations in the early 1700s. The recipes he taught can be traced back to a cooking manual he used in his classes entitled *Receipts of Pastry and Cookery: For the Use of His Scholars*. The book has been found in both manuscript and printed forms and is thought to date from between the 1720s and 1740s. Pastry recipes are definitely the focus. Reflective of the time period, however, most of the pies contain savory fillings, as the use of sugar was just beginning to spread from the upper class to the general public.

Even the dishes under the heading "Sweet Pyes" are what we would consider a main dish today rather than a dessert. Examples include recipes for "A Lamb Pye," "Egg Pyes" and "A Lumber Pye" (which contained minced veal and beef seasoned with spices and pippin apples). He also refers to this type as a humble pie.[1]

It is unclear whether the manuscripts were dictated by Kidder to his students, or copied from one of the printed versions. In any case, this manual was meant to serve as a textbook, and the simplicity of the recipes and lack of detailed instructions suggest

A portrait of Elizabeth Raffald faced the title page of her book, *The Experienced English Housekeeper*, first published in 1769. (*University of Pennsylvania Library*)

that its users already knew or would soon learn the necessary measurements and cooking times for each. The fact that Kidder was able to produce so many copies implies that his activities were successful. In addition to instructing students at his shop, he also advertised that he taught ladies in their own homes.[2]

Twenty years later, the previously mentioned Elizabeth Raffald was another resourceful Briton who shared her pastry-making skills through teaching and writing. She was an extraordinary entrepreneur, sort of an eighteenth-century English version of Martha Stewart, according to University of Pennsylvania professor and folklore, culture, and food historian Janet Theophano.[3] Raffald's recipes were decidedly sweeter in nature, which was not surprising, since just like Mrs. Goodfellow, she operated her cooking school out of her confectionary shop. In addition, sugar was gaining in popularity by this time. Her book, *The Experienced English Housekeeper*, even features a chapter entitled "Observations on Making Decorations for a Table," in which she gives detailed instructions and recommendations on how to fashion dazzling creations out of sugar, including spinning delicate gold and silver webs to cover sweetmeats for the dessert table. She also gives guidance for making fluffy meringue whips and syllabubs, custards and attractive molded flummery, as well as transparent puddings, or jellies that would serve as their quivery base, creating the look of a fish pond or what Eliza Leslie later referred to as a "floating island."[4]

Around this same time, another British pastry cook, Elizabeth Marshall, ran a patisserie and cookery school in Newcastle-upon-Tyne. Like Raffald, she also wrote a book based on her recipes, entitled *The Young Ladies' Guide in the Art of Cookery*, subtitled *Being a Collection of useful Receipts, Published for the Convenience of the Ladies committed to her Care, by Eliz. Marshall*. A significant feature of her book is that it involves large amounts of expensive imported ingredients such as truffles, morels, pineapples, and lemons. So, it is likely that her clientele was upper-class ladies who needed to know how to prepare fancy dishes for their social events, as with Mrs. Goodfellow's students. Marshall also recommends washing butter in order to remove extra salt before using in the cheesecake, pudding, and sweet pastry recipes she taught her pupils to prepare, just as Goodfellow did. Her version, however, contains the interesting twist of washing the butter in rosewater,[5] perhaps to impart some of this delicate taste to the baked goods.

Meanwhile, across the Atlantic in the American colonies, a few lady pastry cooks also began to share their cookery skills, giving wealthy girls and women the ability to learn to make some of these luxuries themselves. In 1731 a woman named Martha Gazley ran an announcement in the

New York Gazette advertising that she taught pastry making.[6] And in early eighteenth-century Louisiana, the
French Canadian governor Jean-Baptiste Le Moyne de
Bienville had the insight to offer cooking lessons to
prospective brides for his colonists taught by his experienced housekeeper, Madame Langlois. The governor's idea
was to give these young ladies the knowledge to modify
unfamiliar American foods into recipes recognizable to the
Old World palate during times when their stock of imported goods might be running low. One can only imagine the
types of French-inspired dishes they concocted, but unfortunately the concept did not stick as the girls staged the
"Petticoat Rebellion" at having to substitute cornbread for
French bread.[7]

There were also classes in cookery taught at the
Moravian Seminary in Bethlehem, Pennsylvania, in the
eighteenth century. The Moravian Seminary was a school
for wealthy girls from all over the country, not only those of
the Moravian faith. Many regional food recipes from this
school, such as Moravian sugar cake, ended up in manuscript cookbooks of wealthy southern ladies.[8]

In colonial Philadelphia Mary Newport was a pastry
cook with a Norris Alley location,[9] who later possibly
moved her business to Dock Street. It is not known
whether she gave pastry-making lessons, but by 1796, her
niece, Elizabeth Sturgis, was advertising that she had taken
over her aunt's business of "pastry cook in all its branches"
and had removed from Dock Street to No. 185, South
Second Street. She includes the following notation at the
bottom of the advertisement: "Young ladies taught by the
month on moderate terms."[10] It is likely Sturgis was a
Quaker as she references her "Friends" in the announcement; it is not known what instruction she provided or if it
encompassed more than pastry making.

In any case, it was not long after when we have our first confirmation that Mrs. Goodfellow had opened her business. She was teaching while she was married to (her second husband) Robert Coane, as per several sources, including a recipe book that dates from the early nineteenth century and is now housed at the Independence National Historic Park Library. This manuscript cookbook contains some recipes for "Mrs. Coanes Puddings," and the unknown owner had written "Mrs. Goodfellow" next to the Mrs. Coane attribution. There is also a date listed—1808— so perhaps this is when the person made the name correction (the same year the widow Coane married William Goodfellow). It is not clear whether the manuscript's owner attended classes given by Mrs. Coane before she was Mrs. Goodfellow, or if she got the recipes in another way. The recipes listed include two lemon puddings, two "Cocoa Nut" (puddings), two almond puddings, orange (pudding), two apple puddings, two citron puddings, two "Potatoe" puddings, and "To Make Paste."[11]

While the exact date Mrs. Goodfellow began teaching or under what name is uncertain (it is possible she began while married to her first husband or soon after his death), she knew that Philadelphians highly valued the handiwork that went into crafting sweets and fine baked goods, and that the city's elite in particular *expected* an abundance of these treats to appear on the tables at their many social functions. So, although most households had servant assistance, women would also make particular dishes on their own, as a way of showing off their talents. The cooking skills that seemed to be the most significant appear to have been making pastry and sweetmeats and preserving fruit, as these were most often mentioned by Philadelphia ladies in their diaries and letters from the eighteenth and nineteenth centuries.[12]

Because sugar was so expensive, sugared fruit was a kind of status symbol, and women would spend long hours over the hot cooking fire producing these confectionaries.[13] They would begin by making a clarified sugar syrup, which required combining large quantities of loaf sugar with fresh spring water and egg whites and boiling the mix over the open fire. Once it was cooked, it could be used right away, or bottled and used at a later date.[14] Such a tricky and time-consuming procedure was considered more of an artistic feat than a lowly household duty. Reputations were made and upheld over colorful, transparent sweetmeats that glittered like stained glass on the banqueting tables of wealthy socialites.[15]

Preserving fruit was also a practical way to enjoy summer and fall bounty such as juicy peaches, plums, and strawberries through the cold winter months, putting color on the table when fresh fruit was unavailable. So even though it is unlikely that these ladies enjoyed the tedious process, the end result was something they could be proud of and at the same time helped cement their social positions.

Pastry making was ranked among the highest of all cooking skills for ladies to master. It was considered on par with other refinements such as having a thorough understanding of literature, learning a foreign language, producing fine needlework, painting, performing music, and dancing. Even the wealthiest women would learn how to make pastry. For some, it may have been one of the few household tasks they did, and even then, they made sure they didn't get mussed.

This point is made clear by Frances Trollope in her book *Domestic Manners of the Americans*. Published in 1832, Trollope describes a typical day of an upper-class Philadelphia lady:

Upon rising, she first spends some time choosing which of her exquisite outfits to wear. After dressing in her finery, she then descends to her parlor for a leisurely breakfast of salt fish, fried ham and coffee prepared by servants and served by her footman. A carriage arrives for her at eleven; but until then she is employed in the pastry-room, her snow-white apron protecting her mouse-coloured silk. Twenty minutes before her carriage should appear, she retires to her chamber, as she calls it, shakes, and folds up her still snow-white apron, smooths her rich dress, and with nice care, sets on her elegant bonnet.[16]

Many Philadelphia girls learned the pastry-making skill as part of their boarding school education. In addition to studying French, art, and literature, they would be sent "off campus" to Mrs. Goodfellow's. The background of these girls varied. Although all were in the upper echelons socially, some may have been the daughters of wealthy Philadelphia merchants, others part of the Quaker circle like the previously mentioned Elizabeth Ellicott Lea, author of the mid-nineteenth-century cookbook *Domestic Cookery*.

It appears that several members of one of Philadelphia's most prominent Quaker families, the Emlens, also probably attended Mrs. Goodfellow's. There are a number of eighteenth- and nineteenth-century manuscript cookbooks with connections to this family, and the latter include Goodfellow recipes. One handwritten recipe book compiled in Philadelphia by an unidentified author lists a recipe for Jumbles attributed to "Mrs. (Elizabeth [Emlen]) Physick from Mrs. Goodfellow's.[17] Mrs. Physick was the wife of the well-known innovative surgeon Philip Syng Physick. Another manuscript cookbook owned by a Margaret Emlen Howell lists Goodfellow recipes including "Jumbles (Mrs. Goodfellow's)," "puff paste," and "buns"

Members of the Emlen Cresson and Prichett families photographed in Philadelphia in March 1844. The Cressons, Prichetts, Physicks, Emlens, and other prominent Philadelphia families intermarried and honored those connections with the names of their children. The Cressons were among the first families to sit for photograph portraits in America. The daguerreotype on the left shows Emlen Cresson standing with (seated, from left to right) his mother, his wife, Sarah Prichett, and her mother, Mrs. Prichett. It is possible that these women, and perhaps the Cresson's daughters, pictured on the right, center and far right, attended Mrs. Goodfellow's school. (*Library of Congress*)

(i.e., Spanish Bunns).[18] A manuscript cookbook compiled by Ellen Markoe Emlen also includes recipes for jumbles and puff paste,[19] seemingly two of Goodfellow's cooking school staples.

As word spread of Mrs. Goodfellow's success, families from miles outside the city's radius began sending their daughters to take lessons at her school, even if they were not attending boarding school. For example, Delaware girls traveled north to attend her classes, where among other things they learned to make "'George Washington's Soup,' a rich blend of crabmeat, sweet cream, bacon, tiny meat balls and hard boiled eggs."[20] Susan Israel, daughter of General Joseph Israel of Revolutionary War fame, was one of Goodfellow's admirers who traveled all the way from Christiana, Delaware, to attend classes in 1807.[21]

There were even some Southern belles that were Goodfellow students. Before the Civil War many Southerners wintered in Philadelphia, soaking up some culture during the colder months and then heading back to their plantations in the summer, or if not there, then the beaches of Cape May, New Jersey. "There was this large class of very well-to-do leisured people who had nothing to do but go to parties and dinners," says food historian William Woys Weaver. "Plenty of Southern women came to these [Philadelphia] boarding schools, and I understand that one of their required courses was to study at Mrs. Goodfellow's. They all essentially learned debutante side-board food—that's what [Eliza Leslie's] *Seventy-Five Receipts* is all about—how to make a good roast standing dish as they were called—things to put on the sideboard during parties and buffets."[22]

Although not much is known about most of them, similar cooking schools eventually sprang up in Philadelphia as other knowledgeable cooks tried to cash in on the concept. In referring to this early nineteenth-century timeframe, Rufus Wilmot Griswold stipulates that the education of women was managed better during this period often called the "golden age of America," than later in the century. "Among the institutions that flourished here then were cooking-schools, in which the most important of sciences was taught in a manner that contributed largely to the comfort of the people," he wrote.[23]

Philadelphia ladies Hannah Widdifield and the previously mentioned terrapin cookery expert Mrs. Rubicam are two that are considered Goodfellow competitors. Hannah

Widdifield was also a Quaker and the matriarch of a family who worked as professional cooks and confectioners in Philadelphia. Like Goodfellow, she expanded on her skills by teaching cookery during the early to mid-nineteenth century, although it is not clear if her instruction was designed for the public like Mrs. Goodfellow's, or if it was set up more as an apprentice system.[24] And unlike Goodfellow, she did produce a cookbook of her recipes, published by her daughters Sarah and Mary after her death.[25] Entitled *Widdifield's New Cook Book: or, Practical Receipts for the House-wife*, the recipes are a diverse collection of what was popular in Philadelphia at that time, featuring basics such as bean soup and boiled fowls as well as the interesting-sounding "salsify dressed as oysters" and "stewed rabbit, French mode" in addition to the rich cakes and pastry favored by the upper class. She also made sure to include directions for the preparation of dishes for the sick and convalescent.[26]

The preface of Widdifield's book states, "The author, in preparing this work, has endeavored to make the contents as plain and explicit as possible, in order that they may be found practicable by the young, as well as the more experienced housewife."[27] Like Goodfellow, she sought to share her cooking skills with young ladies in order to prepare them for marriage and to make them aware of the details they would need to know in order to run an efficient household. Indeed, in nineteenth-century manuscript cookbooks, recipes attributed to Widdifield are often found in close proximity to Goodfellow's, so perhaps girls attended both schools in order to receive the most comprehensive culinary education possible. Or maybe they were simply swapping recipes among their social circle, recording them in their cookery notebooks.

Mrs. Goodfellow wanted to provide her students with a thorough working knowledge of what was wholesome and suitable fare for any occasion. For example, the recipes attributed to her in one manuscript cookbook that dates from the mid-nineteenth century include not only the typical sweet dessert dishes such as almond pudding, gingerbread, and jumbles, but also some savory fare such as a "Ragou of Onions," "Pigs feet souced," and artichokes. In addition, there are instructions for making preparations for the sick, including barley water (a traditional British "soft drink"), tapioca and sago (starches extracted from tropical plants that were boiled with water and flavored with wine, sugar, and nutmeg), and "water gruel," a thin porridge incorporating oatmeal or "Indian" (corn) meal spiked with a little wine and sugar for taste.[28]

This handwritten cookbook is just one example of the collections of recipes likely taught in her school, but it represents the variety of dishes Mrs. Goodfellow was teaching, giving these girls well-rounded culinary training. This fact is affirmed in the 1907 *Colonial Receipt Book*, a collection of nineteenth-century dishes that became popular in and around the Philadelphia area, including "celebrated old receipts used a century ago by Mrs. Goodfellow's Cooking School." In this cookbook's introduction, the Goodfellow experience is described as follows: "Under her able training many of our exquisite yet practical ancestors gained a thorough knowledge of cooking—from soups and the 'Staff of Life' to plum-pudding and Queen cakes."[29] A comparable compilation of recipes, *Famous Old Receipts Used a Hundred Years and More in the Kitchens of the North and the South*, maintains that young ladies learned the *art* of cooking at Mrs. Goodfellow's, "it being the last touch of their education preparatory to entering society."[30]

The memoirs of Philadelphia Quaker Elizabeth W. Levick provide similar and additional insight into Goodfellow's school. Born in 1789 to Isaac and Mary Jones,

Elizabeth was educated very well, receiving instruction in advanced literary works as well as sewing and embroidery from two English women, Ann Gilbert and Elizabeth Pritchard, who had their school in the Pine Street Meeting House. She later continued embroidery lessons with Julia Bader, described as a kind and lively German woman who had received her training at the Moravian school in Bethlehem, Pennsylvania. When Elizabeth was in her mid-twenties she was also fortunate enough to attend botany lectures with a small group of other young ladies given by Dr. Benjamin Waterhouse in one of the rooms of the American Philosophical Society.

While she was not one of Goodfellow's students, her sister Mary was, and Elizabeth would often tag along when Mary attended classes. She describes the cookery school as being very different from that of "Miss Julia," referring to it as "a course of instruction given in pastry and other cooking, by Betsey Goodfellow, a famous maker of cakes and pies at that time. 'Mrs. Goodfellow' was a very respectable, ladylike person, who having been thrown on her own resources, opened a pastry cookery establishment, which soon became famous."[31]

In the memoirs, Levick gives no explanation as to why her sister was a pupil of Goodfellow's yet she was not. However, her narrative seems to indicate that she and Goodfellow had a fairly familiar relationship, as she calls Mrs. Goodfellow "Betsey" and mentions her "need" to work after what she is surely referring to as the consecutive deaths of her husbands.

It is also clear from Levick's tone that she liked and respected Mrs. Goodfellow. She continues her description of Mrs. Goodfellow and the school by claiming that "her pupils were the daughters of our best citizens, and many a household, for years after, bore evidence of her skill in teaching. Her especial talent was in the making of fine

cakes and pastry, though she also gave occasional instruction in the preparing of boned turkey, salads and the like."[32]

As previously mentioned, another difference between
Goodfellow and some of her contemporaries is that she did
not publish any of her recipes herself. The one cookbook
that has been attributed to her, *Mrs. Goodfellow's Cookery as
It Should Be*, was actually published after her death and, as
Eliza Leslie adamantly claimed, many of the recipes it contained were not those of Mrs. Goodfellow.[33] Being a cookbook writer conceivably would have helped Goodfellow
reach an even wider audience, but it appears she achieved
public acclaim and high enrollment in her school regardless.

She encouraged her students to take detailed notes,
which Eliza Leslie famously did and wrote a slew of cookbooks based on them. However, it is unlikely that Leslie's
works had much of an impact on attendance at the cookery
school. Mrs. Goodfellow's school had already been open for
at least two decades by the time Leslie published her first
cookbook, *Seventy-Five Receipts for Pastry, Cakes and
Sweetmeats*, in 1827.

In addition to their own notebooks, it is thought
Goodfellow's students also used cookbooks written by
British authors Maria Eliza Ketelby Rundell and Hannah
Glasse.[34] Although these two never became cooking
instructors (or if they were, it was never recorded), Mrs.
Goodfellow must have highly respected their cooking abil-
ities as she set up her recipes in the same style and used
their books as references for her students.

In America's early days, the cuisine was so highly influenced by the British heritage of its settlers that the
American cookbook was a traditional English cookbook,

with those by Rundell and Glasse the most popular. So although there had been a few published American cookbook authors by the time Mrs. Goodfellow was teaching, she probably was simply following her (assumed) British roots and traditions by borrowing and modifying these two authors' recipes to suit American tastes and ingredients. And while it is unlikely that Mrs. Goodfellow worried about adhering to fashion, she was in fact using the most well-known cookery sources at that time as her textbooks.

British cookbooks were also held in high regard by eighteenth- and nineteenth-century Americans since these authors often boasted of gaining their cookery knowledge and experience through direct assignments in high-ranking, upper-class households. Americans continued to be fascinated and impressed by the European aristocracy, even if they had often journeyed to America to escape the class and religious strictures of one kind or another.[35]

First published in London in 1747, Hannah Glasse's *The Art of Cookery* was widely used throughout the United States and has been referred to as "the most influential cookbook in the English-speaking colonies."[36] In writing about it for a facsimile version of the first American edition in 1805, food historian Karen Hess states, "It was the most English of cookbooks. It was the most American of cookbooks. George Washington owned a copy, as did Thomas Jefferson; indeed, recipes attributed to Mrs. Glasse are included in cookery manuscripts kept by Jefferson's granddaughters, for example."[37]

Then in the early nineteenth century, Maria Rundell's *A New System of Domestic Cookery* became the cookbook of preference, outselling all others at the time. An American edition was first published in 1807, not long after the English version, and was reprinted sixteen times in the U.S. until 1844.[38] In the cookbook's opening remarks, Rundell states that the recipes and advice within should serve as guidance for her children. She also explains that she wanted to create the type of cookery reference book that would have been helpful to her when she was a young lady.[39]

According to food historian Jan Longone, Richard Briggs's *New Art of Cookery* was also used as a teaching tool by Mrs. Goodfellow. "This book was very popular among the Quakers of Philadelphia and influential through its use in Mrs. Goodfellow's Cooking School, which flourished in that city in the early nineteenth century," maintains Longone.[40] The cookbook was an American version of *The English Art of Cookery*, which documented Briggs's inventive recipes while chef of the Globe Tavern in London. (He also did stints at Fleet Street, the White

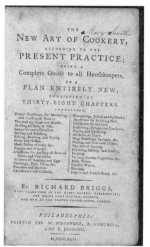

The American edition of *The New Art of Cookery* by Richard Briggs was printed in Philadelphia in 1792 and may have been used in Mrs. Goodfellow's Cooking School. (*PBA Gallery*)

Hart Tavern, Holborn, and Temple Coffee-House.) Originally published in London in 1788, the edition used by Goodfellow and her students (*The New Art of Cookery, According to the Present Practice*) was printed in Philadelphia in 1792.[41]

So Mrs. Goodfellow was definitely keeping pace with the times, teaching recipes and menus that were the most fashionable, both back in Britain as well as locally. She had her finger on the pulse of what young ladies needed to know in order to position themselves favorably in society.

This was not always an easy task, as it appears that these girls were often quite unwilling students. Many times they were forced by their mothers to attend cooking school; they weren't going because they necessarily wanted to.

For example, a nineteenth-century letter written by a young Quaker from Philadelphia named Nancy Howell breezily describes a trip to Wilmington, Delaware, where she stayed with Friends and attended meeting with them. While the letter was addressed to her mother, at the bottom she writes a "Note to Molly and Miss [Sarah] Emlen [perhaps younger cousins or sisters]: 'I heard before I came out of town that Sally intended to go to a cookery school, poor girl.'" She doesn't mention Mrs. Goodfellow's specifically, so it is unknown to which cooking school Nancy refers. However, the previously mentioned handwritten recipe book owned by Margaret Emlen Howell that includes some Goodfellow recipes is part of the same set of correspondence, making it likely some of these family members were Goodfellow students.[42]

This short note illustrates the fact that attending cooking school wasn't exactly the top choice of activities for most girls in the early nineteenth century. Christopher Crag's tongue-in-cheek piece from the 1809 *Tangram, or Fashionable Trifler* goes into vivid detail. Although meant to be pure satire, his deliciously comical interpretation still provides some insight into what these girls thought and felt about this "requirement," and also how Mrs. Goodfellow was viewed by Philadelphia society: as both a skilled, practical cook and a strict and orderly teacher.

In the spoof, Crag refers to Mrs. Goodfellow as

> an ancient *madre* of *five-lorded acquirement*, who had invitingly thrown open the doors of her convent to such of the frolicksome and fashionable belles of this our frugal city. . . . or in the simple terms of the madre's dialect, had opened a cook school for the edification of the pretty fair ones; where, by the assistance of her notable and long experience, she professed to instruct them, in the

art and mystery of pickling cabbages, brewing gooseberry wine, boning turkeys, and making puff paste apple-tarts. To these propositions the young ladies sufficiently testified their abhorrence, maintaining, as such pursuits were unknown in polite literature, they would violently protest against this system of education; but their mamas, kind souls, being determined in this case to *rule the roast*, insisted on their attendance at the epicurean hall.[43]

So, whether they were from a Quaker background or not, these young ladies were testing those in charge; resisting authority while trying to assert their independence. However, Mrs. Goodfellow managed to win them over, as Crag explains:

Convinced at length, of the absurdity of opposition, they were content to call upon the madre, who by an exhibition of unaffected grace, and a no very small donation of oven trumpery, prevailed in determining them upon receiving lessons in domestick accomplishment. Unwilling as they might first have been, to yield to the persuasion of their careful mothers, they were now equally as eager to become the mistresses of cookery, when they received assurance from the madre, that they should not be obligated to acquit the duties of basting, tasting, and pen-feathering.[44]

Eliza Leslie's comments about Mrs. Goodfellow in her books allude to the fact that she did not tolerate sullenness, japery, or dim-witted behavior in her classroom. She strongly felt the skills she was teaching were on par with any of the academic higher learning the girls may have received, and therefore expected them to behave correctly. According to Leslie, if Mrs. Goodfellow's students were acting dull or silly she would quip, "It requires a head even to make cakes."[45]

Through her cookbooks Leslie also reinforced the idea that Mrs. Goodfellow followed a strict regimen regarding using only fine, quality ingredients. In *Miss Leslie's New Cookery Book* (1857), she comments at the end of the recipe for Spanish Buns, "These buns were first introduced by Mrs. Goodfellow; and in her school were always excellently made, nothing being spared that was good, and the use of soda and other alkalis being unknown in the establishment—hartshorn[46] in cakes would have horrified her."[47]

Imagining what her kitchen looked like conjures up visions of a very orderly place where items were laid out before cooking and the ingredients were measured as precisely as possible. In this same tidy and practical vein, she liked to list ingredients first when dictating recipes to her students, as is shown in manuscript cookbooks from her school. Up to this point in time, recipes were usually written out in paragraph form, which could be somewhat confusing and allow more room for error. Through Eliza Leslie's cookbooks, this more useful method of recipe construction was passed on and popularized.

Because Goodfellow started teaching in the early 1800s, it can be assumed her instruction was for open-hearth cooking, as food was cooked over an open fire with heavy kettles and awkward fireplace tools, such as the pivoting crane, until the 1820s, when cast-iron cookstoves were introduced. These new appliances covered and replaced the outmoded fireplaces and burned one-third less wood, which had become increasingly more difficult to obtain as acre after acre of North American forest was cut down. The stoves could also be fueled by coal and made cooking easier because their work surfaces were at waist level, saving housewives from constantly stooping. In the 1830s, most

middle-class families bricked up their fireplaces and purchased the new stoves. By the 1850s, only rural families and
poor Southerners continued with the old ways.[48]

Goodfellow probably taught open-hearth methods of
cooking through the time she was at her Dock Street location, but then switched over to cookstove techniques once
she moved to Washington Square in 1835. (The fire insurance survey from this location indicates that there was
indeed a stove there, as well as two ovens.)[49] So she may
have continued using a brick oven for some of the baking,
as many enthusiasts of baked goods made this way claim it
really is the preferred method (think of the brick-oven piz-
zas many of us find so tasty today).

With their upper-class backgrounds, many of Goodfellow's students probably came to her school with limited
cooking knowledge. As a result, she had her work cut out
for her in order to prepare them to be self-sufficient in
terms of meal planning. It is likely she used a demonstration format, at least at the beginning of a course, doing
much of the work herself while the girls observed.

It is not known if or how Mrs. Goodfellow graded or
tested her students' learning. Although some of her students did write down the recipes they learned in class in
their notebooks, it is doubtful that she gave handwritten
tests given the practical nature of the course. Perhaps she
measured their progress through oral questioning and
"hands-on" assessments as their participation gradually
increased over the course of a semester. This makes the
most sense considering the circumstances as well as Eliza
Leslie's comment that during her time at Goodfellow's she
"took notes of every thing that was made, it being the desire
of the liberal and honest instructress that her scholars
should learn in reality."[50]

Whether they graduated with some sort of certificate or
celebration is unknown, but according to *Famous Old*

Receipts Used a Hundred Years and More in the Kitchens of the North and the South (1908), "boning a turkey gave one a diploma at this celebrated school."[51] Perhaps Goodfellow gave her students this task as a sort of "final exam." And the *Colonial Receipt Book* claims that Susan Israel (who later became Mrs. Thomas Painter) "was graduated [from Mrs. Goodfellow's] with honors, which later grew into widespread appreciation of her recipes, all of which have been carefully preserved by her family, and tested many times before given to the public." Indeed, several recipes in the cookbook were contributed by Mrs. Painter with attribution to Mrs. Goodfellow.[52]

What happened to all the food the ladies created during their lessons is another mystery. It is probable that the students sampled the dishes there as part of the class, or maybe they were allowed to take a portion home, in order to share their handiwork with their families or eat later at their boarding schools. Perhaps it was even sold in the shop if Goodfellow thought the quality was high enough. And items not considered suitable for sale could have been given away to the young suitors who would wait eagerly outside her shop for the pretty girls to emerge, as suggested by Christopher Crag in his sarcastic *Tangram* piece. Crag writes that Goodfellow's shop "was daily honoured with the presence of a score or two of little foplings, who regularly came to storm the crusty wall of mutton pye, and masticate the dainty custard, whose existence was procured by the delicate exertion of these amiable fair-ones."[53]

Although it is not known for sure what happened to the students' creations, it is likely the food was never wasted. Food historian William Woys Weaver feels that if the girls made pound cake at Mrs. Goodfellow's, they took it back to their boarding school and had pound cake for a couple of days with their meals. As he points out, that would make sense, because then it also becomes a reward. "I'm sure that food was not wasted unless of course it was a total disaster," he said. "Boarding schools were on a budget. Girls probably paid a flat fee and that covered the cost of ingredients. You must realize Mrs. Goodfellow was buying her stuff wholesale; they bought items in large quantities in those days, such as thirty pounds of flour at a time, but she still had to watch her costs."[54]

Even though running the school would have required her to buy more ingredients than she needed to make the goods for her shop, the money she earned from teaching must have helped to defray these costs. Having the dual business of pastry shop and school allowed each one to advertise for the other. And the fact that Goodfellow was widowed three times indicates that she needed to support herself and her family, which she did.

Weaver agrees that operating the school must have been lucrative or Goodfellow wouldn't have done it; she and the other cooking instructors took up teaching because they needed the money. The other cookery schools that existed in Philadelphia during Mrs. Goodfellow's period had something to do with the instructors' livelihood so it must have been a critical factor for them. Somebody like the previously mentioned Joseph Head, who was teaching French cooking at the Mansion House Hotel, may have taken up teaching to enhance and maintain his reputation and that of his hotel which had a restaurant. Just like the celebrity chefs on television today, these classes may have served as a form of advertising; a marketing tool.[55]

Crag's *Tangram* essay jokes about yet another way Mrs. Goodfellow may have cleverly endorsed her school. He suggests that in addition to the young beaus who would loiter outside the cooking school gate, waiting for the young ladies to emerge after class, a few gentlemen would actually attend her lessons. Of course this amused the girls a great deal, and Mrs. Goodfellow, with her acclaimed matchmaking abilities, enhanced the lively banter of these young people by proposing the formation of a poetry club. According to Crag, the shrewd Mrs. Goodfellow figured this would also "occasion a more general consumption of her jellies and cheesecakes, and promote the future interest of her establishment."[56]

The students were thrilled at the prospect and so Mrs. Goodfellow began to tag her pastries and custards with little epigrams. The students quickly followed her example and placed poems under the pies and puff pastry to be sold in the shop so that "whatever chance customer came in for a six-penny tart, was sure of receiving three-pence worth of wit or poetry with his bargain, so that, when they had emptied the shell, they might have taught their children to read upon the under crust." Crag alludes that competition raged among the students to best each other with their poems, which entertained city residents a great deal.[57]

In addition to the "poetry contests," Crag implies that the young ladies also amused themselves by making miniature dough figures and placing them on the ledges of the windows.[58] While there are probably few complete truths within his sardonic essay, Crag's tales about Goodfellow and her school do suggest that she was able to engage and hold the attention of her students, no small feat as they were so often unenthusiastic. And the simple fact that he wrote about her shows her respect and renown.

FIVE

Directions for Cookery

Philadelphia, 64 Dock Street
Wednesday, September 20, 1815
11 a.m.

Mrs. Goodfellow grasped her long wooden peel and reached into the bake oven to retrieve one of the lemon puddings. Using it like a shovel, she carefully placed the peel's flat wedge-shaped end under the dish, balanced the pudding on top and pulled it toward her. Once it was within reach, she used a heavy cloth to grip the hot dish and carry it over to the table. As she gently put it down, a delicious sweet-tart aroma steamed up from its shimmering surface, which was a lovely caramel color. The pastry surrounding the filling was crisply baked and its edges nicely browned. She removed the other pudding from the oven in the same manner as her students watched.

After transferring the puddings to the cooling shelf, she ushered the girls over to the fireplace where she swung the pot containing the artichokes toward her and carefully removed each artichoke with a large tin skimmer—a long-handled slotted spoon that let the water drain away. She placed the artichokes on a serving platter and then covered them with a large rounded lid to keep warm.

Next it was time to check on the simmering chickens. Swinging the heavy pot away from the fire, she tested a few pieces for doneness by carefully lifting them out with a long-handled two-pronged fork and then gently pulling the meat apart with a smaller fork to peer at the inside. They were still a little pink in the middle, which she said was just right, as they needed to cook until *almost* done.

She then removed all the chicken pieces from the pot and placed them in a large stoneware dish which she covered with a domed tin lid and set near the fire to keep warm. Gesturing for the girls to follow her to the work table, she portioned off a lump of butter, placed it in a large stew pan, and cut it into small pieces with a knife. She then scooped some flour into the pan and rubbed the butter and flour together until the mixture had the consistency of very coarse crumbs. Picking up the crock of cream, she poured half a pint into the pan and whisked it with the flour and butter mixture. Last, she carried the pan over to the fire where she set it on the hot coals.

Gathering the girls around her, she demonstrated how to stir the mixture until all the butter was melted and the sauce began to thicken. She then added the small cheese-cloth bag of sweet herbs, mace, salt, and pepper that Hannah had prepared earlier that morning, explaining that the blend would infuse flavor without being overpowering, and the sachet would keep the herbs from scattering throughout the sauce, helping to retain the smooth texture and white color.

Next she skillfully transferred the chicken pieces to the stew pan and let the whole mixture come to a boil, stirring occasionally. She let it gently bubble for a few minutes, and then removed the pan from the heat and took the chicken pieces out, placing them on a large pewter serving platter. A spicy-sweet smell from the juicy meat permeated the air. After arranging the pieces attractively, Mrs. Goodfellow ladled the creamy sauce over them, telling the girls that a few small slices of cold ham could be added to enhance and improve the flavor, especially if serving at a dinner party.

She carefully covered the fricassee with a domed lid to retain heat and placed it on a small bench near the fireplace to keep warm. Wiping her hands on her apron, she then led the students over to the large table in the corner where they would be eating.

When the girls reached the dining area, they saw there were actually two tables. The larger one was a gate-leg style—its two drop leaves (one on each end) were up and supported by extra legs in order to open it to maximum size. On the top of the smaller of the two tables Hannah had prepared a tray containing plates, forks, knives, and spoons, some salt cellars, a folded linen tablecloth, and a stack of linen napkins. A few thick oilcloth table mats had been positioned alongside—one held a large glass pitcher of water, and on the others sat some small dishes of colorful preserves and pickles, including mangoes (pickled melons) and tomatoes. Several tumbler glasses were lined up in two rows on another tray, which was perched on top of a tray stand.

Mrs. Goodfellow picked up the linen tablecloth and gestured for the girls to gather around the larger table. She told them that before they could taste and enjoy the various dishes, she would first give them a brief lesson on proper table-setting techniques. A few barely audible groans escaped from some of the now-hungry girls, but Mrs. Goodfellow ignored this and continued, explaining that for each of the ten cookery lessons in the term she would focus on one aspect of dinner party procedures. She asserted that even though they might be delegating some of these tasks to their servants someday, they still needed to know how a proper table was laid and how to plan and properly host a fine party.

She began by stressing that just as with the food preparation, everything needed to be ready and in good order before starting to set the table to avoid having to stop and clean or fix something halfway through. In addition, she told them it is best to use trays to transport as many items at a time as possible to the dining area.

Pointing out the coarse woolen crumb-cloth that was under the table, Mrs. Goodfellow emphasized that this always gets laid down first and serves to catch any crumbs that fall during the meal. She next started to unfold the heavy linen tablecloth, asking a couple of girls to help her shake it out over the table. As they worked to get it properly situated, she carefully ran her hands along the surface, showing them how it should be a good deal larger than the table it is covering, and must be laid smoothly and evenly, so it is does not hang down more on one side than another. She further advised that it is best to get the highest quality table linen that can be afforded, as those that are fine and thick will last much longer and look nicer than those that are coarse and thin. She told them cloth made of double French damask is the most preferable for tablecloths and napkins since this material is not only fine and thick, but also soft and glossy, like satin, and washes very well.

She then walked over to the smaller table to get the tray of napkins, plates, and utensils and carefully carried it to the big table, situating herself at the head. Picking up the pile of napkins, she passed one to each of the girls, and then taking one herself, she slowly demonstrated how to fold it into a diamond shape, asking the girls to follow along step by step. She walked around assisting any of the students who needed help, and as they worked together, Hannah hurried over with two baskets of fresh bread and placed one at each end of the large table.

Once the students had finished creating their "diamonds," Mrs. Goodfellow handed out the plates, asking the girls to place them around the table, one for every person. She instructed them that plates are set for guests only along the sides, with the two ends reserved for the master and mistress of the house. These two positions require some room around them so they can properly carve the meat dishes, she advised. Elaborating on this concept of spaciousness, she recommended that it is always better to set a table "too large for the company," positioning guests a comfortable distance apart rather than crowding them at a table that is too small, particularly in warmer weather.

After the plates were set, she began handing out the eating utensils, explaining that the knife and fork go in front of each plate. As the girls arranged the forks and knives, Mrs. Goodfellow told them that when soup is part of the menu, a spoon is included with the other utensils, and soup plates are placed on top of the dinner plates. She then picked up some spoons and walked around the table, laying two at each corner in criss-cross fashion, asking one of the girls to put a salt cellar between each pair of crossed spoons. She then retrieved a pretty basket of ornamental sugar-work from a shelf and placed it in the middle, telling the girls for a company dinner it is customary to have an elegant centerpiece, such as a vase of flowers, or some other decoration that is functional as well as attractive, like a plateau or an epergne dish to display fruit or sweetmeats. Pieces of fancy sugar-work like the type she put on the table can be hired from a confectioner, she added.

Next she walked back to the small table to retrieve the other tray. After putting it down gently, she began handing out the water tumblers to the girls, asking them to put a glass at the right hand of every plate. She told them if they were setting the table for a true evening dinner party, they would also place one or more wine glasses next to the tumblers, depending on the variety of wines on the menu, as different wines are served in different types of glasses. The wine decanters are situated near the table corners, but the water pitcher or pitchers remain on the sidetable, to replenish the glasses when necessary.

At this point she mentioned that setting the side table is as important as preparing the dining table, especially when serving multiple courses, as its function is to hold the overflow of dishes, serving pieces, utensils, and so on, that are needed throughout the meal. That discussion would be covered in another lesson, she assured them.

For the next step, Mrs. Goodfellow instructed each student to pick up her folded napkin diamond and put it at the right hand side of the plate. She then picked up the bread basket closest to her and showed the girls how to remove a piece of bread with a fork. Lifting it out of the basket, she held it up so the girls could see how Hannah had cut the bread into thick oblong blocks. She warned them never to cut bread into slices except for breakfast or tea, and to make sure the basket holds enough bread to supply all the guests with a second piece if needed. She then showed them how to arrange the bread on the napkin, laying it down in the center, covered by one of the corners. Light French rolls could be served instead of pieces of cut bread, she added.

The whole time Mrs. Goodfellow was giving her dinner party instruction, her student Eliza Leslie was diligently taking notes, just as she had during the cooking lessons. In her late twenties, Eliza was older than the other pupils, and also seemed to be already rather well-acquainted with Mrs. Goodfellow, which piqued the interest of her classmates a bit. This combined with her obvious desire to copy every-thing down caused the other girls to cast sidelong glances her way from time to time, wondering if they were missing something.

As Eliza scribbled furiously, one student could not hold in her curiosity any longer, and she leaned closer to ask Eliza in a low voice why she was keeping such detailed notes. Looking up in surprise, Eliza frowned a bit and whispered back, "There is no loss in having thorough instructions to refer back to when it comes time to prepare a meal."

The girl nodded and shrugged her shoulders, "I guess so," she said. She then turned to the girl to her left and murmured what Eliza had just told her. The other girl whispered back she had heard that Eliza's mother ran a boardinghouse, and guessed that was why she took so many notes—she probably had to help with all the meals. The first girl turned toward Eliza again and gave her a quick sympathetic smile before abruptly lifting her gaze back to Mrs. Goodfellow, who had cleared her throat and said, "Girls, please pay attention."

Actually, the gossipy girl was probably correct—most historians agree that Eliza Leslie's role in assisting with her mother's boardinghouse was likely the real reason she took such copious notes of all Mrs. Goodfellow's recipes during her lessons there. However, it is also a well-known fact that she wanted to be a published author more than anything. Did she have plans all along to try to publish the recipes, or did she seek publication only at the suggestion of her brother (which is what she claimed)? Whatever the case, all her note-taking paid off, as Eliza Leslie ended up writing several cookbooks featuring recipes, techniques, and other household knowledge she learned from Mrs. Goodfellow, making her the most popular cookbook writer in America prior to the Civil War.[1]

Although Eliza Leslie was born in Philadelphia, her parents, Robert and Lydia Baker Leslie, were originally from Cecil County, Maryland. Eliza's paternal great-grandfather, also named Robert Leslie, emigrated to the United States from Scotland around 1745 and took up farming along Maryland's Northeast River, near an insulated hill called Maiden's Mountain. Eliza's mother's parents were Jethro Baker and Ann Gonson, who was of Swedish descent, prompting her to note that she had no English blood in her background,[2] although her brother Charles indicates in his autobiography that his mother's family was from England.[3] (They were both correct in a sense—Ann Gonson was indeed Swedish, but her husband Jethro Baker was British.)

In 1785 Lydia Baker married Cecil County native Robert Leslie. The Leslie family lived about a mile north of the village of North East, described by Eliza as being "over against Bulls Mountain." Not long after their marriage, they moved to Elkton, Maryland, where Robert worked as a clock and watchmaker. After just a year or two in Elkton, the couple moved to Philadelphia in 1786, and Eliza (their first child), was born there the following year.[4]

Eliza had very fond childhood memories of both her parents. She described her mother as "a handsome woman, of excellent sense, very amusing, and a first rate housewife," and she proudly depicted her father as a "man of considerable natural genius, and much self-taught knowledge, particularly in natural philosophy and mechanics." According to Eliza, he was also talented musically and played both the flute and violin, with a special fondness for the Scottish airs he had learned as a child.[5]

Once in Philadelphia, Robert Leslie's clock and watch-making business prospered. A *Pennsylvania Packet* advertisement for his shop in June 1787 listed gold, silver, tortoiseshell, and gilt watches for sale. Another announcement touted "Clocks and Time-Pieces, on a new and improved plan, one of which may be seen at his shop, not subject to any visible variation from the different changes in the weather," as well as clock and watch repairs and improvements.[6]

By 1788 he expanded his services to offer assistance to any gentlemen attempting philosophical or mechanical experiments with small machines or models. A year later he proposed to establish a museum in Philadelphia to house a collection of models of various kinds of machines used in agriculture, manufacturing, and mechanical engineering. His own inventions included a machine for threshing wheat, a horizontal tide-mill (to work with both tides so boats could sail in any direction), a horizontal windmill (so the wind could act on both sides of the wheel at the same time), and an improvement of the common wheat fan (producing more wind with less labor).[7]

Leslie's innovative nature captured the attention of George Washington, Benjamin Franklin and Thomas Jefferson, who became his personal friends, and he was elected a member of the American Philosophical Society as per Jefferson's recommendation.[8] According to Eliza, he suggested a lightning rod improvement to Franklin that was "immediately tested, and afterwards universally adopted."[9] He was also very friendly with Philadelphia's prominent doctors of that time—Benjamin Rush, Benjamin Smith Barton, Caspar Wistar, Philip Syng Physick, and James Mease, and had frequent dealings with the city's illustrious Charles Willson Peale and engineer Oliver Evans.[10]

In an attempt to further promote his business, Robert went into partnership in 1793 with Isaac Price, who stayed behind in Philadelphia while Robert moved his family to London to sell his mechanical inventions there and purchase clocks and watches for both establishments. While in

London, young Eliza took French and music lessons and was given penmanship and drawing instruction by her father.[11] Her mother taught her sewing, and she attended classes to learn ornamental needlework. From an early age her passions were reading and drawing, and she quickly read the few children's books available at the time, thus delving into adult works of literature while still very young.[12]

This love of books then followed her throughout her life, prompting her to first dabble in writing during her preteen years. As she mentions in a letter to her friend Alice B. (Neal) Haven, her earliest writing attempts were verses, specifically songs, tailored to fit the popular airs of the late eighteenth century, about soldiers, sailors, hunters, and nuns. However, by the time she was thirteen or fourteen she began to despise her own poetry and claims to have destroyed it all, abandoning her dream of someday seeing her name in print.[13]

The Leslies lived in London until 1799 when the death of Isaac Price caused the family to move back to Philadelphia. Unfortunately Price had so poorly managed the business during their absence that Eliza's father found himself embroiled in a lawsuit with the executors of his deceased partner. The laborious legal issues added undue strain to Robert, whose health had been failing, and he passed away in 1803 after a week-long illness.[14]

His death left the family in rather dire circumstances, and it was not long after that Lydia was forced to open a boardinghouse in order to support her five children. As the oldest, Eliza helped out by giving drawing lessons and in later years coloring maps and painting feather fans along with her sister Ann.[15] She also did some work copying the pieces of master painters, and her copy of Salvator Rosa's *Banditti in Ruins* was exhibited in 1812 when she was twenty-five.[16] According to Eliza, the family kept their monetary difficulties to themselves and were able to remain debt-free through hard work and perseverance.[17]

Although the family did not ask for any help, it was provided for them in the form of tuition assistance for Eliza's two brothers. Both were able to attend the University of Pennsylvania through the aid of two instructors—Dr. Rogers, who taught English, and mathematics professor Robert Patterson, who had been a friend of their father.[18] Eventually Eliza's four siblings left home, but it appears that she remained with her mother, assisting with the boardinghouse and attending Mrs. Goodfellow's cooking classes.

Eliza described her brother Charles as having an "extraordinary genius for painting," and he went to London to study and enrich his artistic skills. He married while there and became quite successful, rapidly becoming one of the more accomplished painters in Europe. Eliza's sister Ann moved to New York and often visited London, where Charles gave her painting lessons, allowing her to become quite successful at copying pictures. Her other sister, Martha (referred to as Patty), married Henry C. Carey, son of Mathew Carey, founder of one of Philadelphia's earliest publishing houses. Eliza's youngest brother, Thomas Jefferson Leslie, attended West Point Academy and was for many years a paymaster in the U.S. Army, attaining the rank of major.[19]

In the summer of 1820 Eliza moved to Tom's residence in West Point to recuperate after a long illness,[20] and it was this brother who recommended to Eliza that she try to compile a book of the many recipes she had collected while a student at Mrs. Goodfellow's. She forged ahead with the idea, and in 1827 her first book was published, entitled *Seventy-Five Receipts for Pastry, Cakes and Sweetmeats*, "By a Lady of Philadelphia." Although it was very successful and went through several editions, it was not the literary accomplishment Eliza dreamed of producing, and she spoke of it in rather humble terms. She described it as "most *un-parnasseau,*" and says, "truth was, I had a tolerable collection of receipts taken by myself while a pupil at Mrs. Goodfellow's celebrated cooking-school in Philadelphia. I had so many applications from my friends for copies of these directions, that my brother suggested my getting rid of the inconvenience by giving them to the public in print."[21]

These musings were from Eliza's reflective letter to her friend Alice B. Haven, which serves as the most comprehensive existing autobiographical information about her. However, since this letter was dated August 1, 1851 (six months after Goodfellow died), it is possible Eliza never expressed these feelings to her instructor, perhaps preferring to thoughtfully wait until after she was gone to voice her true sentiments.

And even though it might not have been Eliza's genre of choice, she ended up writing a total of nine cookbooks between 1827 and 1857, several of which were reprinted and updated in numerous formats. In fact, these nine cookery books grew into an amazing seventy-two reiterations, according to Eleanor Lowenstein's bibliography *American Cookery Books, 1742–1860.* Furthermore, reissues of Leslie's books continued until the early 1880s, decades after her death.[22]

Leslie became revered and respected for her knowledge and advice regarding cooking and household management. Modern food historians John and Karen Hess assert that "American cookery reached its highest level in the second quarter of the nineteenth century, with Miss Leslie as its guide."[23] In *Nineteenth-Century American Fiction Writers,* Elisa E. Beshero-Bondar describes Leslie as "literally a household word in Victorian America," having "taught generations of American women how to cook, behave themselves in public, and clean their houses."[24]

So even though "home economics" may not have been Leslie's first passion, interest in her cooking techniques has continued to trickle down into every generation since then, even into modern times. Almost two centuries have passed since she first began publishing recipes, but to this day she is widely recognized as one of the most influential American cookbook writers ever.[25] Reprints of her cookbooks and recipes still appear in updated versions, allowing modern cooks to replicate her classic dishes.

And the success of *Seventy-Five Receipts* did get her foot in the door, thus securing a publisher and enabling her to do what she really enjoyed—writing literary works of fiction. In addition to the cookbooks, she eventually wrote short stories and storybooks for young people as well as one novella and a number of short stories for adults. She also served as an editor for *Home Book of Fashion, Literature and Domestic Economy, The Gift* (an annual), *The Violet* (a juvenile souvenir), and briefly her own magazine, *Miss Leslie's Magazine*, in addition to being a regular contributor to *Godey's Lady's Book* and *Graham's Magazine*. These are the achievements she proudly highlights when telling her life story. Ironically though, it is the books on "domestic economy" that she begrudgingly admits were most profitable and successful.[26]

However, the fact that Eliza Leslie kept writing cookbooks shows that she must have appreciated the income and recognition, and came to rely on them for her livelihood. She was sharp enough to be aware of the fact that prior to the publishing of her first cookbook, she was never really able to spread her wings much, as her chief responsibility had been helping her mother, and she had become dependent on her brother Tom's support. The success of *Seventy-Five Receipts* gave her the financial independence and courage to break out on her own, at the age of forty.[27]

Through the 1820s and 1830s Eliza lived with Tom and his family on and off in West Point, and later New York City, when he was transferred there. At this point, New York was already developing into the fast-paced, vibrant city that it is today. As per letters to her friend Abby Bailey, Eliza describes it as much livelier and busier than Philadelphia, but less comfortable, accessible, and functional. She also thought New Yorkers were rather brash and extroverted, less reserved and intellectual than Philadelphians. However, she appreciated their hospitable nature, and thought New York was generally a pleasant

Eliza Leslie (1787–1858), Mrs. Goodfellow's most accomplished student, painted by Thomas Sully in 1844. (*Library of Congress*)

place.[28] So it appears she liked New York's energy and social atmosphere but missed the finer architecture, art, and literature she was accustomed to in Philadelphia.

Leslie also visited Boston in the summer of 1831, finding Bostonians "exactly" to her taste, as this colonial city was more similar to Philadelphia. Not only were the ladies "well-educated, intelligent and of frank and polished manner," but many prominent residents showered her with attention. She was pleased that it was a city of readers and writers, both male and female, and felt that nobody was trying to put on false airs,[29] a trait she detested. She liked it there—she fit in.

These experiences undoubtedly gave her additional material regarding social customs for her behavior book and fiction sketches, allowing her to compare and contrast what was popular in these cities with Philadelphia style and norms. She may have also picked up different recipes and techniques for her cookbooks from these places.

Eventually she made her way back to Philadelphia and appeared to again receive instruction and guidance from Mrs. Goodfellow. However, for some reason she does not acknowledge her mentor in her cookbooks until the late 1840s, not long before Goodfellow died. Considering the respectful way Miss Leslie *does* reference her, it is hard to imagine that she was trying to take all the credit on her own. Perhaps Mrs. Goodfellow didn't think it would have been proper for Eliza to give her attribution, although it would have been terrific advertising for her school and shop. When Eliza does mention Mrs. Goodfellow, it is always in a favorable light. For example, in *Miss Leslie's New Cookery Book*, she begins her pound cake recipe by stating, "One of Mrs. Goodfellow's maxims was, 'up-weight of flour, and downweight of everything else'—and she was right, as the excellence of her cakes sufficiently proved, during the thirty years that she taught her art in Philadelphia, with unexampled success."[30]

Did Eliza Leslie ever use the knowledge she learned from Mrs. Goodfellow to teach as well, either teaming with Mrs. Goodfellow or on her own? There is no existing evidence that she did, and food historian William Woys Weaver does not believe so, due to these revered declarations and asides about Mrs. Goodfellow and her methodology that Leslie makes in some of her cookbooks.[31] So although Leslie was essentially educating women about many aspects of cooking techniques through the detailed recipes and instructions in her books, she appeared to leave the hands-on teaching to Mrs. Goodfellow.

The true relationship between the two women has never been plumbed. At the very least, it is clear Mrs. Goodfellow was Eliza's mentor and an indispensable resource for her writing. Although Eliza did publish three cookbooks after Mrs. Goodfellow died in 1851, they were basically revisions and updates of the original recipes, mixed with "new receipts" she credited to other sources. For example, *Miss Leslie's New Receipts for Cooking*, published in 1854, includes recipes of "French origin" as well as some "obtained from the South, and from ladies noted for their skill in housewifery."[32]

It is possible that Leslie was running her recipes past Mrs. Goodfellow the whole time she was writing (or at least until the time of Goodfellow's death in 1851). The fact that Leslie was living in a hotel for several years later in life[33] meant that she was most likely eating her meals in the hotel dining room, and would have had no place to test her recipes, although the publisher's description at the beginning of *Miss Leslie's New Cookery Book* (1857) claims that all its receipts are new and have been "fully tried and tested by the author since the publication of her former books."[34]

In any case, Leslie became famous for her cookbooks, household advice, and short stories depicting domestic conventions and behavior, even though she never managed her own home or became a wife or mother. In fact, her rather nontraditional living accommodations for an unmarried woman at that time created quite a stir, causing some of the Philadelphia high society ladies to dislike and distrust her. Well known for her opinionated comments which could escalate into heated discussions at parties, Eliza didn't hide behind a veneer of propriety.[35] And while some people were intimidated by her often acerbic remarks and unconventional behavior, others admired her honesty, loyalty, and generosity.[36] An acquaintance referred to her as "the stiffest, though most companionable, of the three Leslie girls."[37]

For her first book (*Seventy-Five Receipts*), she published as "A Lady of Philadelphia," as it was a common practice for female writers at that time to withhold one's identity. However, once she gained some notice, she instead deliberately signed her true name to her books (either Eliza Leslie or Miss Leslie), another example of her boldness. And she peppered her writings with her opinions and double entendres.[38]

These bits and pieces of satire and wisdom brought a humorous and interesting quality to her cookbooks, giving them a more readable quality than a typical collection of recipes. And while her style may have offended some, it undoubtedly added to the books' popularity, as she was still able to sell thousands of them to women of various economic levels, thus spreading Goodfellow's advice and instructions across the country.

Eliza Leslie's success stemmed from the skillful way she was able to address the needs of the wide variety of cultures and social classes that were meshing together in nineteenth-century America. This could have been a result of Mrs. Goodfellow's influence, but it also helped that Leslie had experienced the culinary styles of a number of large cities during her lifetime, including London, Philadelphia, New York, and Boston, in addition to the influence of relatives from Maryland. While other cookbook writers at the time focused mainly on the regional foods they were familiar with, Leslie had the foresight to take a more cosmopolitan approach to American cooking. Her cookbooks provided recipes representing all parts of the country—from Carolina punch to Yankee pumpkin pudding, as well as everything in between.[39]

By the time her third cookbook, *Directions for Cookery, in Its Various Branches*, was published in 1837, she had expanded her subject matter to include all sorts of cookery (not just pastry and sweetmeats), which were "particularly adapted to the domestic economy of her own country." In the preface she explicitly explained that she designed the book "as a manual of American housewifery," avoiding recipes that required European utensils and ingredients difficult to find in America. She had also begun to follow the increasingly popular trend of suggesting the use of chemical leavenings such as pearlash and saleratus, although she sometimes preceded these directions with the advice "not to use too much as it gives an unpleasant taste."

Often considered Leslie's most significant work, *Directions for Cookery* had the highest number of printings of any cookbook in nineteenth-century America, with every run producing at least one thousand copies.[40] In its heyday, it was recommended by fellow cookbook author Sarah Rutledge in *The Carolina Housewife* (1847) for general-purpose kitchen instructions. And modern culinary experts John and Karen Hess rank it along with Mrs. Randolph's *Virgina House-wife* as one of the two best American cookbooks ever written, possessing a "concern for quality that now seems almost alien."[41]

In *Directions for Cookery*, Mrs. Goodfellow's influence and Leslie's writing combine to create a comprehensive cookery manual—complete with specific, straightforward instructions and suggestions, discussions about the significance of fresh ingredients, and details of proper technique.[42] Leslie stresses that "accuracy in proportioning the ingredients is indispensable to success in cookery"; and therefore recommends that scales and weights and a set of tin measures (from a gallon to half a gill) are extremely important. She warns her readers that cooking, especially cake baking, can be difficult, perhaps even disastrous, without proper tools. A failed cake was both a disappointment and an expensive waste[43]—no doubt topics she had heard Mrs. Goodfellow lecture about in her classes.

For her fellow Philadelphia readers, Leslie even mentions where to purchase all the utensils necessary for cake and pastry-making (and the other branches of cooking)— Gideon Cox's household store located at 335 Market Street. "Everything of the sort will be found there in great variety, of good quality, and at reasonable price," she says. She also gives a few examples of where to find specific ingredients in the city's famous markets, including rennet (for making curds and whey), unskinned calves' feet (for jelly), and cream cheese.[44]

When she produced a revised version of this book in 1851 entitled *Miss Leslie's Complete Cookery: Directions for Cookery, in Its Various Branches,* she targeted a range of household incomes with her recipes, stressing the same guidelines for good wholesome ingredients that Mrs. Goodfellow preached. "By judicious management, and by taking due care that nothing is wasted or thrown away which might be used to advantage, one family will live 'excellently well,' at no greater cost in the end than another family is expending on a table that never has a good thing upon it," she remarks in the opening.[45]

Leslie learned from Goodfellow how to find the middle ground between frugality and excess in meal preparation— a balanced approach her cookbooks conveyed through the way she presented her recipes. In *Miss Leslie's New Receipts for Cooking,* she explains that many of the dishes "are designed for elegant tables, and an equal proportion for families who live well, but moderately." Expanding upon this concept of appealing to a wide audience, she includes a chapter for young readers in which she lists specific menus for various meal types, situations, and family sizes, specifying what items best enhance each other and are in season at the same time.[46] Although designed to assist newlyweds with household management, these helpful tips were undoubtedly a good reference for seasoned housekeepers as well.

By the mid-nineteenth century Leslie's cookbooks had become a leading source of cooking advice and information for American women from all levels of society. These "manuals" were standard fixtures not only in the established communities on the East Coast; but they also traveled westward along with pioneers. As Barbara M. Walker notes in *The Little House Cookbook—Frontier Foods from Laura Ingalls Wilder's Classic Stories*, Eliza Leslie's *Directions for Cookery* was one of the most popular cookbooks among these frontier women, who lived an often isolated and nomadic existence. The author even surmises that if Laura Ingalls Wilder had a copy, Leslie's guidance would have probably helped her in her newlywed years.[47] Although pioneer women learned many cooking techniques directly from their mothers after they married, they often moved to farms and settlements miles away. Without telephones, they did not have quick access to the maternal advice they may have craved. Cookbooks with detailed instructions and suggestions such as Leslie's would have helped fill this void.

Leslie's cookbooks were also indispensable for women from the middle and upper levels of society who were not lucky enough to attend Mrs. Goodfellow's or similar classes like herself. For example, Mary Todd Lincoln had led a rather indulgent childhood in Lexington, Kentucky, with nannies and cooks. Although some of her contemporaries did learn culinary and domestic arts so they could later direct their servants on how to properly perform these tasks, it appears that Mary did not. Therefore, she had no cookery or housekeeping training when she married Abraham Lincoln. Money was tight at first for the Lincolns, and Mary got by with household assistance from relatives and limited domestic hired help. Eventually, however, Miss Leslie came to her aid.

The Lincolns had been married four years when one of them purchased a copy of *Directions for Cookery* from the John Irwin & Company store in Springfield, Illinois, for eighty-seven cents, as well as Leslie's *The House Book: or, a Manual of Domestic Economy for Town and Country*.[48] From Leslie, Mary learned to make some of her favorite dishes from her Kentucky upbringing, including waffles, batter cakes, egg cornbread, and buckwheat cakes. She also became adept at preserving fruit, making cheese, roasting coffee, and baking bread, pies, and cakes. She developed a special skill for making white cake (a classic layer type with hints of vanilla and almond flavors), which she sometimes served with fresh strawberries, but never frosted. It ended up being one of Abe's favorites and she made it often for him, causing him to comment, "Mary's white cake is the best I've ever eaten."[49]

Leslie's approach of casting such a wide net was rather innovative. Until this point in time, many cookbook writers appealed to singular groups—such as the upper class with its taste (and budget) for pastries and sweetmeats, or the thrifty women Lydia Maria Child targeted in *The American Frugal Housewife*. But Leslie found a way to capture the attention of a wide audience.

As Patrick Dunne and Charles L. Mackie assert, through the success of Leslie's cookbooks, Goodfellow and Leslie essentially changed the way American women viewed food preparation. Leslie's recipes had much clearer instructions than those of her predecessors, listing specific quantities and making it much easier for those with less-developed cooking skills to re-create popular dishes of the time.[50]

So she included women from all walks of life in her intended audience. She assured her readers (reflecting the attitudes of her day) that her receipts were written in a style "so plain and minute, as to be perfectly intelligible to servants, and persons of the most moderate capacity."[51] The level of detail in Leslie's directions conjures up images of her as a student inside Mrs. Goodfellow's "classroom" writing down her teacher's instructions verbatim, as if she was taking notes for an absent schoolmate.

This clarity in Leslie's recipes is apparent from the very beginning; in the preface of *Seventy-Five Receipts* she reassures her readers: "The following Receipts for Pastry, Cakes, and Sweetmeats, are original, and have been used by the author and many of her friends with uniform success," she boldly states. "All the ingredients, with their proper quantities, are enumerated in a list at the head of each receipt, a plan which will greatly facilitate the business of procuring and preparing the requisite articles."[52] Prior to this, recipes were commonly written out in paragraph form. Leslie made things easier by listing ingredients first, something we take for granted when reading a recipe today, but at that time it was a novel approach, and an influence of her mentor, Mrs. Goodfellow.[53]

Eliza also had a knack for seeing a need and interest for various cooking techniques and methods, and then introducing them to the American public. It is likely Mrs. Goodfellow had some input here as well, perhaps suggesting what types of recipes Eliza could include in her cookbooks.

For example, Leslie's second book, *Domestic French Cookery*, "chiefly translated from Sulpice Barué," which was published in 1832, was especially well-received in the South, where there was a sizable interest in French cooking.[54] As Leslie indicates in the book's preface, her purpose in writing *Domestic French Cookery* was to provide a select variety of recipes for French specialties that were adapted to products and ingredients found in America. She included only dishes that she felt were well-suited to American palates and the country's diversity of foods, making subtle changes and substitutions in her versions.[55]

Leslie's savvy in knowing how to adapt and "Americanize" French cookery in order to make it viable in this new nation differentiated her work. She realized many people did not speak or read French, so she interpreted the terms and directions. Her goal was to make a book available for people who appreciated fine French foods, but perhaps did not have the culinary skills required to create them. She was also hoping that exposure to these dishes would help improve American cookery, and suggests "this little work may be found equally useful in private families, hotels, and boarding-houses."[56]

A great deal of mystery surrounded this cookbook for many years, in particular the background of Monsieur Barué and how Leslie obtained these recipes. Leslie makes no mention in any of her writings about who he was, any relationship they may have had, or how this book even came to be published. Historians often wondered if they were authentic or simply contrived, especially since Katherine Bitting's *Gastronomic Bibliography* (published in 1939) maintains that there is no listing of a Sulpice Barué in Vicaire's well-known French cookbook reference book, *Bibliographie Gastronomique*.

However, through meticulous research, food historian Jan Longone revealed that Barué was indeed the editor of several editions of Louis-Eustache Audot's *La Cuisinière de la Campagne et de la Ville* (1827–1829), and had also contributed 150 recipes of his own to the volumes. Leslie's cookbook was simply a translated compilation of these receipts, as duly noted on the book's cover. She never mentioned this work in her autobiographical letter because she evidently never considered it to be anything more than a translation.[57]

According to William Woys Weaver, Leslie's *Domestic French Cookery* came about as an attempt by Philadelphia publishers to establish more control over the West Indian and Latin American trade (since Boston monopolized the U.S. book market at the time). Publishing this volume in Philadelphia was a way to infiltrate the New Orleans market (with its large French influence). He maintains its success had nothing to do with the high-class (French) cooking that was popular in Philadelphia, because the recipes chosen by Leslie were more bourgeois (middle or merchant class) in nature, not the elaborate French cuisine produced in Philadelphia at that time by French-trained chefs and caterers.[58]

The fact that Leslie made any type of French recipes available to the general public was quite remarkable, especially for a woman. Male professionals dominated French cooking from its earliest days, with creative chefs striving to concoct luxurious dishes for royal families, aristocrats, and wealthy merchants. Their handiwork eventually trickled down into a number of other food service occupations such as catering, pastry and confectionary making, and restaurant work. For a long time French cookbooks were written by men, mainly for other men employed in these positions.[59]

The French Cook by Louis Eustache Ude had been reprinted in America before Leslie's *Domestic French Cookery*, and although Ude's intention was to produce an easier method of French cookery for cooks of all levels, his writing style was less direct than Leslie's. But after Leslie's *Domestic French Cookery*, more adaptations of French cookbooks were introduced to the American public, including one produced by J. M. Sanderson of Philadelphia's Franklin House in 1843[60] and Charles Elme Francatelli's *The Modern Cook*, published in 1846.

Then Pierre Blot, a Frenchman who came to the United States in the 1850s, published his first book in 1863, *What to Eat and How to Cook It.* Similar to Leslie, his recipes were "systematically and practically arranged, to enable the housekeeper to prepare the most difficult or simple dishes in the best manner." Two years later he opened with much fanfare what many food experts consider the first school of French cookery in the U.S.—the New York Cooking Academy, and in 1867 authored the *Hand-book Of Practical Cookery, For Ladies and Professional Cooks.*[61] We'll visit him again later in our story.

So although Leslie was among the first of American cookbook writers to offer French cooking instructions for the masses, it is not known which (if any) of these French cooking techniques came from Mrs. Goodfellow's lectures. More than likely, Mrs. Goodfellow taught the "Anglicized" versions of French recipes, which had been popular in England and printed in the British cookbooks Goodfellow used as textbooks.

For example, there is a recipe for "Ragou of Onions" attributed to Mrs. Goodfellow in a manuscript cookbook compiled in Philadelphia. The directions call for browning onions in a stew pan with butter; then adding flour, gravy, cayenne pepper, salt, and mustard and cooking until the mixture is thick.[62] *Ragout* is a French term for a rich stew of meat and vegetables, particularly one with a highly flavorful sauce added near the end of the cooking time. It was adapted into English as *ragoo* in the seventeenth century,[63] and according to Andrew F. Smith, ragout recipes were published in the United States beginning in 1828.[64]

The "Queries and Answers" column from the January 1931 issue of *American Cookery* magazine provides additional insight into some of the French techniques that may have been taught by Mrs. Goodfellow. In explaining the differences between ragouts and salmis, the columnist says (facetiously), "A hundred years ago, more or less, when we went to cooking school, we learned that a salmi is a stew of game; a ragout is a stew with either vinegar or wine added while cooking." According to the article, the wine or vinegar served to soften the tough connective tissue of any meat that needed it, whether game or butcher's meat.[65] As the receipt attributed to Mrs. Goodfellow did not contain any meat, the softening agents were not required.

In *Domestic French Cookery*, Leslie lists recipes for "Ragooed Cabbage," "Ragooed mushrooms," and "Ragooed Livers." Fittingly, the "Ragooed Livers" call for white wine, but the vegetable recipes do not. The other recipes for similarly cooked dishes are all labeled "stewed," in line with Leslie's translations of French cooking for the American public. The Game and Poultry section also includes receipts for "A Salmi" and "Cold Salmi," [66] and a recipe for "Salmi of Partridges" (French dish) is found in *The Lady's Receipt-Book: A Useful Companion for Large or Small Families* (1947).[67]

In *Directions for Cookery*, Leslie includes the recipe for an often unpredictable French dish, omelette soufflé. She includes such strict instructions that it should have a disclaimer attached. Perhaps this was one technique not typically taught by Mrs. Goodfellow, or maybe Leslie had little confidence in her readers' ability to replicate the light, fluffy delicacy. Either way, her description makes it sound like something only the most daring housewives would want to try; even modern home cooks who have attempted this dish can attest to its level of difficulty.

She warns not to begin to make an omelette soufflé until guests have finished their dinner, so that it may be ready to serve as soon as the meat course is removed. "Send it immediately to table, or it will fall and flatten," she cautions. "An omelette soufflé is a very nice and-delicate thing when properly managed; but if flat and heavy it should not be brought to table." To prevent this horrid scenario from happening, her final bit of advice provides less adventurous cooks with a way to opt out altogether. "If you live in a large town, the safest way of avoiding a failure in an omelette soufflé is to hire a French cook to come to your kitchen with his own utensils and ingredients, and make and bake it himself, while the first part of the dinner is progressing in the dining room."[68] One can only imagine what Mrs. Goodfellow thought of that suggestion; it seems unlikely that she would have advised Leslie to print this in her cookbook, but perhaps even she realized there were limits to the cooking abilities of nonprofessionals.

Another of Leslie's cookbooks that smartly filled a market niche, yet had long baffled food historians, was *The Indian Meal Book*, first published in 1846 in London. In this cookbook, Leslie provides recipes that feature cornmeal as a main ingredient, designed to be a nutritious and less expensive substitute for wheat flour during the time of the potato famine in Ireland. The purpose of this book was to educate the Irish and British about the versatility of maize, or Indian corn, as it was called, thus helping them survive the potato crop failure.[69]

Americans had been experimenting with cornmeal for years and knew how to incorporate it into palatable baked goods. Indeed, "Indian Pound Cake" was considered one of Mrs. Goodfellow's signature recipes. Leslie included it in many of her cookbooks, and permutations of the recipe also found their way into Philadelphia area manuscript cookbooks of the time.[70]

It had been assumed that *The Indian Meal Book* had been first published in 1847 by the Philadelphia publishing house Carey and Hart, as Leslie had worked with them on several of her books, a relationship fostered by her sister Patty's marriage to Henry C. Carey. However, once again, sleuthing by Jan Longone found the two earlier editions published in London. What has never been determined is how Leslie was chosen to write the book. Was it her idea (or even Goodfellow's), or was she commissioned to write it by the London publisher or some other? It remains a mystery.[71]

The many uses of cornmeal adopted from the Native Americans are just one example of how ingredients and flavors from other cultures were integrated with foods widely available in North America. In *New Receipts for Cooking* (1854), Miss Leslie's recipe for "Guisada or Spanish Stew" calls for "hare, rabbit, partridges, pheasants, or chickens," all of which were popular fare in the United States at that time. Stewing was a common cooking method, especially for game meat, but one thing that differentiated this recipe was Leslie's suggestion at the end: "It will be improved by the juice of one or two oranges, squeezed in toward the last."[72]

Citrus fruits like oranges were just one of the numerous exotics that were shipped to Philadelphia and other American ports from warmer climates including Spain, India, and the Caribbean. Diverse flavorings such as West Indian molasses, turmeric, cayenne pepper, rose and orange flower water, nutmeg, and cinnamon were among the many others. As a result, recipes such as West India Cocoa-Nut Cake, chicken curry, Alpistekas (Spanish cakes), and Pollo Valenciano were included in Miss Leslie's cookbooks, helping to familiarize Americans with a variety of taste combinations.[73]

Sauces and condiments using these imported spices and seasonings were central to these multicultural dishes, and Leslie's cookbooks featured instructions for different versions, including what foods they go best with and how to serve them. Her "East India Sauce for Fish" recipe says to "mix well together a jill of India soy; a jill of chili vinegar;

half a pint of walnut catchup, and a pint of mushroom-catchup. Shake the whole hard, and transfer it to small green bottles, putting a teaspoonful of sweet oil at the top of each, and keep the sauce in a cool dry place. When eating fish, mix a little of this with the melted butter on your plate."[74]

The "catchups" she is referring to were salty, spicy liquids, thinner than the thick tomato "ketchup" we slather on our hamburgers today. More like a soy sauce, there were versions made from walnuts, mushrooms, cucumbers, lemons, and lobster, as well as grapes and tomatoes. Leslie even had a recipe for "camp catchup" that was made out of ale or porter, white wine, shallots or onions, nutmeg, and ginger.[75]

All these varieties originated from Asian cuisines, introduced to Europe by Dutch traders. The word *ketchup* derives from the Chinese word *kêtsiap*, a fermented fish sauce, which was most likely originally the Malay word *kechap*, (now spelled *kecap*), or soy sauce. Common features included their salty taste, concentrated consistency, and long shelf life.[76] Although rather time-consuming to prepare, they provided interesting preserved seasonings at the ready, especially in the days before refrigeration. Up until about 1850, when ketchup was listed as an ingredient in an American recipe, it most likely was referring to those sauces made out of mushroom, walnut, or oyster. The use of these savory flavor enhancers continued throughout the second half of the nineteenth century, mostly owing to the continued popularity of Miss Leslie's cookbooks.[77]

Also from India, spicy curries were not unfamiliar to Americans, especially to those of English descent, as recipes for them had been included by British cookbook authors such as Hannah Glasse and William Kitchener beginning in the eighteenth century.[78] In America, *The Virginia House-wife* (1824) by Mary Randolph has instructions regarding "To Make a Curry of Catfish" and "To Make a Dish of Curry After the East Indian Manner," as well as a general recipe for curry powder that she says can be "used as a fine flavoured seasoning for fish, fowls, steaks, chops, veal cutlets, hashes, minces, alamodes, turtle soup, and in all rich dishes, gravies, sauce, etc."[79]

Eliza Leslie also incorporated several curry recipes in her cookbooks, stating that in its homeland of India, curry powder is "much used as a peculiar flavoring for soups, stews, and hashes." Like Hannah Glasse, she used a curry powder made of freshly ground spices to season these dishes. Her instructions say to "pound in a marble mortar three ounces of turmeric, three ounces of coriander seed, and a quarter of an ounce of cayenne; one ounce of mustard, one ounce of cardamoms, a half ounce of cummin seed, and half an ounce of mace. Let all these ingredients be thoroughly mixed in the mortar, and then sift it through a fine sieve, dry it for an hour before the fire, and put it into clean bottles, securing the corks well. Use from two to three table-spoonfuls at a time, in proportion to the size of the dish you intend to curry."

She states that this very pungent powder (with turmeric as a core ingredient) is indispensable to all curries, which may be made using any meat, poultry, game, or even oysters. Onions and boiled rice are also vital to the authenticity, she maintains, adding "in India there is always something acid in the mixture, as lemons, sour apple juice, or green tamarinds." As a suggestion she recommends adding two ounces of finely grated coconut, a "pleasant improvement to curried dishes, and (is) universally liked."[80]

Persons of African descent were another group that had a huge influence on the cuisines of the southern United States and Caribbean, and Leslie paid homage to their expertise as well. She is the first white author to openly acknowledge African American women as the source of

some of her recipes.[81] As previously mentioned, in the preface of *New Receipts for Cooking* (1854) she credits Southern
women as contributors of several of the cookbook's recipes,
claiming that "many were dictated by colored cooks, of high
reputation in the art, for which nature seems to have gifted
that race with a peculiar capability."[82] Her "compliments"
seem back-handed today, but were reflective of the time;
the idea of racial subordination surfaces in several of
Leslie's fiction books as well.

The recipe for Filet Gumbo is one she describes as "a
genuine southern receipt," instructing the reader to "cut up
a pair of fine plump fowls into pieces, as when carving," but
that actually "filet gumbo may be made of any sort of poultry, or of veal, lamb, venison, or kid." The seasonings
include chopped marjoram and two heaped teaspoonfuls of
sassafras powder; but if that is unavailable, she suggests a
clever substitution—stirring the gumbo frequently with a
stick of sassafras root. As with other receipts, she recommends including three or four thin slices of cold boiled ham
to improve the flavor. Adding a dozen fresh oysters and
their liquor to the stew toward the end is another optional
enhancement.[83]

By including recipes and instructions from all these different cultures, Leslie was able to boost exposure to what
was becoming established as "American cookery." She also
sought to strengthen America's position as a recognized
culture in *Miss Leslie's Behavior Book*, a guide for ladies in
regard to their conversation, manners, dress, introductions,
entry to society, shopping, and so on. In this handbook she
is not afraid to criticize long-established European traditions, explaining how and why things are done better in
America. For example, in her chapter on how to behave
while dining in a hotel, she instructs, "Abstain from picking
your teeth at table. Notwithstanding that custom has
allowed this practice in Europe, (even in fashionable socie-

ty,) it is still a very disagreeable one, and to delicate spectators absolutely sickening to behold. Delay it till you are alone, and till you can indulge in it without witnesses."[84]

And although she does admit "the English travellers who visit America are often right in their remarks on many of our customs" (such as eating food too fast, chewing loudly, and not allowing enough time to enjoy meals), she recommends that instead of being offended by these comments, Americans should gain from this "constructive criticism" by choosing to reform their ways. She goes on to compare Americans to the French, who she says eat even faster (than Americans), ingesting "a surprising quantity of food in less time than any people in the civilized world." She advises that the English are the better of the two nations to serve as a model for refined table manners, but "the best class of Americans are unsurpassed in the essentials of all these observances." She claims that "the English attach too much importance to ceremonies merely conventional, and for which there seems no motive but the ever-changing decrees of fashion."[85]

Even though *The Behavior Book* was intended for upper-class ladies (usually in urban areas), its popularity spread throughout the nation. Perhaps the American public was so eager to be wealthy that they devoured this guidebook. It was as if Leslie were instructing the middle class on how to climb the social ladder to success, a theme that has embodied the "American dream" since the country's beginnings.

Another of Mrs. Goodfellow's maxims that Leslie cleverly followed was advising women to learn to cook properly in order to please their husbands and families. In the preface of *Miss Leslie's Complete Cookery* (the revised edition of her best-seller *Directions for Cookery*), she claims that many women "who have entered into married life with no other acquirements than a few showy accomplishments" had informed her that *Directions for Cookery* helped shape them into practical housewives. "Gentlemen, also, have told me of great improvements in the family-table, after presenting their wives with this manual of domestic cookery," she boasts; "and that, after a morning devoted to the fatigues of business, they no longer find themselves subjected to the annoyance of an ill-dressed dinner."[86]

Leslie conveys this concept and other social conventions of the time through her fiction works as well. She was a keen observer, basing characters and settings on her own experiences and dealings with people she likely met through the cooking school and her societal circle. Appropriate education for young ladies and their ability to capture the attention and esteem of eligible bachelors were common plot points, with characters that did not live up to the standards of proper decorum and housekeeping ability considered flawed.[87] Leslie surely had a good deal of exposure to all these notions through Mrs. Goodfellow's teaching as well as watching the behavior of her classmates. She borrows from this experience by actually referencing Mrs. Goodfellow in her stories, depicting her and her confectionery products as the culinary benchmark ladies strived to measure themselves against.

Leslie's fellow Philadelphians were especially proud of her achievements. In their 1884 *History of Philadelphia*, Scharf and Westcott refer to her as "one of the most popular female writers that has risen in any part of this country. The works of no other female American author have ever sold so well as those of Miss Leslie."[88] Over two decades since her death had passed at this point and she was still considered a best-seller.

Leslie's character can perhaps best be summed up in an entry written about her by Sarah Josepha Hale in the 1855 publication *Woman's Record*. Subtitled *Sketches of All Distinguished Women, from the Creation to A.D. 1868*, the book is arranged in four eras, each containing biographies of women who made a difference: the varied entries include Cleopatra, Joan of Arc, Anne Boleyn, and Abigail Adams, to name a few. Leslie was still alive when this book was published, and is described as having "quick observation, a retentive memory, a sprightly fancy, and a persevering mind. She has also the great merit of being free from affectation; her purpose is always to be useful. Miss Leslie is such a truehearted American, that she earnestly desires to aid her countrywomen in becoming perfect, few of our female writers have wielded so powerful an influence, or been more widely read."[89]

It is interesting to note that this book contains only one other cookbook writer—Betty Gleim, a German self-taught educator who opened Bremen's first private school for girls in 1806 and wrote two cookery books. Since Hale's book was published, many women have provided innovation and expertise on cooking and domestic economy (Fannie Farmer and Julia Child are just two). Their achievements were possible because Leslie and Goodfellow helped pave the way.

Lemons and Sugar (1822). Charles Willson Peale's son Raphaelle Peale made a number of paintings of food during his short career, including this still life of one of the most popular but still exotic fruits found in early nineteenth-century Philadelphia. Raphaelle Peale's paintings also featured cakes and pastries of the kinds made by shops such as Mrs. Goodfellow's. (*Reading Public Museum*)

SIX

Lemon Meringue Pie

Philadelphia, 64 Dock Street
Wednesday, September 20, 1815
Noon

A quiet murmur could be heard among the restless girls standing around the dining table awaiting their next instruction. Clapping her hands together to get their attention, Mrs. Goodfellow explained they needed to finish a few last-minute things before they ate, and proceeded to guide the group back to the kitchen work table. Taking a large hunk of butter from the butter kettle, she flipped it into an iron saucepan and carried it over to the fire. Placing it on top of the coals, she stirred it around until the butter melted. She then promptly poured the melted butter into a china sauceboat, explaining that this was to be served with the artichokes.

While the students had been learning table-setting techniques from Mrs. Goodfellow, Hannah was busy making the custards for the order that had come in earlier in the week. She was now standing at the work table, whipping up egg whites at a rapid pace. As she quickly worked the hickory egg beater, she told Mrs. Goodfellow that the custards were cooling on the larder shelf, the kisses (meringue cookies) were in the oven, and the egg whites she was beating were for the icing that would top the custards. "But please, ma'am, what shall we do with the little bit of egg white left over?" she said, nodding her head in the direction of a small dish. "I have already iced the Queen cakes . . . they are drying near the fire."

Mrs. Goodfellow thought for a moment, and then walked over to the work table, gesturing for her students to follow. "We never want to waste something as valuable as some extra egg whites," she told them. "Since we have no way to preserve them, we will have to use them right away. I have an idea."

First she poured the extra egg whites into the bowl Hannah had been using for the custard topping, added a pinch more sugar, and proceeded to beat the mixture until it stood up in soft peaks. She then got the custards from the larder and spooned a generous mound of icing on top of each one, finishing them off by placing a dot of red nonpareils in the middle of each icing stack. Next, she took one of the lemon puddings and spread the rest of the egg whites on top with a small flat wooden paddle. She swirled it around decoratively, making a very pretty, lacy pattern, like icing on a cake, and then placed it near the fire so the topping would set and harden a little. For the other lemon pudding, she just grated a little loaf sugar over the surface, as was customary. She then moved the custards back to the cool larder until it was time to package them up for delivery, and put the other lemon pudding back on the shelf.

Wiping her hands on her apron, Mrs. Goodfellow told the girls that they were now ready to carry the serving dishes over to the table. Hannah had already retrieved the now-empty trays from the dining area, and carefully held one out in front of her while Mrs. Goodfellow first put the sauceboat's saucer on the tray, and then gently placed the sauceboat of melted butter on top. Mrs. Goodfellow then grabbed a kitchen towel for each hand so she wouldn't burn them on the hot dish, and set the platter of artichokes on the tray next to the butter, making sure the cover was still on tightly.

Firmly grasping the tray with both hands, Hannah headed over to the dining area, put it down on the tray stand and then took one of the kitchen towels and a round silver hand-waiter and stood behind the foot of the table and a little to the left of the chair. Taking two more cloths, Mrs. Goodfellow positioned the hot fricassee platter on the other tray and picked it up herself, nodding for the rest of the girls to make their way over to the table as she followed.

When they got to the table, Mrs. Goodfellow put the chicken down at the foot and remained standing behind it. Once the girls were all seated at their places, Hannah leaned over and removed the dish cover, releasing the chicken's savory, peppery smell. She put the cover upside down on the tray, careful not to let any moisture get on the tablecloth, and then walked around to the left side of the girl nearest to her, picked up her plate, put it on the hand-waiter, and carried it over to Mrs. Goodfellow. She then held the plate while Mrs. Goodfellow lifted up a piece of chicken with a serving fork, placed it on the plate, and then spooned a bit of the gravy over it. She handed it to Hannah, who put it back on the hand-waiter, and then carried the plate back to the student and set it down in front of her. She then proceeded to the next student, serving each one in turn.

While the chicken was being dished up, Mrs. Goodfellow explained that when the menu contains a meat dish, it is placed at the foot of the table in front of the man of the house to carve. If soup and fish are on the menu, the mistress of the house serves the soup from her place at the head of the table, and the fish is placed in front of the master. If there is only one of these items, it goes in front of the lady, and the largest dish of meat or poultry is placed at the foot, as is the case with today's chicken fricassee, she said, nodding her head toward the platter.

For their "classroom" purposes, she explained that Hannah was taking the role that would usually be filled by a waiter at a dinner party. If there is only one waiter, he normally takes his position behind the person who is carving in order to determine what might be needed. When there are two waiters at a party, the second one stands near the lady of the house, she continued, and if there are four, two should stand at the sides of the table. She told the girls to notice how Hannah reached around the left side of each person to take their plate and put it back, always putting it on and taking it from the small server. This is proper decorum for table attendants, she explained. If there are men and women eating together, the ladies are always served first, she added.

Mrs. Goodfellow stressed that even though the girls would not be performing these tasks themselves, they would need to know these skills when seeking servant assistance. She added that a dinner party's success hinges on all these factors coming together—food, table setting, service, even the guest list and careful seat assignments.

Once the chicken was served to all the girls, Hannah took the cover off the artichoke platter and put it on top of the tray. She then transferred the platter and the sauceboat to the hand-waiter and began to move around the table, serving Mrs. Goodfellow and each girl an artichoke dressed with a little melted butter. As a last step she placed the small dishes of colorful preserves and pickles on the hand-waiter and walked around the table, offering the sweet and tart accompaniments to those who wanted to taste a spoonful or two.

Once Hannah was finished serving, Mrs. Goodfellow finally said that the girls could begin eating. They gladly tucked into the tasty dishes they had watched being transformed from basic simple foods into fare worthy of a dinner party, and under Mrs. Goodfellow's watchful eye they made sure they used their best table manners.

Hannah counted the dessert forks and plates, making sure all would be ready when the girls were finished the main course. Then she went back to the kitchen to finish up with the kisses and packaging orders for delivery.

While the students were eating, Mrs. Goodfellow worked in a little instruction about appropriate dinner-party conversation for young ladies. Looking around the table at each girl in turn, she said that they must keep in mind that it takes time and experience to develop into a lively and respectable conversationalist. Ticking off the necessary components on her fingers, she first listed the importance of having well-rounded knowledge about books and the world, and being able to talk intelligently about these things. It is also key to have a fresh and imaginative mind, combined with a good memory and an intuitive perception of what is best to say, and what should be left unsaid. Good taste, an even temper, and proper manners are other appealing attributes. In addition, a clear, distinct voice is indispensable—ladies who speak in too low a tone will sound unintelligible. Last, the ability to quickly and seamlessly change topics and dialogue is very important—not laboring over any one subject as to bore the other guests. All these things will make a young lady a successful and sought-after dinner-party companion, she emphasized.

As far as what topics should be discussed at a party, a little common sense goes a long way, Mrs. Goodfellow continued. First of all, never ask a gentleman about his profession unless he mentions it himself. Also, women who had formerly lived under more modest circumstances do not like to talk about their prior experiences. Instead of questioning them about domestic economy, speak with them as if they had always been living in comfort, she advised.

It is also best to stay away from malicious behavior and speech, Mrs. Goodfellow cautioned. If a gentleman speaks highly of a lady whom you do not think deserving of his praise, nothing will be gained by trying to disagree; especially if she is attractive. It will only make you appear spiteful and envious, tainting his impression of you. Even if you dislike the lady, ignore her faults and try to think up a few positive traits, agreeing cordially with the gentleman.

And avoid talking about religion—it is too sacred a subject for discussion at balls and parties, Mrs. Goodfellow warned. As her final piece of advice, she told the girls to be very cautious if asked for a candid opinion of someone, as it may lead to unpleasant consequences. Even close, lifelong friends are not always to be trusted—a bit of conversation meant to be told in confidence can sometimes be revealed to others later on.

She then began to do a bit of her famous match-making, asking the girls questions about their current beaus—particularly their family backgrounds and ambitions. Most of the girls squirmed in their seats, too shy to reveal details of any blossoming romances. Some of the bolder ones, however, did disclose a few tidbits of information, and Mrs. Goodfellow nodded her head if she knew the family, or pressed for more specifics if she didn't.

She once again voiced her opinion, telling the girls that here in America, nearly every young man must make a living in some way. Few can afford to spend most of their time lolling around engaging in flirtatious behavior, and those who make this a habit are not worth having. A man who is a deserving match has something purposeful to do with his day, she advised.

While they were eating and having their lessons in deportment, Hannah had come back over to the dining area a few times to refill water glasses and see if anything else was needed. As the girls finished up, Mrs. Goodfellow gave her the signal to clear the plates and dishes, and Hannah began to remove them, placing the larger items on the tray, and the forks and knives in the knife-basket, each in their separate compartment. She next went around the table and collected all the pieces of bread that were left, and then brushed off all the crumbs with a crumb-brush and a small server.

Finally it was time for the lemon pudding. Hannah hurried off to retrieve the one topped with meringue drying in front of the fire, and brought it into the dining area, placing it on the side table. She then cut the pudding into wedges, putting a slice and a small fork on a dessert plate. She arranged them on the hand waiter and went around the table, carefully serving every student. As she passed them out, Mrs. Goodfellow explained that this was a very rich pastry, pure dinner-party fare, and not appropriate for children or invalids. Just a taste for each one of them would be enough, she cautioned.

The tiny golden triangles capped with a fluff of white meringue looked almost too lovely to eat, but the girls were eager to try the luxurious treat. They all waited until everyone was served a piece, and then each took dainty bites of the glistening custard accented by the airy "icing." The sweet, light topping melted in their mouths, a perfect accent to the smooth, lemony custard. As they savored the richness, they all nodded around the table to each other with expressions of delight, raving about how incredibly delicious it was. Mrs. Goodfellow also took a small forkful and agreed that adding a sweet, delicate top layer to the thick, rich pudding was a tasty contrast.

The description above is just one possible scenario of how lemon meringue pie first came to be, as no one knows for sure exactly how and when it was originally conceived. However, according to food historian William Woys Weaver, we can thank Mrs. Goodfellow for inventing this popular dessert. Lemon pudding was known as one of her signature confections, but it is not clear how and when the meringue topping was added. The rich sweet-tart pudding was either spooned into a pastry crust before baking (like a pie), or simply poured into a dish and baked without a bottom shell. Lemon puddings existed before her version, but as we know it in America, lemon meringue pie is a Goodfellow creation. The English made lemon curd, and her rendering is essentially lemon curd baked in a piecrust.[1]

In America, lemon pie adaptations eventually emerged where lemons were sliced like in an apple pie, and sometimes a top crust was added. But the most popular style eventually evolved into a pie of layers. The contrasting texture of a slightly crispy shell covering very sweet pillowy meringue balances the tart, thick, custardy lemon filling perfectly. The flaky pastry crust holds it all together.

How and why did Mrs. Goodfellow think to pair these flavors that are different and complementary at the same time? Cooks have been flavoring custards, puddings, and pies with lemons and other citrus fruits since medieval times. The acidic lemon was valued for both its flavor as well as its preservative effect, which made it a sought-after ingredient for many recipes. An expensive commodity, lemons would be preserved by drying or made into a liquid flavoring or essence like our baking extracts today.[2]

As many cooks know, adding lemon to a recipe brings out the flavors of the other ingredients and makes everything taste fresher and brighter. Think of how just a squeeze of lemon enhances the mild taste of flaky, white fish or jazzes up fresh-picked vegetables. Like salt, the lemon's balancing quality works in both savory and sweet dishes. Because lemons taste good with almost everything, they can be paired with herbs, spices, fruits and vegetables, meats, and so on, resulting in endless combinations of recipes.[3] In baking, lemon's acid content sets it apart from other flavors. Although sour by itself, when paired with butter, sugar, and eggs it results in a product that tastes tangy and pleasantly astringent.[4]

Mrs. Goodfellow used this knowledge to her advantage, especially in her pastries and cakes. Her lemon pudding recipe says to sprinkle some white sugar over the top after baking. And since her lemon custard recipe calls for the yolks of ten eggs, it is likely that at some point she poured the custard into a piecrust and then cleverly whipped the whites with this sugar to create a meringue for the top, instead of letting them just go to waste. How pretty and tasty it must have been for those lucky enough to have the first taste of this new delicacy.

What is unclear is exactly when Mrs. Goodfellow first introduced lemon meringue pie to the public. The use of whisked egg whites in dishes can be traced to Renaissance cooks, but it wasn't until the seventeenth century that they perfected meringue. Although there are recipes for decorating cakes, tarts, and custards with sweetened and flavored egg whites from that time forward, adding meringue to a pudding (pie) doesn't seem to appear until the nineteenth century.

Using Eliza Leslie's cookbooks as a timeline of what Mrs. Goodfellow was teaching in her classroom, we can see that starting in 1827 with Leslie's earliest cookbook, a

Meringue is simply a mixture of stiffly beaten egg whites and sugar. European cooks first discovered in the sixteenth century that whisking egg whites with birch twigs (for the lack of a better utensil), created an appealing frothy mixture. They used this method to make what they called "snow," a whipped dish combining the beaten egg whites with cream. The term *meringue* likely came to France from Germany, initially appearing in writing in 1691, although recipes for these combined ingredients had appeared earlier. Not long after, the word spread to England, showing up in print around 1706. It was eventually discovered that when meringue is baked at a low temperature (or even just left out in the air to dry), it hardens. In the seventeenth century this was often called "sugar puff," which was sometimes flavored with caraway seeds, a tradition that continued to evolve with other flavorings, creating a large number of taste combinations. Today there are three distinct types of meringue: French, Italian, and Swiss, depending on the method used to mix in the sugar. For French (also called "ordinary") meringue, dry sugar is beaten into whipped egg whites, whereas Italian meringue uses hot sugar syrup. Swiss meringue combines the egg whites and sugar at the beginning and then calls for them to be whipped over low heat.[5]

recipe for "Fine Custards" which requires topping them with an egg white "icing" after they are baked is included. In addition, the recipes in this book for "Rice Custards" and "Almond Custards" recommend embellishing the final product with a froth of stiff egg white (beaten with a few drops of lemon essence and a tiny bit of powdered loaf sugar). However, unlike the crisp layer that tops lemon meringue as we know it, the egg whites in these dishes were not cooked at all, and probably would have tasted more like foamy whipped cream.[6]

In this same cookbook, Leslie's Queen Cake recipe also calls for a beaten egg white and sugar icing, flavored with rosewater or lemon essence. However in this case, the egg white topping would have been more like a true meringue, as she says to set the cakes in a warm place to dry after they are iced, "but not too near the fire, as that will cause the icing to crack." She recommends icing them twice, spreading the mixture very thin the first time.[7] This technique would be similar to drying them in an oven that has been turned off or set at a very low temperature, as we do today with meringues in order to achieve that familiar light, hardened texture.

Kisses were also featured in *Seventy-Five Receipts for Pastry, Cakes and Sweetmeats*. In this recipe the whites of four eggs are beaten until they stand alone, then a pound of powdered and sifted loaf sugar is added, one teaspoonful at a time, and finally twelve drops of lemon essence, all beaten together very hard. To form the cookies, the egg white mixture is spooned on top of small mounds of stiff currant jelly which have been spaced an equal distance apart on the bottom of a paper-lined baking tin. They are then set in a cool oven, and considered done when they are a pale yellow color, at which point they are taken out. After cooling briefly, the flat undersides are joined together, laid lightly on a sieve, and dried again in a cool oven, until the two bottoms are firmly stuck, creating a ball or oval shape.[8]

So even though the concept of meringue must have been part of Goodfellow's curriculum, the actual term doesn't show up in Leslie's cookbooks until the 1840 publication of *Directions for Cookery, in Its Various Branches,* when she lists a recipe for "A Charlotte Polonaise." She says, "Have ready the whites of the six eggs whipped to a stiff froth, with which have been gradually mixed six ounces of powdered sugar, and twelve drops of oil of lemon. With a spoon heap this meringue (as the French call it) all over the pile of cake, and then sift powdered sugar over it. Set it in a very slow oven, till the outside becomes a light brown colour."[9]

After this point, Leslie uses the word *meringue* more frequently in her cookbooks (sometimes interchangeably with icing), but lists no specific recipe for lemon meringue pie. The meringue-topped recipes featured in Leslie's cookbooks are initially paired with flavors other than lemon, such as almond, coconut, or apple, as in the recipe for Meringued Apples from *The Lady's Receipt-Book: A Useful Companion for Large or Small Families* (1847).

Leslie also makes the comment in this book: "Any very nice baked pudding will be improved by covering the surface with a meringue." So by mid-century it appears that Eliza Leslie (presumably through Goodfellow's influence) was introducing the concept of puddings topped with meringue to the American people, including those with a lemon component in the filling or base.

This idea of baked puddings or crèmes iced with meringue increases through the next few decades. Lemon flavor continues to play an increasing role in the pairing, such as the crème meringue recipes found in the 1852 cookbook *The Ladies' New Book of Cookery* by Sarah Josepha Hale as well as an 1855 cookbook simply titled *Cook Book* by Debbie Coleman. (Coleman was possibly a Goodfellow student as her cookbook includes recipes for jumbles and cocoanut pudding attributed to Mrs. Goodfellow.) In place of lemon juice, crème meringue infuses a bit of lemon rind in cream in order to capture a lemon taste.[10]

Rice is also often added to these "meringued puddings," most likely a Southern influence. The recipe for meringue rice pudding featured in *Mrs. Putnam's Receipt Book* (1867) includes "one teacup of rice boiled soft in milk; a pint of milk; a piece of butter the size of an egg; the yolks of five eggs and the rind of two lemons grated."[11]

During this final transitional stage, lemon meringue was sometimes called iced lemon pie, lemon cream pie, or lemon custard pie. In fact, lemon custard pie as made by Nancy Breedlove was a favorite of Abraham Lincoln. Mrs. Breedlove kept a hotel in Illinois in the mid-1800s, and Lincoln stayed there for weeks at a time when involved in court trials. He liked her lemon custard pie so much that he requested that she write out the recipe for him, and he told her years later that it was the favorite White House dessert.[12]

Lemon pie thrived in the South, where lemons became a favorite ingredient. In addition to the region's numerous port cities that would have received imported lemons (such as Charleston, Savannah, and New Orleans), the citrus fruit was also successfully grown in Florida, close enough to transport to the southern states. One version that became a Southern specialty is lemon chess pie, basically a lemon meringue pie without the meringue. The term "chess" is a derivative of the word "cheese," a reference to the custards and puddings preferred by the English and French in the seventeenth and eighteenth centuries which were created by heating milk until it curdled or turned into clabber, the first step in making cheese. Eggs were added, along with a flavoring such as orange, lemon, vanilla, brandy, or rosewater. Even when made without milk, the words "cheese" and "curd" referred to thickening eggs by heating them.[13] As noted by Southern food expert Bill Neal, "lemon meringue pie has been around a long time in the South and most likely grew out of the vast repertoire of puddings, whose popularity pies eclipsed in the late nineteenth century."[14]

By this point, lemon pie was much closer to what we are familiar with: the combination of a pastry undercrust, a lemon custard filling, and the lightly browned meringue "frosting." But it wasn't really until the last few decades of the nineteenth century that lemon meringue pie as we know it fully entered into American food culture.

Despite these successes and the public's obvious adoration for this tasty treat, the high cost and limited sources for its ingredients kept it from becoming universally available. Mrs. Goodfellow's baked lemon pudding "was at one time a mark of great luxury in the high cookery of Philadelphia and New York, requiring as it did many fresh eggs, sweet-cream butter, and fresh lemons—and thus considerable expense." In fact, vinegar pie became a substitute for lemon pie at some hotels and boardinghouses throughout the upper Midwest in the second half of the nineteenth century because it was expensive to transport lemons so far from coastal port cities. In this version, which could be called poor man's lemon meringue pie, the "lemon" is just a hint of grated zest, and the juice is actually vinegar. The resulting pie looked like lemon meringue, but did not taste like it.[15]

Once lemon meringue became more available and mainstream, its acceptance spread rapidly throughout the nation, with the American people developing a passion for the tasty dessert. In addition to Lincoln, President Calvin Coolidge was also known to favor a simple lemon custard pie. It became an American classic served at Boston's Parker House, and is often featured on Thanksgiving tables in California instead of the traditional pumpkin pie, as it better represents the local harvest.[16]

Recipes evolve and change with the times. Many factors can be involved in this process: ingredient availability, people's tastes, cooking methods, and equipment. This is exactly what happened with Goodfellow's lemon pudding as well as some of her other recipes, techniques, and philosophies, which were made available mostly through Eliza Leslie, but also through some of Goodfellow's other students, who copied and handed them down to future generations who in turn adapted them to suit their needs. These recipes credited to Mrs. Goodfellow can be found in any number of nineteenth-century manuscript cookbooks, by women who were presumably her students, or perhaps even friends or relatives of those who attended her classes.

Published cookbooks also contained recipes attributed to Mrs. Goodfellow by women other than Eliza Leslie, the most well-known being the previously mentioned *Cookery as It Should Be*, which was first available in 1853, and later reprinted in 1865 as *Mrs. Goodfellow's Cookery as it Should Be*. As noted earlier, the true author of this cookbook has never been identified. The author does emphasize some of Goodfellow's values, such as using only the best quality ingredients: "there is no economy in employing inferior butter in cooking, as good materials are often spoiled and rendered unpalatable, and in fact unwholesome, by bad butter and stale eggs," she says in the "Preparations of Puddings" chapter. But her advice on quick rising agents is rather contradictory. In one sentence she describes the use of saleratus as an "injurious habit," and then in the next she advocates that "a little best quality soda, in judicious hands is not hurtful." She even has a recipe for a saleratus cake. And several of this book's recipes call for chemical leavens such as baking soda and cream of tartar.[17]

Although Eliza Leslie points out that Mrs. Goodfellow would never have used unnatural ingredients of this type, quite frankly Leslie herself included some of these "alkalis," as she referred to them, in some of her recipes, stating that "pearlash, saleratus, soda, and sal-volatile will remove acidity, and increase lightness." But, she warns, "If too much is used, they will impart a disagreeable taste."[18] Starting with her very first cookbook (*Seventy-Five Receipts*), a few recipes call for pearl-ash as an ingredient, including Dover cake, common gingerbread, and sugar biscuits. And there are recipes in her later cookbooks that feature baking soda or saleratus, such as Indian cupcakes, sweet potato pone, and New Year's cake.

It is really rather puzzling—did Leslie make these substitutions on her own? And if so, what did Mrs. Goodfellow think of this? Or is it possible Mrs. Goodfellow occasionally tolerated the time-saving assistance these products provided, maybe even privately endorsing their use to Miss Leslie, her star pupil? This seems highly unlikely from what we know of Goodfellow's dislike of these products and their artificial taste.

The most reasonable explanation why Miss Leslie and the author of *Cookery as it Should Be* both included quick rising agents was probably simply as a way to keep up with the times. They and their publishers may have thought their cookbooks wouldn't sell as well if they didn't include at least some recipes that incorporated these modern innovations, especially since American bakers had been using quick rising agents since the late 1700s when pearl-ash became available. They likely assumed many women would compromise a little natural freshness for the assistance and time savings these newfangled additives provided. Really, what hard-working housekeeper isn't interested in making her job easier? Especially when a simple recipe such as Milk Biscuits says to knead the mixture for 40 minutes![19]

When baking powder came on the scene in the late 1850s, quick breads became popular, and sky-high layer cakes could be produced with much less effort. Recipes for baked goods that formerly called for eggs and yeast to make them rise replaced these traditional ingredients with this new time-saving substance. In addition, baking powder manufacturers pushed the idea that it was healthful, inexpensive, and fast-acting, referring to it as "nutritive yeast powder"[20] and even publishing pamphlets of recipes featuring the ingredient.

A new era in baking was born, and many of the older recipes were restructured to incorporate the substitute. In addition to the recipes Leslie published, two others attributed to Goodfellow were found to contain chemical rising agents (both soda and cream of tartar). One was for "quick waffles" in the 1907 *Colonial Receipt Book* cookbook. Contributed by Mrs. Ebenezer Greenough of Sunbury, Pennsylvania, the cookbook states that the recipe was from Mrs. Goodfellow's Cooking School in Philadelphia and that Mrs. Greenough was a pupil.[21] It is unknown whether Goodfellow actually ever taught this version, and actually rather improbable since all the other waffle recipes attributed to her are leavened with yeast. The other recipe is for "Goodfellow's Spanish buns" in Mrs. Fred Patterson's manuscript recipe book housed at the Winterthur Library in Delaware. They were called "Spanish" because they were similar to a cake made in Latin America.[22] As previously mentioned, Eliza Leslie claimed that "these buns were first introduced by Mrs. Goodfellow; and in her school were always excellently made,"[23] although the recipe has also been attributed to the Pennsylvania Germans.[24] A tea-time favorite, the yeasty, rich buns were often iced or glazed after baking, and had a delicate cake-like texture which featured nutmeg,[25] cinnamon, and mace, and sometimes rosewater flavoring and raisins or currants. Mrs. Patterson's recipe also calls for cream of tartar and soda.[26] Once again, it is not known if this was copied from her classroom or handed down to Mrs. Patterson by a friend or family member. The latter is more likely as the date range for the book is 1870–1879, and just like the waffles, every other recipe for Spanish buns attributed to Goodfellow says to use yeast as the rising agent.

Eliza Leslie was adamant that the best fresh brewer's yeast be used to make them. "If you cannot procure yeast of the very best quality, an attempt to make these buns will most probably prove a failure, as the variety of other ingredients will prevent them from rising unless the yeast is as strong as possible," she warned.[27] The buns could be baked either all in one pan like a cake, or in individual tins. The main factor was the time involved—planning ahead was necessary as it could take up to five hours for the batter to rise high enough and produce the tell-tale airy bubbles on the surface indicating it was ready to bake. "Buns wanted for tea should be made in the forenoon," advised Miss Leslie.[28]

So, it is no surprise that the yeast was replaced with baking soda, powder, or both when these time-saving ingredients became available. Other substitutions throughout the nineteenth century included exchanging the nutmeg for other spices (mace, cloves, or cinnamon), using brown sugar instead of white, and combining molasses with sour milk and baking soda in order to make the buns rise. There were also recipes for "Philadelphia buns," which were basically the same type of sweet bread as Spanish buns but without a spice like nutmeg, cinnamon, or mace.

By the late 1800s recipes for Spanish buns appeared to evolve into a one-pan "Spanish bun cake," which can be found in cookbooks from the early twentieth century. The cake was probably another time-saving adaptation as it was always baked in one pan, doing away with the concept of individual tins. Then eventually this version was found less and less throughout the twentieth century, perhaps due to the rising popularity of other types of sweet breads and coffee cakes such as Philadelphia sticky buns—gooey, yeasty rolls swirled with cinnamon and dripping with caramelized brown sugar and walnuts. So while true Spanish bun recipes do crop up occasionally in modern recipe listings (usually in a retrospective section), Goodfellow's recipe reinforced the baked goods popular today as coffee-break and breakfast foods. Present-day recipes for these types of sweet breads often feature sour cream instead of the milk or cream found in the original Spanish buns recipe in order to create a soft, rich dough.

Other Goodfellow recipes can also be found in published cookbooks and magazines all the way through the beginning of the twentieth century, decades after her passing. While some of these look like they were printed essentially as Goodfellow must have recited them, others were altered to take advantage of modern innovations. In addition to substituting for yeast, chemical leavenings also took the place of eggs in many recipes. Original Goodfellow recipes (and others from the nineteenth century) often call for an enormous number of eggs by today's standards—sometimes upward of a dozen for one cake, such as the recipes for black cake (or plum cake), sponge cake, and jelly cake found in Miss Leslie's *Seventy-Five Receipts*. (The French almond cake recipe in this cookbook requires fourteen eggs.[29]) So many eggs were needed to make the cake rise, and at that time eggs were much smaller than today.

The precursor of modern cupcakes, Goodfellow's fashionable Queen cake recipe, commonly called for ten eggs, beat "very light" or "to a froth" in order to produce a light, airy textured product which was baked in small tins and then fancifully iced. The term "cup cake" was actually first mentioned in print by Miss Leslie in *Seventy-Five Receipts*. Her cup cake recipe was more of a spice cake or muffin, however, and not iced like the Queen cake recipe listed in the same cookbook.[30] "Cup cake" was likely coined from the "Queen cakes" version listed in Maria Rundell's *A New*

System of Domestic Cookery which actually suggests baking the cakes in little teacups or saucers.[31] Since this book was supposedly one of Goodfellow's "textbooks" for her students, perhaps she was even the one who came up with the catchy new name.

Although the recipe continued this way through much of the nineteenth century (using several eggs and baking in small tins), by 1896 the version in Fannie Farmer's *Original Boston Cooking-School Cook Book* says to use just six egg whites and 1/2 teaspoon soda, and to bake it in a long, shallow pan.[32] Then by the turn of the twentieth century, references to Queen cake are not as prevalent. When listed in cookbooks or magazines, the recipes usually call for making the cake in a single pan as Farmer did, pairing baking powder with just a couple of eggs as leavening ingredients. A one-pan cake was quicker and easier for cooks, and using fewer eggs would have been cheaper. However, the idea of fancy individual cakes did not go away, and when made this way they were at first sometimes called Queen *cakes* (plural), before fully evolving into the widely accepted name of cupcakes, or even fairy cakes, the more diminutive form that are common party-fare in England.

Another signature Goodfellow recipe that had roots in her school and became wildly successful throughout America was jumbles (sometimes spelled jumbals). A delicately spiced butter cookie, it was one of the first cookie types popularized in America. Although the name "jumbles" is now unfamiliar to most of us, the taste and concept of these treats has become hugely popular, as billions of cookies are devoured every year by over 95 percent of American households. Cookies were first brought to America by Dutch and British immigrants in the 1600s. The English referred to

Still Life with Cake (1822) by Raphaelle Peale. This painting features a decorated Queen cake and gives us the relative size and appearance of these popular baked goods at the time of Mrs. Goodfellow's School. (*Brooklyn Museum*)

them as small cakes, sweet biscuits, or tea cakes, but it was the Dutch term koekjes, which means "little cakes," that Americans adapted as "cookie" or "cooky." Amelia Simmons's *American Cookery* (1796), which has two recipes for cookies, is generally considered the first American cookbook to use the term.[33]

Originally shaped like a figure eight or double ring, the name jumbles comes from the Latin word *gemel*, which means "twin." To make preparation quicker and easier, it became customary for Americans to form the dough into single rings.[34] By the late nineteenth century, further shortcuts were taken by enterprising cooks who would roll out the dough, cut it into round shapes and then stamp out the middles (like doughnuts). Eventually the ring shape fell out of favor, and jumbles were often simply rolled out and cut into circles.[35]

Rich with generous amounts of butter, egg, and sugar, the dough was often seasoned with fresh grated nutmeg (sometimes with cinnamon or mace), as well as rosewater or lemon essence for additional flavoring. In fact, they were sometimes called "rose jumbles," or "Waverly jumbles," which was apparently the favorite cookie of President James Monroe.[36]

A common fixture in nineteenth-century American cookbooks, jumbles are also one of the most widespread recipes scattered through manuscript cookbooks from the same timeframe. Sometimes several are grouped together with just slight variations, and many are attributed to Goodfellow, so surely they were taught in her school. As expected from Goodfellow's typical approach of following tradition and not cutting corners, her instructions were to form jumbles into the customary ring shape. She must have also used the term "cookies," since a recipe by this name cites her as the source in the *Colonial Receipt Book*— although it sounds very similar to jumbles, calling for "a teacup of butter, one of sugar, one egg and flour to roll very thin; flavor with nutmeg. Roll only a few at a time."[37] The small quantities of ingredients show that these cookies were sometimes made in modest batches.

"Apees" were a type of butter cookie also taught by Goodfellow. According to Eliza Leslie, "Apees were first made by Ann Page, who lived in a small frame house in Second Street, two doors north of Carter's Alley. The name originated from the fact that she marked the cakes with her initials A.P."[38] A nineteenth-century street food sold by Philadelphia vendors, apees were flavored with caraway seeds, wine, cinnamon, and nutmeg. They were actually thick round little cakes similar to German springerle,[39] a biscuit-like cookie featuring an embossed design which was made by pressing a mold into rolled dough and then letting it dry before baking. However, instead of the traditional elaborate springerle designs such as wedding scenes, animals, or fruit prints, apees were simply stamped with the letters "A.P." These types of molded or stamped cookies are not as popular today, at least in the United States, probably because of the amount of time involved to make them.

Although some years may have been leaner than others for Mrs. Goodfellow, her business was ultimately a successful one—she was even able to expand to a larger and grander Washington Square location in 1835 after a brief stint on South Second Street (her shop and school were there for about five years). At this point she was in her late sixties and likely ready to turn over the reins of her business, or at least get some support with it. Once situated there a few years, she brought her son Robert into the confectionery business, and as partners they transformed the shop into a fancy cake bakery and ice cream saloon. Having her son as a partner may have freed her up from doing some of (or even all) the baking, allowing her to focus solely on the cooking school. In any case, it is likely that she stepped back in some capacity, or perhaps even retired from the business altogether once they formed the partnership. Surely she still offered advice and input, as well as her famous Goodfellow name, which undoubtedly helped retain and bring in customers.

Goodfellow had always had upper-class clientele, but this move to Washington Square no doubt increased her business options. With a larger kitchen she and her son could accept more orders, and the eating area would have allowed them to serve a greater number of customers—for example, businessmen and politicians from nearby banks, offices, and government buildings, as well as young couples and families craving an ice cream treat.

Undoubtedly a pleasant change of scenery for Mrs. Goodfellow, South Sixth Street at this point was residential and parklike, shaded by cool trees and lined with elegant homes, very different than the crowded, noisy, and smelly Dock Street area where she had lived and worked for so many years. Although formerly a potter's field, Washington Square had by the time she moved there in the 1830s become part of Philadelphia's most prosperous neighborhood and the gathering place for the city's elite residents.[40]

So the announcement of "E. Goodfellow & Son's Confectionary, Pastry, and Fancy Cake Bakery" in 1837 was timed perfectly with the square's refined new image. The verdant setting would have been ideal for leisurely strolls, with the splendid new store providing a welcoming stop for a refreshing ice cream or pastry as well as a chance to socialize.

To passersby, the shop would have appeared as an attractive and inviting three-story brick building with beautiful large cased windows featuring double-hung sashes and windowboxes bordered by Venetian shutters. The window sills and front step were made of marble, and the paneled entry door (which was on the north side of the building) featured a glazed transom window over the top. Upon entering the building, customers would have stepped into a vestibule with a marble mosaic-patterned floor set in stone and a Venetian door with a transom and sash widow above that led to the interior of the shop.

After passing through the entryway, a visitor took a small step up to enter the spacious area which was divided into two rooms (store and saloon) with a neat wooden counter extending across the entire front. Overhead, the high paneled ceilings featured rich stucco molding. The building's windows were expansive, plentiful, and elegant, including an "angle end bulk window having a large light of plate glass" and other windows had many lights (individual panes of glass) within each sash. They must have provided a bright and sunny atmosphere, casting quite a glow on the cypress and pine floorboards and the curving spiral stairway with mahogany post, rail, and balusters which led to the second story. The second and third stories also featured luxurious touches such as marble columns and ornamental wood frieze fireplace mantels, several closets (both side and recessed), a small second-floor balcony and heart pine stairs with rich mahogany newel posts, rails, and balusters. The second floor probably contained bedrooms for Mrs. Goodfellow and the Coane family, with servants taking up residence in the garret rooms on the third floor.

Descriptions of the rest of the property sound equally impressive, including extravagances such as a piazza and two-story frame bath house. There was a sizable back building behind the store that may have provided more living space for the two families, workspace for the confectionery business and cooking school, and/or additional servant quarters. The survey diagram and description shows a dining room and kitchen on the ground floor with a niche for the stove and a kitchen dresser with doors and drawers. There was a window to provide some light and a back door with a transom window over it. Perhaps this cheery area was where Mrs. Goodfellow provided her cooking instruction; it was no doubt brighter and roomier than her former Dock Street location.

A flight of winding stairs led down to a large two-room cellar that had two ovens, a kitchen dresser with drawers, and a furnace for warming the stove. This was most likely where the shop's baking, confectionery, and ice cream making took place. (There must have been some sort of refrigeration or icebox for storing the ice cream, fruit, and blancmange, but this is not mentioned.) The back building's second- and third-story rooms included a nursery, another kitchen, and even a room with a bath and water closet and windows framed with Venetian shutters. As with the main building, all rooms are depicted as having many windows, closets, and fancy woodwork.[41]

Robert Coane must have been pretty well off to afford this and the similarly lavish house next door, which also featured intricate woodwork, rich marble accents, and impressive windows.[42] It is unclear if this provided additional living space for his large household (which numbered seventeen people at the time of the 1850 census—including family, servants, and three professional confectioners) or perhaps he rented it out for extra income. The site of the shop (91 South Sixth Street) is listed as his residence at the time of Goodfellow's death in 1851, and this is probably where she had lived as well.

After his mother's death, it appears Robert retained the business at this site for just another five years or so, keeping the Goodfellow & Coane name, most likely because it was so well-known. Then for some reason he left the confectionery business in the mid-1850s, perhaps preferring to focus on other interests such as community service and political affairs.[43] In the mid-1870s, a few years before he died, he was one of several people who petitioned the Philadelphia Court of Common Pleas to straighten and open Girard Avenue and Twenty-Second Street through the grounds of Girard College in order to help improve and increase property value in the area.[44]

So although no other family members continued Mrs. Goodfellow's pastry-making legacy, at least the knowledge was not lost, as her recipes and techniques were passed down by those whom she taught over the years. In addition, the success of her cooking school helped set the stage for other cooking instructors who followed her—from the 1850s up to the present.

SEVEN

Modern Cooking Schools

A city of the palate, Philadelphia has always loved fine food and drink, which represent friendship and hospitality.[1] In its early days while it was still the center of American cookery, what happened there (in terms of gastronomy) was watched by everyone else, even New Yorkers.[2] But by the time of Mrs. Goodfellow's death, New York had slowly been creeping up behind Philadelphia to take the position of America's premier food city. Pierre Blot, the Frenchman who immigrated to the United States in 1855, took advantage of the city's burgeoning role, carefully exploring its residents' interest in food by giving lectures on the culinary arts and publishing a book in 1863, *What to Eat and How to Cook it; Containing over One Thousand Receipts*. Then in 1865, he launched the New York Cooking Academy, designating himself as the professor of gastronomy.[3]

Blot was determined to raise cooking in America to an art form, using the school (dubbed Blot's Culinary Academy of Design in a *New York Times* article) as an opportunity to share his ideals. With his sophisticated manner and French education, he quickly became a self-professed authority on the art of cooking. He claimed not only that his dishes were better tasting than typical American fare, but also they were more wholesome and economical. And in the customary French style, he put a great deal of emphasis on plating his recipes attractively before presenting them on the table.[4]

Blot has been described as America's first celebrity chef, and indeed he seemed like quite a showman in his teaching manner, although perhaps not quite as animated as the professionals on television today. He was described as pleasant, conversational, and attentive and always ready to take questions from the audience. He explained things simply and clearly, and as noted by a *New York Times* reporter who sat in on one of his lectures: "He knows, in fact, *how* to teach." His classrooms were set up accordingly—the "Academy's" front room on the ground floor (which functioned as a lecture hall) was organized like a stage, with a work table, range, and fireplace at the front. Settees were placed around the lecture area at intervals so all could see, and the day's menu was neatly written on a blackboard above the fireplace.[5]

His second-floor kitchen classroom was also orderly and practically arranged with a large stove on one side of the room and cooking utensils laid out on a side table. The central work table which contained the chicken, fish, and meats (prepared by Blot's female assistant) was in clear view of the wooden benches where the students sat and observed. Different recipes were demonstrated each day, increasing in difficulty as the lessons progressed. A sample menu for one class included: pot au feu; striped bass;

Hullandar's (perhaps hollandaise?) sauce; filet of mutton, larded and braised; roasted chicken au jus; spinach à la crème; turnips (as a garniture for the beef); genoises, with almonds.[6] Quite an enterprising agenda for one afternoon.

The enrollment for Blot's first series of classes was sixty-two students, most of them rich, intelligent women eager to learn not only how dishes should be made, but also how to prepare them for their own families. This was a similar demographic to the pupils who attended Goodfellow's except that Blot's students seemed to *want* to be there, having signed up on their own accord, not at the urging of their mothers. Another difference was that Blot offered three classes, two for "ladies" of this type and one for servants.[7] Domestics might have attended Goodfellow's now and then, but if so, they were probably mixed in with the rest of the students, not in separate classes. (To be fair, Goodfellow did not have a very large operation and she was also running her pastry shop at the same time.) In addition, Blot's attention to budget-conscious cooking eventually attracted women from less affluent households.

Blot soon became hugely popular, teaching and giving demonstrations throughout the Northeast as well as writing a number of articles on a variety of culinary topics. Unfortunately his reign did not last very long. While his articles were well-received at first, they increasingly depicted American cuisine in a negative light, often with degrading descriptions and comparisons to French cookery, which he considered superior. Blot fell out of favor with the American public by the early 1870s and died in 1874.[8]

Just as Blot's popularity was declining, his concept of opening cooking school doors to more than just the wealthy was beginning to expand. The theory of home economics was in its developmental stages and the number of cooking schools soon surged in response to its popularity.

The idea of "domestic science" came about as a way to increase opportunities for women through formal education and the creation of a profession that understood their responsibilities. Early campaigners for this concept included Catharine Beecher and her sister, abolitionist and author Harriet Beecher Stowe, both having come from a religious family of activists that highly valued female education. Catharine was educated both at home and in a liberal private school for girls until she was forced to end her studies at the age of sixteen when her mother passed away. She then (with some assistance from an aunt) took over as caretaker for the rest of her family until her father remarried, crediting her mother, aunt, and stepmother for her extensive homemaking skills.[9]

Perhaps a as result of the direct experience she gained, Catharine felt that American housewives suffered from poor health, largely due to the arduous nature of housework. Like her sister, she was also a successful author, and spread her ideas though her writing and promotion of domestic education in schools.[10] She aspired to make domestic economy a viable career path managed by well-educated, experienced women. Her popular books covered topics ranging from healthful living and interior design to original recipes she claimed were "tested by superior housekeepers and warranted to be *the best*."[11]

Around the same time, in 1862 the U.S. government devoted federal lands to support the development of colleges focused on agricultural and mechanical arts courses through the Morrill Act. This gave home economics a further boost as farm wives enrolled in these land-grant colleges at the same time as their husbands.[12] Even though the Morrill Act did not target women specifically, it boosted their education opportunities by enrolling female students and introducing relevant topics to them.[13] Iowa Agricultural School at Ames (later Iowa State University) is considered the first college to provide cooking classes, which were offered through its domestic economy course in 1876. Similar programs appeared in other states, including Kansas State Agricultural College at Manhattan (later Kansas State University) and the Illinois Industrial University, which started a School of Domestic Science in 1878. Courses included dietetics, household science, and the chemistry of bread making, among others.[14]

Ellen Swallow Richards (1842–1911) was the first woman to earn a bachelor of science degree from the Massachusetts Institute of Technology and was instrumental in the formation of the American Home Economics Association. (*Library of Congress*)

This increased interest in the science of food and housekeeping, particularly incorporating new technology, was a big factor in the home economics movement, and women such as Ellen Swallow Richards helped drive the curriculum. Considered the founder of home economics, Richards hugely influenced women's household tasks and roles. Her unrelenting drive and intense interest in science led her to become the first woman to earn a bachelor of science degree at the Massachusetts Institute of Technology in 1873 (after first obtaining an A.B. degree from Vassar College in 1870).

Richards then worked in a number of different settings, instructing women from all levels of society about science and its impact on their daily lives. She helped spread the word about subjects ranging from nutrition and cost-effective meal planning to food chemistry and the effect of germs in the kitchen. Her efforts were finally rewarded by

MIT in 1882 when the school allowed women to enroll on a regular basis. Two years later she was hired as MIT's first female instructor (in sanitary chemistry), and taught courses in the radical new subjects of air, water, and sewage analysis, as well as assisting in several research projects, until her death in 1911.

Throughout her life, Richards worked tirelessly to create courses in domestic science as part of her vision to establish a new profession for women. In September 1897 she invited twelve women who had influenced domestic science to join her in Lake Placid, New York, to discuss ways to promote the field of study. The meeting was so successful that the group met annually for ten more years, and then in 1908 decided to form the American Home Economics Association, which is still a vital force today.[15]

At the same time Richards was forging ahead with these new philosophies and concepts, cooking schools were also going through a number of changes, particularly in large cities. As Laura Scheone says in her book *A Thousand Years Over a Hot Stove*, "During the late 1870s, a collection of energetic and determined cooking teachers provided the greatest firepower for the domestic science movement by founding three highly influential schools: the New York Cooking School, the Philadelphia Cooking School and the Boston Cooking School."[16]

The women associated with these schools were dynamic trailblazers. They worked hard to generate a genuine interest in cooking for women from all walks of life, showing them how meals could be prepared easily and within a budget, yet still in a tasteful way—making it less the chore it had always been. They knew how to market themselves and their ideas, influencing millions of women across America through writing cookbooks, home economics texts, and magazine articles. Like Eliza Leslie, many served as writers and editors for widely circulated new women's magazines such as *Ladies Home Journal* and *Good Housekeeping*. And as Pierre Blot had done, some traveled around the country giving public cooking demonstrations which were very well attended. This early example of the celebrity chef concept took off in the twentieth century and is hugely popular today.[17]

This new way of looking at food and meal preparation had its start in 1874, when cooking classes were offered in New York as part of the Free Training School for Women, an offshoot of the Women's Educational and Industrial Society of New York, organized to give women the training and education they needed to find employment. The cooking class was headed by Juliet Corson, who taught herself French and German culinary techniques that she passed on to her students.[18]

Over 200 people attended lectures the first year, and Corson organized the "ladies' cooking class" the following year. Then in 1876 she launched the New York Cooking School out of her home, and in 1878 the "plain cook's class," which taught the principles of simple family cooking for housewives, young women employed as domestics, and the wives and daughters of working men. These lectures were so popular that Corson made this topic a significant focus in her work, publishing and distributing 50,000 copies of a pamphlet called "Fifteen Cent Dinners for Workmen's Families." She also started giving public cooking lessons outside the school to working people as well as their children.[19]

Under the influence of the home economics movement, cooking classes and instructors branched out in many different directions from what Mrs. Goodfellow had offered more than a generation ago. The study of cookery had become more affordable and suited to a much wider student base. Lesson structure was changing and evolving in order to fit these various niches. Whereas Goodfellow's concentration was primarily teaching daughters of the wealthy to prepare dinner-party fare, Juliet Corson conceived a system of graded levels within cooking schools, providing many more options for potential students of various backgrounds.

In addition to the introduction of classes in plain cooking and those for the children of working people, this four-tiered approach also included instruction in fancy cookery.[20] Unlike Goodfellow's lessons, however, these "cooks' classes" were geared toward both men and women with the goal of learning more sophisticated techniques so they could serve as professional cooks. As per a description in the *Christian Union*, these classes were taught by a French cook, referred to as "Monsieur," who skillfully demonstrated the cooking tasks while the students observed and took notes.[21] Other classes were designated as "normal schools of cookery," where ladies learned the theory of domestic economy in order to practice it in their own homes and/or to be able to teach it to others.[22] Both of these latter two were kind of a conglomeration of what Goodfellow had started.

The Philadelphia Cooking School also developed out of a women's group—the New Century Club, which was founded in 1877. The club encouraged free-thinking, creativity, and charitable work among women and the promotion of science, literature, and art within a comfortable and convenient meeting place. Committees and subgroups on a variety of subjects were formed, including education, poetry, foreign languages, household sciences, and cookery, with the New Century Cooking School opening in 1878.[23]

A cooking lesson at a women's school in New York City in 1890. (*New York Public Library*)

In an effort to reach women from all economic levels, the school aimed to set reasonable fees, with prices starting at fifty cents for a single lesson, and one dollar for the "special dishes" curriculum. A series of twelve lessons in plain cooking was five dollars, and a course of twelve "ladies' classes" was ten dollars. Twenty-five dollars secured a yearly subscription, which enabled the subscriber to enroll three students, helpful for families who had several daughters and/or domestic servants they wished to send. Top of the line was the life membership for a hundred dollars, allowing subscribers to send one pupil every year.[24] For those who could not afford the tuition, assistance was available, in the true benevolent nature of the New Century Club. This generous offer would have allowed many women to take formal cooking lessons who would not have been previously able to do so.

One of the school's first students was Sarah Tyson Rorer, who was at the time studying chemistry and medicine.

Rorer signed up for the cooking school at the urging of her cousin and took the "full course—two practical lessons a week for three months and a course of twenty-four demonstrated lectures." Although it ended up being her only formal training in cookery, she became so enthusiastic and mastered the lessons at such a fast pace that she was elected to replace the school's principal when she resigned the following year.[25]

Her teaching method was to first tell the class what she was planning to do before actually performing any cooking tasks. Then after showing the technique(s), she would explain why it was done, answering any questions that arose. She would not demonstrate the entire recipe at once, but instead walked the class through all the steps in a detailed manner to make sure it was easily understood.[26]

It appears the types of dishes she prepared during a lecture were actually very similar to those taught by Mrs. Goodfellow, with one exception being that the New Century Cooking School did not permit the use of liquor in any of its recipes. One account from an 1880 *Philadelphia Inquirer* article listed soupe à la reine, puff paste, and chicken patties as the day's lesson. As per the reporter, the soup included "the meat of a chicken, well boiled and shredded fine; three quarts of water, half cup rice, salt, pepper, two bay leaves, one carrot, one gill of cream, very small onion, three tablespoons of butter and one of flour, and four cloves." In keeping with the rules of the school, Sarah Rorer did not enhance her soup with any wine or sherry (as Mrs. Goodfellow would have done), a point noted by several women attending the lecture who felt the dish would have tasted even better with that addition. Mrs. Rorer agreed, telling the women they could make that change when they prepared it at home.[27]

The puff paste segment of the lesson was taught with the same degree of reverence and detail as in Goodfellow's school. Mrs. Rorer also stressed the importance of quality ingredients, in addition to the consistency of their combination, showing the audience that the pastry should resemble a thick paste rather than a thin dough. She also spent time emphasizing the extensive method of rolling it out in pieces, placing the paste set on the side on ice to toughen. Like Goodfellow, she suggested the use of a marble pieboard, and also mentioned a new technological marvel for the time—a glass roller that could be filled with ice, thus eliminating the long waiting time for the paste to harden. Mrs. Rorer then took the chicken that was left over from the making of the soup, mixed it with some butter, flour, salt, and cream, and positioned spoonfuls of the combination on the rolled-out puff paste circles, pinching the edges to make some attractive pasties.[28] Such a recipe was typical of her talent for creatively stretching meals.

Sarah Tyson Rorer (1849–1937) was a student and then became the principal at Philadelphia's New Century Cooking School until she opened her own cooking school in 1883. She gave cooking demonstrations at the 1893 Chicago World's Fair and became a popular figure on the national lecture circuit. (*George H. Buchanan & Co.*)

In addition to Rorer's New Century Cooking School assignment, she combined her knowledge of hygiene and nutrition with cooking to teach at the Women's Medical College and also appeared at the Franklin Institute in 1880 in connection with a course on household science. From then on, her expertise was in high demand and she followed a number of different pursuits within the field.[29]

After she had headed the New Century Cooking School for just a few years, several Philadelphia physicians were so impressed with her knowledge and success that they asked her to resign in order to open her own school, which she did in 1883, calling it the Philadelphia School. Seventy-four students, including homemakers, cooks, and young women, enrolled the first year. Eventually teachers of domestic arts signed up for her classes as well. Rorer also gave four public lectures each week, with audiences of up to five thousand people.[30]

These personal appearances and cooking demonstrations ultimately became Mrs. Rorer's bread and butter. An energetic and gifted speaker, she was very much at home on the stage, and as a result, "never wanted for an audience," as she acknowledged in her own words.[31] After appearing at the 1893 World's Fair in Chicago, she became a household name and traveled throughout the country to personally demonstrate cooking techniques to one packed auditorium after another.

Rorer also published books, articles, and testimonials to complement her lecture circuit. Capitalizing on her scientific and medical knowledge, she was very outspoken about promoting health and nutrition. She personally often suffered from digestive issues[32] and was quite critical of the typical American diet, shunning sweets, fried foods, and meats like pork which she considered not easily digested. Rather ahead of her time, she was a huge proponent of salads, stating that a salad should be included as part of every dinner meal. She claimed greens were "nature's lubricant, purifying the blood and clearing the complexion." She also felt most Americans wasted incredible amounts of food, and preached about topics that pop up in cooking magazines and websites all the time today: meal planning, budget cooking, and creative ideas for crafting new meals out of leftovers.[33]

This practical advice and over-the-top showiness enraptured her audiences, which often included people from all classes of society. Since seating was strictly general admission, attendees would take their seats hours ahead of time, patiently waiting for Rorer to emerge and begin bustling about the model kitchen set up on the stage. Her engaging and dynamic manner was similar to Julia Child's on her television cooking programs decades later. Like Child, Rorer was also a rather imposing figure—a full-figured, middle-aged-woman of above average height with wavy blond hair, bright blue eyes, and creamy skin. However, one difference between the two ladies was that Mrs. Rorer preferred to deck herself out in fancy clothing during her cooking demonstrations. Her outfit was always a silk dress with protective sleevelets and a sheer white apron with lace edging, topped off with a tiny lace cap. She claimed that by wearing this type of finery, it proved to her audiences the ease and simplicity of cooking.[34]

*T*he most well-known of the big three cooking schools of this era was undoubtedly the Boston Cooking School, largely because of its connection with Fannie Farmer, who took over as the school's fourth principal in 1893 and later wrote the *Boston Cooking-School Cookbook*, which is still available today in reprint and updated versions. However, there were actually a number of women who worked together to make the Boston Cooking School successful, ultimately transforming the way women viewed cooking in the process.

The school was formed out of the Women's Education Association, founded in 1872 by Boston-area activists and philanthropists. The endeavor was financed by subscribers (like today's public television model) and generous donations.[35] Similar to the Women's Educational and Industrial

Society of New York and Philadelphia's New Century Club, the association aimed to develop better education for women, establishing committees on subjects including fine arts, intellectual and industrial pursuits, philosophy, and physical education. In 1879 the Committee on Industrial Education started a cooking school, which was formally designated as the Boston Cooking School four years later.[36]

The school's founding was championed by its first president, Sarah E. Hooper, chairman of the Industrial Committee and a vital force in shaping this famous institution, known as the first incorporated cooking school in America.[37] Hooper had observed classes at the South Kensington Cooking School in London, and had returned to Boston filled with ambitious ideas for establishing a similar school there. In particular she wanted the school to foster culinary knowledge among the underprivileged and help the working class attain employment in the field.[38]

The first classes were small (just seven students), but by 1882 the school's enrollment numbered two thousand— much, much larger than what Mrs. Goodfellow had managed decades before. The curriculum was also very different; fine pastries and dinner-party fare were not the focus. Instead, its emphasis was on home economics, with pupils receiving course work in more than just cooking, including subjects such as chemistry, anatomy, and hygiene. The aim was to make domestic science an accepted and established concept in homes throughout America, raising the bar for cooking standards in the process. As noted by cooking expert Christopher Kimball, "this was a social, not just a culinary, movement."[39]

Hooper hired the school's first teacher, Johanna Sweeney, a mostly self-taught cook who had a true knack for culinary skills with experience teaching private cookery lessons.[40] Hooper also called on the services of home economics advocate Maria Parloa, who embraced the idea of technology in the kitchen and stressed the importance of nutrition and home organization.

Parloa had honed her skills by working as a cook in private homes and as a pastry chef at a number of summer resorts in New Hampshire. By the time of the Boston Cooking School founding, she was already rather well-known in the New England area from giving public cooking lectures and teaching domestic science at Lasell Seminary, now Lasell College. She soon established her own school on Tremont Street in Boston and was so popular that she could charge impressive fees for her services.[41]

Asked to serve as principal at the Boston Cooking School, Parloa turned down the offer as she was involved in other endeavors and commanded a much larger salary than the school could pay her. However, she was hired to train a group of teachers prior to the school's opening, and later gave public lecture-demonstrations on weekends.[42] She also wrote several cookbooks, including *Miss Parloa's New Cook Book and Marketing Guide* (1880), which gave advice on shopping as well as cooking, and *Miss Parloa's Kitchen Companion* (1887), which was the first volume in America to go into such detail regarding kitchen equipment and design.[43]

Instead, Mary Johnson Bailey Lincoln, a former school-teacher and housekeeper, ended up taking the important role as the school's first principal. In 1879 her sister's friend suggested she apply to the Boston Cooking School as a teacher, but she initially declined due to her lack of formal culinary training. However, she was prompted by her husband's increasingly ill health to find lucrative employment. After taking a few lessons "in fancy dishes" from Sweeney, attending one of Parloa's lectures, and falling back on her own domestic experience, she was able to convince herself and the hiring committee that she was suited to be principal.[44]

At first it was not an easy road for either her or the students, as her lack of cooking experience was evident at times, but she persevered, receiving additional training from Sweeney and Parloa. She was more familiar with "plain" cooking, and especially in the beginning tended to focus on simpler preparations. However, she learned quickly, eventually becoming familiar with more elaborate cooking techniques, although she continued to tout the benefits of unfussy dishes.[45]

In a speech delivered at the 1893 World's Fair, she claimed, "Women would lessen the labor of cooking greatly if they would cease making mixtures of food materials which require much time and labor in their preparation, and also the expenditure of great digestive energy. Why should we take anything so simple and delicious as a properly roasted or boiled chicken, and expend time and labor in chopping it, mixing it with so many other things that we cannot detect its original flavor, then shaping, egging and crumbing it, and making it more indigestible by browning it in scorching fat?"[46]

So although perhaps she did not always see the virtues of gourmet cookery with its more involved procedures and flavors, she soon developed into a respected teacher, lecturer, and author, publishing her first cookbook in 1884, *Mrs. Lincoln's Boston Cook Book: What to Do and What Not to Do in Cooking*. A precursor to Fannie Farmer's *Boston Cooking-School Cook Book*, this fresh and creative guidebook was chock-full of practical details, essentially giving readers a "behind the scenes" look into cooking schools. It contained not only all the information a cooking school graduate would need to know, but also the requirements for getting a cooking school started, including proper utensils, lecture topics, textbooks, test questions, and the actual Boston Cooking School curriculum.

It seems Mary Lincoln put together the exact type of manual she wished she could have consulted before taking the job at Boston Cooking School. According to one review at the time: "It is the trimmest, best arranged, best illustrated, most intelligible, manual of cookery as a high art, and as an economic art, that has appeared."[47]

Lincoln continued to serve as Boston Cooking School principal for another year, when she resigned following the death of her sister. She then began teaching classes at Lasell Seminary while also compiling her second book, the *Boston School Kitchen Text-Book* (1887), to be used in public schools, as educators began to add home economics to elementary- and secondary-level curricula. This book, as well as her earlier one, soon became source manuals for coursework taught in private and public schools throughout the United States, Canada, and England.[48]

By this time her expertise was in high demand, and like Sarah Rorer, she hit the lecture circuit, speaking at cooking schools, colleges, women's clubs, and even department stores. She also co-founded the *New England Kitchen* magazine, later renamed *American Kitchen* magazine, and continued to write articles and books as well as several promotional pamphlets for food and cooking equipment companies. She was so well-known and revered in the field that she was quite sought after for endorsements, and even gave her support to Mrs. Lincoln's Baking Powder Company, which flourished in Boston at the turn of the century.[49]

Although ultimately successful, Boston Cooking School did suffer through some fits and starts, experiencing many changes in both curriculum and faculty along the way. Most important, when the school became incorporated in 1884, it broke away from the Women's Education Association, losing the funding and support of its benefactors. As a result, the admirable concepts of giving free cooking lessons to the poor and teaching women to become professional cooks created a great financial strain.[50]

As Mrs. Goodfellow had perceptively realized long before, it was the fancy cooking techniques that really brought in the students. After all, plain cooking was not as exciting or interesting, and besides, many women probably knew at least a bit about the kitchen already. While it was fine to offer basic cooking methodology, especially for beginners, providing the ability to impress one's peers with culinary knowledge and skill was a marketing tool the school's leaders realized they needed to use. So they developed the popular concept of "ladies' practice classes," a three-tiered approach that included course work in "plain cooking," "richer cooking," and "fancy cooking."[51] These classes were limited to eight students and were held once a week from 9 A.M. to 12:30 P.M.; afterward students could sample the food that had been prepared. The cost of the lessons ranged from twelve to eighteen dollars, with a materials fee of three dollars.[52]

In 1885, the Boston Cooking School lost the popular Mary Lincoln. At this point, Ida Maynard (a recent graduate of the program) took over as principal, but Lincoln was difficult to replace. As a result, the unknown Miss Maynard was not very well received and failed to bring in many students, which added to the school's economic woes. The crisis was averted, however, by several wealthy Boston-area supporters who helped bring the school out of debt. Then Maynard was replaced by another alumna, Carrie Dearborn. Like Lincoln, Dearborn quickly became well-respected in the field and began giving cooking demonstrations in addition to her duties as principal. This change in leadership, combined with a new advertising campaign launched by the school, began to renew the public's interest.[53]

Mrs. Dearborn was much admired during her tenure as principal, but she voluntarily resigned in 1893 due to health problems. At this time, the Boston Cooking School was still getting its finances back in order, so finding a strong leader to replace her was critical. Luckily there was another former student who had shown a great deal of promise— Fannie Farmer. Well aware of the culinary preferences of her Boston contemporaries, Farmer had already been assisting Dearborn. The board of trustees promptly elected her to the position.[54] Farmer ended up being the most famous of the culinary greats associated with the Boston Cooking School, and she greatly boosted the program with her dynamism and modern ideas.

Born in 1857, Fannie Merritt Farmer either contracted polio or suffered a mild stroke when she was just a teenager. This left her at first paralyzed in her left leg; she eventually regained use of the leg but walked with a limp from then on, preventing her from finishing high school and dashing her hopes for a college education. She found work as a mother's helper, but her inquisitive and ambitious nature made it clear that she could handle a more challenging position. Through her sister, she found out about the Boston Cooking School and signed up for a two-year course in 1887 at the age of thirty.[55]

Working as assistant to Dearborn after she graduated enabled Farmer to expand her culinary knowledge even further. The position also surely helped develop the keen marketing and management skills she so famously employed after becoming principal in 1893. Under Farmer's direction, the Boston Cooking School reached the height of its popularity and success. In spite of her physical handicap, she ran the school with seemingly boundless energy and proficiency. She was a perfectionist who viewed food on a scientific, experimental level, constantly guiding her students to tweak and test recipes. After putting a dish through a series of tests, she would frequently ask them if it could be made even better, often to the point of their frustration.[56]

At this time, the students attending the Boston Cooking School were a mix of young single women preparing for marriage, housewives, and cooks working in private homes. The school had four kitchens and ten instructors on staff. Beginners' classes started out with easy-to-follow recipes generally geared toward feeding a family of six who employed one servant. Such interesting options as "how to shop" courses that included off-site excursions to Faneuil Hall were also offered, as well as a "crash course" featuring a month's worth of daily lessons.[57]

It was during this time as principal that Farmer began her crusade to develop the clear, concise recipe instructions with level measurements by volume we are so familiar with today. Although she has been referred to as the "mother of level measurements" due to her persistent quest for accuracy, this is a title often disputed among historians. A movement toward recipe clarity and consistency had already been developing throughout the nineteenth century. For example, Eliza Leslie listed ingredients at the beginning of a recipe and stressed the importance of accurate proportions—no doubt a lesson learned from Mrs. Goodfellow—including a guide to both liquid and dry weights and measures in her cookbooks. However, many recipes were still written in paragraph form, often using such arbitrary quantities as heaped teaspoons, pinches of seasoning, "wineglasses" of liquid, and "butter the size of an egg." In addition, the cookware industry didn't offer standard measuring equipment until the late nineteenth century, so it was often difficult for home cooks to correctly duplicate ingredient quantities.[58]

As previously mentioned, it was Mary Lincoln (Farmer's Boston Cooking School predecessor) who took things to a whole new level with her cookbook, *Mrs. Lincoln's Boston Cook Book: What To Do and What Not To Do in Cooking.* Her detailed explanations emphasized the science of cookery, including focus on proper measurements and specific ingredient descriptions. Even though this cookbook was hailed as revolutionary and became extremely popular both at cooking schools and with the general public, Farmer still found fault with it. She felt the directions were insufficient and the number of recipes lacking. Just as with her relentless recipe testing, she thought it could be better.

Fannie Farmer (1857–1915) became principal of the Boston Cooking School in 1893. She revised her predecessor's *Mrs. Lincoln's Boston Cook Book* which ultimately became the *Fannie Farmer Cookbook*, one of the most famous and influential cookbooks ever published. (*Boston Public Library*)

Farmer's obsession with precision led her to revise and elaborate on Lincoln's version, with the objective of ensuring easy recipe directions and standardizing measurements once and for all. The result of her hard work was *The Boston Cooking-School Cookbook*, a massive 831-page cooking reference manual published in 1896. Fannie's chosen publishing house (Little, Brown) was initially doubtful that the book would sell. However, they eventually agreed to serve as her agent and distributor, giving Farmer the responsibility for publication costs. This arrangement eventually worked to Farmer's advantage as she ended up owning the copyright on one of the most popular cookbooks ever published in the United States. And because she was the author (not the Boston Cooking School), the name of the book was soon changed to *The Fannie Farmer Cookbook*. This is how it is known today, having gone through numerous reprints and revisions in the hundred-plus years since its initial publication.[59]

Farmer went on to write several more cookery books before her death in 1915, although none of them was as successful as her original. She continued working at the Boston Cooking School until 1902, when she resigned in order to open her own school, Miss Farmer's School of Cookery. Soon after, the Boston Cooking School closed its doors as a separate institution and became part of Simmons College.[60]

Now in charge of her own school, Farmer remained vital and focused on her teaching, giving popular biweekly demonstration lectures for a student base of mostly housewives and society ladies that often numbered two hundred. She also taught evening lessons geared for professional chefs.[61] Still her energy level did not wane; she moved around the lecture hall's kitchen platform at a swift pace, her bright blue eyes and red hair matching her vibrant personality. Although she always had help from an assistant (even in her early years) in order to save her strength, this was as much due to the fact that she was often an impatient cook and had difficulty remaining in one place. Even when her health was failing toward the end of her life, she continued to lecture from her wheelchair.[62]

Probably as a result of her own health challenges, she also worked on creating special diets for those recovering from illness, publishing *Food and Cookery for the Sick and Convalescent* in 1904, a book she considered her most important. She even gave training to nurses and dietitians on this topic, providing demonstrations in hospital wards. And she wrote a regular magazine column with her sister for *Woman's Home Companion* from 1905 to 1915.[63]

However, even with all these impressive accomplishments, Farmer's legacy is not without controversy. She has been faulted for her lack of originality, including revising Mary Lincoln's earlier work without giving her predecessor any credit, although as Laura Shapiro notes in her book *Perfection Salad*, Farmer did change the style significantly, swapping Lincoln's chatty, more personable approach for her own methodical, more concise instructions.[64] As a result, this crisp reference manual format has been criticized for the lack of detail in its directions and explanations. However, Farmer wanted to design it as a cooking school textbook, not a novel to be read cover to cover. She wanted cooks to learn by observing and doing, not reading.[65]

In addition, Farmer's technical approach to cooking was sometimes deemed too bland and tasteless, as if mealtime was simply a requirement to be fulfilled, not an experience to be savored. She also had a tendency to use copious amounts of flour and butter to thicken sauces, which would have resulted in a thick, pasty texture. (When trying to duplicate Farmer's recipes for his book *Fannie's Last Supper*, Christopher Kimball found her typical formula was to combine one quarter cup of butter and a sizable half cup of flour with only six cups of stock.)[66]

But this type of food was characteristic of the time, so perhaps Farmer didn't have much of an idea how else "good food" could be prepared, even though she was so constantly striving to make recipe improvements. The recipes studied in the first cooking schools were not necessarily innovative, at least in the beginning. Fannie and the other early cooking-school leaders are often criticized for their reliance on the simple and hearty New England-style fare that they knew best. Lincoln especially focused more on the American basics, avoiding rich foods and complicated sauces. Farmer did however, try branching out into what *she* considered more daring territory; for example, adding oysters and canned tomatoes to augment a classic French bouillon.[67]

But no matter how you look at her, Fannie Farmer had a significant impact on modern cooking. Her condensed "formula" recipe made it easier for busy women to put meals on the table more quickly and efficiently, preparing them for the changes the twentieth century would bring. Indeed, in an overview of Western culinary history written by Anne Willan (founder of the French cooking school La Varenne), Farmer is the only American mentioned on the list of fourteen "most influential chefs since the fourteenth century."[68] And although some food historians may not consider her to have been the most skillful cook, most acknowledge that her enthusiastic style and business sense made up for her lack of cooking ability. In fact, she often thought of herself as primarily a businesswoman.[69] Like Goodfellow, she knew her market and used this knowledge to her advantage.

A common thread among early cooking school innovators is that they were all essentially marketing their talent and services, hoping the public would be interested in what they were selling. Each had a specific agenda—from Eliza Goodfellow and her insistence on wholesome, fresh ingredients to Fannie Farmer and her passion for precision. It helped that they were energetic, convincing speakers—like actors on a stage, holding the rapt attention of their audience.

But their target market was primarily housewives and domestic servants; restaurant training still used the apprenticeship model, with hands-on instruction the norm. As the century progressed, support for vocational schools began to increase and the idea of teaching cooking as a professional trade slowly gained acceptance.[70]

Becoming a restaurant chef is such a widely recognized career path today that it is almost unbelievable to realize that schools offering this type of culinary training have only been around since World War II, when veterans began to take advantage of the G.I. Bill for education assistance. Seeking to provide professional training and viable employment for returning veterans, the New Haven Restaurant Institute (now known as the Culinary Institute of America) opened its doors in 1946. It was the first school in America to award degrees focusing on culinary arts. Now students can choose from hundreds of institutions that provide a range of offerings—from hospitality industry certification through advanced academic degrees in gastronomy and nutrition.[71]

Another trend that exploded during the second half of the twentieth century was the idea of cooking as a leisure activity. As technological innovations made food preparation less time-consuming, women began to view cooking as an enjoyable pastime rather than a necessary chore or a way to impress one's social circle. Better and more efficient transportation led to increased cultural awareness and the mingling of different culinary flavors and techniques. Likewise, food that previously wouldn't have been available in one region could suddenly be flown by plane across the globe, allowing cooks to experiment with exotic ingredients and dishes. Cookbooks that featured international cuisines became popular. Television also became an important avenue for cooking instructors, allowing them to showcase their skills to a much wider market than the ladies from the home economics movement were able to achieve with their popular traveling cooking demonstrations. As a result, savvy marketers began to develop a whole new culinary model—recreational cooking classes.

In a way, this is the type of cooking the proto-celebrity chef Pierre Blot tried to introduce to New York City a hundred years before. And while he did attract sizable interest and had a good run with his French cooking classes, his success was rather short lived. If television had been available during Blot's lifetime, it would have undoubtedly enhanced his celebrity status even more. One could picture him broadcasting his epicurean techniques from his cozy bistro-like Academy. But the invention of television would have to wait almost another century; and once it came on the scene, New York area chefs took advantage. In 1946, James Beard was featured on television's first cooking show on NBC, and after that continued as a vital force on television and radio. He opened the James Beard Cooking School in New York in 1955. Starting in 1947, Dione Lucas juggled a television program, restaurant, and cooking school.[72]

But it was another French cooking expert who really roused the public's interest in making gourmet food—Julia Child. Recreational cooking in America truly began to take off soon after the famous cookbook Child co-wrote with her colleagues Simone Beck and Louisette Bertholle, *Mastering the Art of French Cooking* was published in 1961. Child (an American citizen) charmed the country with her thorough knowledge of French cookery techniques, acquired from the renowned Cordon Bleu cooking school in France. The television programs she began to host a few years later (starting with *The French Chef,* which premiered in 1962) increased her exposure even more. With her sing-song voice and chatty style, she awakened a whole generation of women to the fact that gourmet cooking could be interesting and fun. By the end of the 1960s, there were fifteen cooking schools in New York City; today there are hundreds of recreational cooking schools or programs in the United States.[73]

Unlike the often reluctant well-to-do young ladies who attended Mrs. Goodfellow's school, the students taking these recreational culinary programs are genuinely interested in cooking. Cooking as a hobby and creative outlet was unheard of in Goodfellow's time, but many twentieth-century innovations helped drive the appeal—from globalization trends to labor-saving kitchen appliances and utensils. Classes are still informational, but in a different way. Mrs. Goodfellow was giving her students the cooking skills they would need to succeed in their upper-class married lives. Her curriculum was targeted to their lifestyle and probably didn't vary much from year to year. But with recreational cooking, a variety of topics can be explored—regional cooking, nutritional and health aspects, specific baking or cooking techniques, and the list goes on. And classes aren't limited to an exclusive group. Those with little or no cooking background might be in the same class as experienced cooks, as long as they share an interest in the specific theme being covered.

Once the public started picking up on the idea of cooking for fun, other types of culinary education began to crop up, including in-home instruction, cooking class parties, programs for children, and the increasingly popular cooking classes available through supermarkets, specialty food, and department stores. Culinary tourism is another emerging offshoot for those who wish to immerse themselves in a specific regional cuisine while on vacation. And celebrity chefs can be seen on every available media outlet demonstrating and promoting their latest concoctions.[74] These types of learning are usually rather abbreviated—designed to scratch the surface and introduce interested cooks to one or two particular culinary topics as well as to provide entertainment. So again, the format differs from the series of lessons Mrs. Goodfellow and the other early cooking schools offered, where each class built on the previous one.

Although cooking schools have experienced such diverse changes and growth since Mrs. Goodfellow's time, the same important principles that she preached have remained through the years. Many people welcomed the new technologies that made cooking and baking easier such as quick-rising agents, cook stoves, and eventually processed foods such as boxed, canned, and frozen goods, but some still held tight to the notion Mrs. Goodfellow constantly emphasized to her students—using quality, fresh ingredients to create a wholesome and superior product.

James Beard was one of the best communicators of this concept. Well-known for unpretentious, hearty, and natural good cooking, Beard dedicated his remarkable food bible of American specialty dishes, *James Beard's American Cookery* (1972), to his "favorite great ladies of the American kitchen." On his list are seven celebrated women who helped shape cooking in the United States, with Eliza Leslie at the top. The other luminaries are: Mrs. T. J. Crowen, author of *Every Lady's Book* (1845); Philadelphia Cooking School founder Sarah Tyson Rorer; Boston Cooking-School's Fannie Merritt Farmer; Irma Rombauer, author of *The Joy of Cooking* (1931); Helen Evans Brown, food writer and consultant; and June Platt, food writer and designer.[75]

Although Mrs. Goodfellow is not listed in this elite group, Beard refers to her and her school in the book. His views on cookery were strikingly similar to Goodfellow and her protégé, Eliza Leslie. Like Goodfellow, he preached the merits of simplicity through his recipes and classes. And although his cookbooks were published over a century after Miss Leslie, they are comparable to hers—practical, basic teaching manuals. By highlighting simple, unfussy cooking methods, he was able to emphasize the benefits of these early American cooking concepts, showing the public that taste doesn't have to be artificial. As pointed out by Betty Fussell in *Masters of American Cookery*, Beard expressed disappointment over the disappearance of many American regional foods, but he did "more than anybody to stalk the wild traditions of our past and honor earlier giants."[76]

Although Beard was probably the best known cooking expert in recent years to thoroughly explore and revitalize the concept of home cooking, many others also have rediscovered its delights. As a result, the idea that Mrs. Goodfellow so adamantly preached continues to spark interest. A number of cookbooks today focus on simple, wholesome cooking with natural ingredients, such as *American Home Cooking* by the husband-and-wife team of Bill and Cheryl Alters Jamison, which celebrates the modest yet hearty "comfort food" that Americans turned to since the first settlers arrived and that is having a renaissance.[77] And in *Baking in America: Traditional and Contemporary Favorites from the Past Two Hundred Years*, baking expert Greg Patent carefully studies and tests classic baking recipes from old American cookbooks, including several attributed to Goodfellow and Leslie. By making the necessary conversions to contemporary ingredients and methods, he gives present-day cooks a chance to make and enjoy many traditional baked goods that have been largely forgotten.

Mrs. Goodfellow and other cooks from her time often planned their menus according to what they knew would be fresh, frequenting open-air markets which provided a wealth of local, seasonal produce. James Beard also saw this benefit, and we can thank him in part for the revival of the farmer's markets in towns and cities across America today.[78] Many, many people are now "buying fresh, buying local," perhaps influenced by the early culinary greats. For others, it makes sense for any number of reasons. To cookbook writer Diana Kennedy, "eating well means supporting local farms. . . . It's good for the environment, it's good for communities and culture, it's good for your health."[79]

Trends in cooking are always changing. However, as food writer Mark Bittman notes in his foreword to the 2007 re-issue of *Beard on Food: The Best Recipes and Kitchen Wisdom from the Dean of American Cooking*, "Beard's approach remains invaluable to real people cooking real food."[80] So does Mrs. Goodfellow's, as her insistence on wholesome, fresh ingredients is echoed on many cooking programs on television. Yet as much as she represented her time, in her influence on her students and later cooking teachers, Mrs. Goodfellow was also well ahead of it.

Epilogue: The End of the Day

Philadelphia, 64 Dock Street
Wednesday, September 20, 1815
7 p.m.

Mrs. Goodfellow retrieved the last slice of apple pudding, the rest of the Spanish buns, and the remaining two Queen cakes from the shelf behind the counter and carefully placed them in a basket lined with a clean towel. She then scooped up the half dozen or so jumbles that were left and transferred them to a small tin, which she nestled in the basket next to the other items. These leftover treats would be shared among her family and servants.

While her servant Mary was busy sweeping the floor, Mrs. Goodfellow dipped a soft flannel cloth in a bowl of warm soapy water and began to wipe down the shelves and counter. She then rinsed off the surfaces with plain water and dried them with a linen cloth. When they were both finished their cleaning tasks, Mrs. Goodfellow lit a candle and then carefully closed the shutters in the front of her pastry shop, making sure they were secure for the night. She then shut the heavy front door and locked it. It was now quite dark inside the shop so they were both grateful for the candle's soft glow.

Mary held the candle while Mrs. Goodfellow emptied the money from the cash box and put it inside the pocket she wore around her neck. Grasping the basket in one hand and the cleaning bowl and cloths in the other, she followed Mary down the steps to the kitchen, where Hannah was busy washing up the dishes and kitchen utensils.

Mrs. Goodfellow put the bowl and cloths on the table and asked Mary to get out the ingredients she would need to prepare some tins of Spanish buns for the morning. She then went back upstairs where her husband, son, and daughter were sitting near the fireplace reading. Taking the pocket from around her neck, she handed the day's earnings from the pastry shop to her husband William to count and then offered each of them one of the leftover baked goods. Robert and Sarah thanked their mother, both eagerly choosing a colorful Queen cake. William decided on the slice of apple pudding. She kissed each of her children good-night and took the rest of the bakery items back down to the kitchen.

Placing the basket on the end of the table, Mrs. Goodfellow told Mary that she and the other servants could help themselves to the remaining pastries when they were done. Hannah had finished the dishes and was busy gathering wood for the oven so it would be ready in the morning.

Mrs. Goodfellow then headed over to the work table and proceeded to finish mixing the Spanish buns so they could rise overnight. Mary was grating a nutmeg and had already set out a bowl of eggs, a jar of yeast, a demijohn of rosewater, small paper sacks of cinnamon and mace, and a wooden box containing the remaining sugar that Hannah had

pounded to a fine consistency earlier. Mrs. Goodfellow
went to the cooling shelf to retrieve a soup plate of butter
and milk that she had set near the fire to soften and then
moved to cool once it had melted. Working quickly, she
broke each of four eggs one at a time into a dish, checking
for freshness, and beat them very light. She then added the
milk and butter combination; when it was well blended, she
poured the frothy yellow mixture into a broad pan of flour
Mary had just sifted. To this she added two wine glasses of
strong yeast, a tablespoon of rosewater flavoring, the grated
nutmeg, and a large teaspoon each of powdered mace and
cinnamon. She started adding some sugar a little at a time
while stirring the mixture very hard with a knife—she
knew if she added the sugar too quickly, the buns would
become heavy. Then she gradually sprinkled a little more
flour and stirred the dough well. Finally she buttered a
square pan and added the dough, covering it with a cloth
and setting it on a stool near the fire to rise.

Once Mrs. Goodfellow and Mary were done, Hannah
began to wash the dishes and baking implements while
Mary carefully wiped down the work surfaces with a clean
cloth and Mrs. Goodfellow put the ingredients away, making sure they were in place for the morning. She checked
the kitchen dresser and larder to see if any supplies were
needed and that the scales had been put away properly.

While she was doing these final checks, Mary briskly
swept the floor and Hannah carefully began closing the cellar windows in order to prevent rats and mice from coming
in overnight. Once the windows were shut tightly, she went
over to the fireplace and removed a few long sticks that
were on the fire and carried them out into the yard, pour-
ing water on them to extinguish them completely. She then
used the fireplace tongs to pick up a few wood chunks and
hot coals and placed them in the very back of the oven,
shoveling ashes over them until they were totally buried.

This would keep the fire smoldering until the morning, when Mary would uncover it and add the kindling to get it going quickly.

Finally, they all neatly hung up their aprons and Mary and Hannah said good night. Mary lit a candle and they both thanked Mrs. Goodfellow for the basket of baked goods which they carried with them up to the servants' quarters. Mrs. Goodfellow also took a candle and made her way back upstairs. Sarah and Robert were already in bed, but William was still sitting near the fire, smoking a pipe. He had already counted the shop money and locked it away in a desk drawer. She asked him for the figure, and then walked over to the desk and carefully entered it into the correct spot in her ledger. They spoke briefly about the day's happenings, and then, exhausted, she told him she was heading up to bed. She needed to be rested, as very early the next morning the baking process would begin all over again.

Recipes

The following recipes are those that we can confidently attribute to Mrs. Goodfellow's Cooking School. The recipes are taken from primary sources and were developed for eighteenth- or nineteenth-century ingredients and kitchens. Present-day ingredients and cooking techniques could produce varying results.

Listed below is a guide to "Weights and Measures" taken from Eliza Leslie's first book, *Seventy-Five Receipts for Pastry, Cakes, and Sweetmeats*. It can be presumed that these are similar to what Mrs. Goodfellow taught in her classes.

As all families are not provided with scales and weights, referring to the ingredients generally used in cakes and pastry, we subjoin a list of weights and measures.

WEIGHT AND MEASURE

Wheat flour	one pound is	one quart.
Indian meal	one pound, 2 ounces,	is one quart.
Butter—when soft	one pound, 1 ounce,	is one quart.
Loaf-sugar, broken	one pound is	one quart.
White sugar, powdered,	one pound, 1 ounce,	is one quart.
Eggs	ten eggs are	one pound.
Best brown sugar	one pound 2 ounces	is one quart.

LIQUID MEASURE

Sixteen large table-spoonfuls are	half a pint.
Eight large table-spoonfuls are	one gill.
Four large table-spoonfuls are	half a gill.

——-

A common-sized tumbler holds	half a pint.
A common-sized wine-glass holds	half a gill.

Allowing for accidental differences in the quality, freshness, dryness, and moisture of the articles, we believe this comparison, between weight and measure, to be as nearly correct as possible.

☞ Bread, Hot Cakes, and Cereals

BARRINGTON RUSK

(*From Mrs. Goodfellow's Cooking School, Philadelphia, Pa.*)
1 cup of sugar, 1 cup of milk, 1 cup of yeast, 1 cup of flour. Mix overnight. In the morning add 1/2 cup of sugar and 1/2 cup of butter, creamed light, two eggs, reserving the white of one, beaten to a stiff froth with 1/2 cup of sugar and spread over the top of the rusk. Bake in a quick oven.
(Source: *Colonial Receipt Book.* Recipe from a Pupil, Mrs. Thos. Painter, Sunbury, Pa.)

POTATO BISCUIT

(*From Mrs. Goodfellow's Cooking School, Philadelphia, Pa.*)
Boil mealy potatoes very soft, pare and mash them to four good-sized potatoes. Put a piece of butter the size of an egg and a teaspoonful of salt. When the butter has melted put 1/2 pint of cold milk. If the milk cools the potatoes put in 1/4 of a pint of yeast and flour to make them of the right consistency. Set them in a warm place. When risen mold them with the hands. Let them remain ten or fifteen minutes before baking.
(Source: *Colonial Receipt Book.* Recipe from a Pupil, Mrs. Thos. Painter, Sunbury, Pa.)

GOODFELLOW'S BUNS

A pound and quarter flour, 3/4 white sugar, 1/2 butter, 6 eggs. Half a nutmeg-wine glass of brandy, handful currants. Half pint new milk, half tea cup yeast.
(Source: Receipt Book for Cooking 1811–1824, Hannah Marshall Haines, American Philosophical Society)

GOODFELLOW'S SPANISH BUNNS

Mix 6 oz. butter in cup of cream or rich milk 1/2 pound of sugar. Beat 6 eggs, 3/4 lb flour mix the flour and eggs in alternatively. 1 teaspoonful of cream of tartar two-thirds full of soda put the soda in a cup the acid on it dissolve with rose water a little nutmeg.

(Source: Doc. 391, Mrs. Fred Patterson recipe book, Winterthur Library)

GOODFELLOW'S SPANISH BUNS

3/4 lb. flour, 6oz. butter, cut up fine in it, 4 eggs beaten well, 1 tea-spoonful of mixed nutmeg, mace and cinnamon, 3 wine-glasses baker's or brewer's yeast, 3 wine-glasses milk; mix it with a knife; add the sugar. Place it in the tins, and let it rise 2 to 3 hours; then sprinkle 2 oz. cleaned currants over the batter, pressing them lightly below the surface. Bake in a slow oven; when done, ice or sprinkle sugar over, and cut in squares.

(Source: Nicholson, *What I Know; or Hints on the Daily Duties of a Housekeeper*, 55)

SPANISH BUNS

(Mrs. Goodfellow)

4 eggs, 3/4 of a lb of Flour, 1/2 a lb of Sugar, 2 1/2 wine glasses of rich milk, 6 oz of fresh Butter, 1 tablespoonful of Rose-water, 1 grated nutmeg, 1 large tea-spoonful of pow-dered mace and cinnamon. Sift 1/2 a lb of flour into a broad pan and put a 1/4 of a lb separately into a deep plate and set it aside. Put the milk into a soup plate, cut up the butter and set it near the fire to warm. When the butter is soft stir it all through the milk and set it away to cool. Beat the eggs very light and mix the milk and butter with them all at once, then pour all into the pan of flour. Put in the fla-

voring add the yeast, stir the whole very hard with a knife add the sugar gradually, because if it be not stirred in slowly a little at a time the Buns will be heavy. Then by degrees sprinkle in the remainder of the flour and stir it well; butter a square pan and put in the mixture cover it with a cloth and set it to rise for perhaps 5 hours when it has risen very high and is covered with bubbles bake it in a moderate oven about a quarter of an hour or one this quantity will make 12 or 15 buns; if you choose to bake them separately in small square tins adding to the batter 1/2 lb of chopped raisins or currants floured and stirred in at the last. Stir your yeast well before using and pour off the beer and their part from the top; if not good do not attempt to use it as they will not be light. Buns may be made in a plainer way with 1/2 lb of Flour (a quarter set aside to sprinkle in at the last), 3 eggs, 1/2 a lb powdered sugar, 3 wine glasses of milk, 1 1/2 of yeast, 1 large teaspoonful of cinnamon, 1/4 lb of butter cut up and warmed in the milk and mixed as above.
(Source: Manuscript Recipe Book written by Henrietta "Hetty" Ann Bellah [b. 1809] for Martha Canby Morris, 1860, p. 29, Independence National Historic Park Library)

WAFFLES

3 pints of milk, 3/4 lb butter put into the milk and warmed, then add 3 pints flour and beat it up together, beat 7 eggs and put in 2 table spoons full of yeast, set it to rise moderately warm; when you bake them, so not stir them, bit take the top after they are baked set them before the fire to dry. Have melted butter ready to put over them with powdered sugar and cinnamon.
(Source: Recipe Book: Manuscript, 1841–1862; Ms. Codex 884. Rare Book & Manuscripts Library, University of Pennsylvania)

WAFFLES

(From Mrs. Goodfellow's Cooking School, Philadelphia, Pa.)
Take 1 quart of flour and a teaspoonful of salt, 1 quart of milk with 1 tablespoonful of melted butter, and mix the flour gradually until perfectly smooth. Add 3 tablespoonfuls of yeast, let rise until light. Bake in a waffle iron.
(Source: *Colonial Receipt Book.* Recipe from a Pupil, Mrs. Thos. Painter, Sunbury, Pa.)

QUICK WAFFLES

(From Mrs. Goodfellow's Cooking School, Philadelphia, Pa.)
1 quart of flour, 1 quart of sour milk, 2 tablespoonfuls of melted butter, 5 eggs beaten separately until light, 1 teaspoonful of soda dissolved in the milk. To 1 heaping teaspoonful cream of tartar, add the flour, the yolks of the eggs and the whites of the eggs thoroughly beaten just before baking.
(Colonial Receipt Book. Recipe contributed by a Pupil. Mrs. Ebenezer Greenough, Sunbury, Pa.)

☞ Vegetables

ARTICHOKES

Wring off the stalks, pull out the strings & wash them in water–have a large pot of water, when it boils, put in some salt, throw them in tops downwards, boil them gently 1 1/2 hour, you will know when they are done by pulling out the leaves, if they come out easily they are done, take them out let them drain & eat them with melted butter.
(Source: Recipe Book: Manuscript, 1841–1862; Ms. Codex 884. Rare Book & Manuscripts Library, University of Pennsylvania)

Ragou of Onions

Peel a pint of small onions, chop 1 or 2 large ones fine, put 1/4 lb. butter into a stew pan, when it is melted and done hissing, put in the onions and fry them brown, put in a little flour and shake them round till they are thick, then add 1 pint of gravy, a little cayenne pepper, salt and a teaspoon full of mustard and when they are well tasted put them in a dish.

(Source: Recipe Book: Manuscript, 1841–1862; Ms. Codex 884. Rare Book & Manuscripts Library, University of Pennsylvania)

☞ Meats/Main Dishes

White Fricassee Chickens

Take 3 chickens, cut them up, take off the skin, throw them into cold water and let them lay some time, then put them over the fire in boiling water and keep them boiling till they are almost done; then take them off and put them in a dish. Take 1/4 butter rubbed in flour with 1/2 pint of cream. Put them over the fire—keep stirring it till all the butter is melted then tie a little sweet herbs with a little mace, whole pepper and salt in a bag and put into this mixture. Put your chickens in and let them boil a few minutes, when done, take the chickens out and place them on a dish and pour the sauce over.

(Source: Recipe Book: Manuscript, 1841–1862; Ms. Codex 884. Rare Book & Manuscripts Library, University of Pennsylvania)

To Stew Veal

Put a lump of butter into a stew pan set it over the fire and let it brown, add 1/2 pint of water, lay the veal in it & let it stew. Turn it on all sides that it may be well browned, then pour on a quart of water, add some mace, cloves, pepper salt

& sweet herbs—cover it close & let it stew gently 3 hours, when done lay the veal on a dish & pour the gravy over it. (Source: Recipe Book: Manuscript, 1841–1862; Ms. Codex 884. Rare Book & Manuscripts Library, University of Pennsylvania)

To Cook Terrapin

(*Mrs. Goodfellow*)

To 1 large sized terrapin take 1/4 of a pound of butter, 1/2 a gill of cream, the same of wine, cayenne pepper, salt and flour to your taste; a little water must be mixed with it to prevent your butter going to oil. Just before you take them up stir in the cream. The boiling of the terrapin depends on the size.

(Source: *Famous Old Receipts Used a Hundred Years and More*, 84)

☞ Preserves and Pickles

Mangoes

Take as many melons as you wish, slit them two thirds up the middle and take all the seeds out, put them into strong salt and water for 24 hours and drain them on a sieve; mix 1/2 lb mustard seed, 2 oz. pepper, 2 oz. allspice, 2 oz. mace and cloves, a large quantity of garlic and horseradish cut in pieces and quarter of an ounce cayenne pepper fill the melons full of this mixture close the hole and tie it with thread and put them in a jar, boil some vinegar with some of the mixture in it and pour over the melons and cover them close.

(Source: Recipe Book: Manuscript, 1841–1862; Ms. Codex 884. Rare Book & Manuscripts Library, University of Pennsylvania)

PIGS FEET SOUCED

After cleaning the feet, boil them till tender, then boil as much water with salt and vinegar, allspice and pepper in it as will cover them, when both are cold put the feet into a jar, and pour the pickle over them and when you use them fry them in a batter of eggs and lard.

(Source: Recipe Book: Manuscript, 1841–1862; Ms. Codex 884. Rare Book & Manuscripts Library, University of Pennsylvania)

☞ Cookies

COOKIES

(*Mrs. Goodfellow's Cooking School, Philadelphia, Pa.*)
1 teacup of butter, 1 of sugar, 1 egg and flour to roll very thin. Flavor with nutmeg. Roll only a few at a time.

(Source: *Colonial Receipt Book*. Recipe from Mrs. Thos. Painter, Sunbury, Pa. Recipe contributed by Miss Mary E. Painter.)

GINGERBREAD

3 pds of flour, 1 lb of butter, 1 lb of sugar, 1 qt of molasses, 7 dos of cloves pounded fine, a little cinnamon, work it in a 1/4 of a lb of flour

(Source: Recipe Book: Manuscript, 1841–1862; Ms. Codex 884. Rare Book & Manuscripts Library, University of Pennsylvania)

GINGERBREAD

(*From Mrs. Goodfellow*)
1 1/2 pounds of flour, 1/2 pound butter, 1/4 pound sugar, 1 pint of molasses, spice to taste. A little black pepper improves.

(Source: *Colonial Receipt Book*. Recipe contributed by Mrs. Craig D. Ritchie, Philadelphia, Pa.)

Gingerbread Spiced, Mrs. Goodfellow's Receipt

1 lb. of sugar rolled fine, 1 pound of butter, 1 oz. of ginger, 1 oz. of cinnamon, 4 dosen cloves, 12 dosen allspice mixed in 3 pounds and a half of flour with as much molasfes as will make it into dough roll thin, keeping out a half pound of the flour for rolling.

(Source: Doc. 1381, Recipe books, ca. 1829–1884 [unknown, possibly Quaker], Winterthur Library)

Jumbles

(Mrs. Physick's recipe from Mrs. Goodfellow's)
Take 1 lb of butter, 1 lb of powdered white sugar, 1 lb of flour, a wine glass full of rose water, the yolks and whites of 4 eggs, beaten separately—the butter and sugar must be beat together and the other ingredients added afterwards.

(Source: Recipe Book: Manuscript, 1841–1862; Ms. Codex 884. Rare Book & Manuscripts Library, University of Pennsylvania)

Jumbles

(Mrs. Goodfellow)
1 lb. flour, 3/4 lb. sugar, 3/4 lb. butter, 4 eggs and some spice to suit your taste. Roll them out in fine sugar.

(Source: Coleman, *Cook Book*, July 16, 1855)

Goodfellow's Jumbles

1 lb. flour, 1 lb. sugar, 1 lb. butter, 1/2 glass rosewater, a little spice, 12 drops Essence of lemon, 4 eggs

(Source: Receipt Book for Cooking 1811–1824, Hannah Marshall Haines, APS)

Spice Nuts

1 lb. flour, 1 lb. sugar, 3/4 lb. butter, 1 pt. molasses, 3 table-

spoons full of ginger, 1 tablespoon allspice, 1 tablespoon cinnamon, 2 tablespoons orange peel, 1/2 oz. caraway seeds.

(Source: Recipe Book: Manuscript, 1841–1862; Ms. Codex 884. Rare Book & Manuscripts Library, University of Pennsylvania)

☞ Pastry, Puddings, Pies

ALMOND PUDDING

1 lb. butter and 1 lb. sugar beaten to a cream, 1/4 lb. almonds blanched and beaten in a mortar with 1/2 glass of rose water, 1/2 glass of wine or brandy, 9 eggs beaten very light (for 4 puddings).

(Source: Recipe book: manuscript, 1841–1862; Ms. Codex 884. Rare Book & Manuscripts Library, University of Pennsylvania)

TWO ALMOND PUDDINGS

(*Mrs. Coane's/Mrs. Goodfellow's—1808*)
Beat quarter and a half of butter and the same of sugar to a cream, four eggs beaten light and added to the cream with half a glass of brandy. Take half a pound of almonds weighed in the shells, when shelled and blanched put them into a mortar and wet them with rosewater, pound them until they become a paste, add a little more rosewater to them to prevent their oiling—add all this together and beat them well before you put them in the paste.

(Source: Manuscript Recipe Book, Catalogue No. 3696, Independence National Historic Park)

APPLE PUDDING

4 apples, stew them well, throw in a small piece of lemon peel, when done add 1/2 lb. butter, 1/2 lb. sugar well beaten together till the butter becomes a cream, 5 eggs, beaten to

a froth and 1 wine glass of brandy, 1 of wine, 1 tablespoon rose water (for 2 puddings).

(Source: Recipe Book: Manuscript, 1841–1862; Ms. Codex 884. Rare Book & Manuscripts Library, University of Pennsylvania)

Two Apple Puddings

(Mrs. Coane's/Mrs. Goodfellow's—1808)

Pare six pippins and boil them gently in a little water when soft take them out and pulp them through a colander, add to this the skin of one orange, boiled in three different waters and pounded fine, also the juice of it. One wine glass of brandy and one of wine as much cinnamon and nutmeg as would fill a teaspoon and a tablespoonful of rosewater— have the butter and sugar a quarter and a half of it each beaten to a cream, four eggs beaten light and added to the cream—and mix by degrees the apples when prepared as above. Have ready the paste before all the ingredients are mixed together.

(Source: Manuscript Recipe Book, Catalogue No. 3696, Independence National Historic Park)

Two Citron Puddings

(Mrs. Coane's/Mrs. Goodfellow's—1808)

Beat a quarter and half of butter the same of sugar to a cream and four eggs beaten light and half a glass of brandy and half as much of rose water two teaspoons full of the grated skin of a lemon and the juice, beat these ingredients well together and put them in the paste—weigh two ounces of citron and cut it in thin slices and lay it on the top of the pudding. Take a knife and press it down so that the batter may cover it.

(Source: Manuscript Recipe Book, Catalogue No. 3696, Independence National Historic Park)

Cocoanut Pudding

(Mrs. Goodfellow)
1/4 lb. of cocoanut grated, 1/4 lb. of sugar, 3 ozs. of butter, and 6 eggs, the whites only to be used and to be beaten very stiff; 1/2 a wineglass of brandy, 1/2 a wineglass of wine and 1 spoonful of rose water. Beat the butter and sugar to a cream and then mix all together and bake in puff paste.
(Source: Coleman, *Cook Book,* July 16, 1855)

Two Cocoanut Puddings

(Mrs. Coane's/Mrs. Goodfellow's—1808)
Take quarter and a half of butter the same of sugar and beat to a cream—the whites of six eggs well beaten add these altogether, then add half a wine glass of brandy and half as much rosewater. The cocoanut must be added the last thing when properly prepared which is by weighing quarter and a half of cocoanut and grating it fine it must be mixed with the other ingredients and stirred but gently after it is in then put it in your paste.
(Source: Manuscript Recipe Book, Catalogue No. 3696, Independence National Historic Park)

Lemon Custard

(Mrs. Goodfellow's Cooking School, Philadelphia, Pa.)
Beat the yolks of 10 eggs very light. Strain them, beat again, and beat with a pint of cream. Sweeten the juice of 2 lemons, add to the mixture, and stir over a slow fire to the usual thickness of a custard.
(Source: *Colonial Receipt Book,* 108. Recipe contributed by Mrs. Thomas Painter, Sunbury, Pa.)

Lemon Pudding

1 lb. butter, 1 lb. sugar well beaten together, 1 wine glass wine, 1 of brandy, 1 tablespoon rose water, mixed with 10 eggs (originally called for 9, but the 9 was crossed out and the number 10 written on top) beaten very light, the juice and grated rinds of 2 lemons (for 4 puddings).

(Source: Recipe Book: Manuscript, 1841–1862; Ms. Codex 884. Rare Book & Manuscripts Library, University of Pennsylvania)

Mrs. Goodfellow's Lemon Pudding

Take of butter (the very best) and loaf-sugar, each half a pound, beat them to a froth as or pound cake, add five eggs, the juice of half of a large or the whole of a small lemon. Grate into it the outside yellow rind, but not an atom of the white—half a glass of Madeira, a teaspoonful of orange-flower water, pour it into your paste, and bake with a moderate oven.

(Source: *Godey's Lady's Book*, January 1874)

Two Lemon Puddings

(Mrs. Coane's / Mrs. Goodfellow's—1808)

Take a quarter and a half of good butter, the same of sugar—beat until they become a cream—have ready four eggs beaten light, pour them into the cream by degrees—grate the peal of one lemon, add its juice to that of an orange and half a glass of brandy. Stir these well together and put them into the paste.

(Source: Manuscript Recipe Book, Catalogue No. 3696, Independence National Historic Park)

Mince Meat

(*Contributed by Mrs. Goodfellow*)

One lb. of beef or tongue or heart, 1 lb. of suet, 1 lb. of sugar, 1 lb. of raisins, 1 lb. of currants, 1/2 lb. of citron, 2 lbs. of apples, 1 pt. of wine, 1 pt. of brandy, 1/2 oz. of cinnamon, 1 whole nutmeg, 1/4 oz. cloves, 1/4 oz. mace, the rind of 1 orange pounded. Boil the meat before chopping, seed raisins, wash and pick the currants, slice citron, pare, core, and chop the apples. Mix together the liquids last. The weight is for the articles after they are prepared for mixing.

(Source: *Famous Old Receipts Used a Hundred Years and More*, 218)

Two Orange Puddings

(*Mrs. Coane's / Mrs. Goodfellow's—1808*)

Peal one orange and put the skins on to boil—changing the water three times, when they are tender, take them off and pound them in a mortar, add to this the juice of the orange with that of one lemon squeezed through a grater, put this to a quarter and a half of butter, the same of sugar beaten to a cream, also four eggs and half a glass of wine and the same of brandy. It must be stirred very gently after the orange is in or else it will be heavy—have your paste ready before the orange is put to the butter and sugar.

(Source: Manuscript Recipe Book, Catalogue No. 3696, Independence National Historic Park)

Two Potato Puddings

(*Mrs. Coane's / Mrs. Goodfellow's—1808*)

Boil half a pound of potatoes with the skins off, wash them through a colander and add them to a quarter and half of butter the same of sugar beaten to a cream and four eggs beaten light. One wine glass of brandy, the same of wine

and half as much rosewater, a teaspoonful of cinnamon and nutmeg, mix these together and put them in a paste.
(Source: Manuscript Recipe Book, Catalogue No. 3696, Independence National Historic Park)

WHITE POTATO PIE

(*Mrs. Goodfellow's Recipe*)
1/2 pound of butter, 1/2 pound of sugar creamed together; add 1/2 pound of white potatoes boiled and grated, 4 eggs well-beaten, a gill of cream, a glass of wine, brandy and rose-water mixed. Flavor with cinnamon or nutmeg. Bake in puff paste.
(Source: *Colonial Receipt Book*, 131. Recipe contributed by Mrs. William Henry Kennedy, Philadelphia)

TO MAKE PUFF PASTE

(*From Mrs. Goodfellow*)
Take a pound and quarter of flour, dry and sift it. Weigh out half, and divide it into two parts on the table, cut a pound of butter into four equal parts, take one quarter, and mix it up with a knife, and role it in, then roll it in the other two quarters, and keep it as cool as possible.
(Source: *Margaret Coxe Burd Receipt Books*, 1801–1852. (Phi) Am.912339, Historical Society of Pennsylvania)

TO MAKE PASTE

(*Mrs. Coane's / Mrs. Goodfellow's—1808*)
Weigh one pound and two ounces of flour, one pound of butter—have the butter well washed—the flour dried and sifted. Divide the butter into four quarters and the flour in half. Take half the flour and one quarter of the butter and mix them together in a pan with some cold water, mixing it

with a knife all the time then put it on the paste board or marble, dip your hands in the flour. [Cut off from here.]

(Source: Manuscript Recipe Book, Catalogue No. 3696, Independence National Historic Park)

PASTRY

This will make puff paste for 2 puddings, or for one soup plate-pie or for four small shells.

Weigh 1/2 a lb and 2 oz of flour, and sift it through a hair sieve into a large deep dish. Take out one fourth of the flour, place it aside on one corner of your paste board, to roll and sprinkle with.

Wash in cold water 1/2 lb of the best fresh butter squeeze it with your hands, and make it up into a round lump: divide it into four equal parts, lay them on one size of your paste board and have ready a glass of cold water. Cut one of the four pieces into the pan of flour as small as possible: wet it gradually with very little water as too much will make it tough and mix well with the point of a large knife but do not touch it with your hands; then sprinkle the board with some of the flour laid aside and turn the dough out with a knife. Rub the rolling pin with flour and sprinkle a little on the lump of paste. Roll it thin and evenly pressing very lightly. Then take the second of the four pieces of butter and with the knife stick it in little bits at equal distance, all over the sheet of paste. Sprinkle on a little flour and fold up the dough flour the board and pin and roll out a second time stick the third piece of butter—fold and roll out again and stick on the fourth and last piece of butter, fold it up and then roll it out in a large round sheet pressing lightly with the pin every time.

When preparing it for the pudding plate roll with a short quick stroke pressing the pin rather harder than when putting the butter in. If the paste rises in blisters it will be light unless spoiled in baking. He cut the sheet in half, fold up each piece and roll out once more separately, in round sheets the size of your plate making it thinner in the middle than at the edges: if the edges are not thick enough put the trimmings together, roll them out, cut in slips the breadth of the rim of the plate joining them nicely and place round evenly then notch the rim handsomely; fill the dish with the pudding and bake in a moderate oven. The paste should be a light brown color. If the oven be too slow it will be soft and clammy if too quick it will not have time to rise as it ought. IN making the best puff paste try to avoid using more flour to sprinkle and roll with than the small portion you have laid aside. It is difficult to make puff paste in the summer unless in a cellar, a very cool room, or on a marble table, your butter should be kept cool and your water with ice in it. After the paste is mixed it should be set in a cool place or in cold water till you are ready for the last rolling.

"With all these precautions to prevent its being heavy, it will not rise as well, or be in any respect as good as in cold weather."
~ Mrs. Goodfellow ~

(Source: Manuscript Recipe Book written by Henrietta "Hetty" Ann Bellah [b. 1809] for Martha Canby Morris, 1860, p. 59, Independence National Historic Park Library)

☞ Cakes

CHEESE CAKE

(Mrs. Goodfellow)

Four eggs well beaten, stirred into two cups boiling milk; then put your pan containing the milk and the eggs on some coals or a stove, stir them until it curdles, then strain off the whey, and let the curd cool; grate six ounces of sponge cake, or any other light cake that is stale, and mix with the cold curd; cream half a pound of butter, and half a pound of sugar, add a wine-glass of brandy and wine mixed; spices and rose water then mix all the ingredients together; add the rind and juice of one lemon, just before putting into paste. Have ready a nice puff paste, put in the mixture and bake in a slow oven. One pint of cottage cheese may be used if at hand, instead of preparing the curd as above. Rub it very smooth before mixing it, or sift it through a small strainer.

(Source: *American Kitchen Magazine* 14 (October 1900–March 1901): 32)

INDIAN POUND CAKE

Eight eggs; the weight of 8 in sugar-the weight of 6 in Indian meal sifted, 1/2 lb of butter, one nutmeg grated or one teaspoonful of cinnamon, stir the butter and sugar to a cream, then put the meal and eggs alternately into the butter and sugar, grate in the nutmeg and stir all well; butter a tin pan put in the mixture and bake in a moderate oven.

(Source: Bellah Manuscript Recipe Book, 40, Independence National Historic Park Library)

MRS. GOODFELLOW'S QUEEN CAKE

One pound of butter and one pound of sugar beat to a cream, a wineglass of brandy and rose water, put with the sugar and butter, ten eggs beat to a froth, one pound of flour—beat the flour and eggs in by degrees, then add a teaspoonful of cinnamon and nutmeg mixed, beat the cake well. (From Mrs. Claypoole)

(Source: *Eliza Kane Recipe Book,* New York circa 1847–1852, William L. Clements Library, University of Michigan)

QUEEN CAKE

(Mrs. Goodfellow's Cooking School, Philadelphia, Pa.)

2 1/2 pounds of flour, 1/2 pound of butter, 2 gills of yeast, 1 saltspoon of salt. Rub the butter, flour and salt together, then add the yeast with as much milk as will make it into a tolerably soft dough. Knead it well and replace in the pan to rise. This must be done in the evening. Next morning knead it lightly. Make it into small round cakes; place them on tins. Prick them with a fork and put them in a warm elevated place to rise. As soon as light bake in a quick oven. When done wash the tops lightly with a little water and cover with a towel to make them soft. In these biscuits always boil the milk, and when the weather is cold use it while tepid.

(Source: *Colonial Receipt Book.* Recipe from Mrs. Thomas Painter, Sunbury, Pa., 1811)

☞ Other Desserts

FLOATING ISLAND

(From A Pupil Of Mrs. Goodfellow)

To the white of every egg, add a tablespoonful of currant jelly and the same of white sugar. Beat until perfectly stiff. Float it on milk. Cover with flecks of currant jelly. Eat with rich cream.

(Source: *Colonial Receipt Book,* 108. Recipe from Mrs. Thomas Painter, Sunbury, Pa., contributed by her daughter, Miss Mary E. Painter, Muncy, Pa.)

SWISS CREAM

(*Mrs. Goodfellow's Cooking School, Philadelphia, Pa.*)

Take 1 quart of sweet rich cream and add 1 teaspoonful of vanilla. Let it come to a boil. Take off the stove; beat the whites of 6 eggs very, very light. Set the cream which must be nearly cold on the fire, stir the eggs slowly in and keep stirring 1/2 minute. Take from the fire, turn into a mold and stand in a cool place.

(Source: *Colonial Receipt Book,* 108. Recipe from Mrs. Thomas Painter, Sunbury, Pa.)

☞ Preparations for the Sick

BARLEY WATER

Put 1/4 lb barley into 2 qts water, let it boil, skim it clean, boil half away and strain it off; sweeten to your taste and add a little wine.

(Source: Recipe Book: Manuscript, 1841–1862; Ms. Codex 884. Rare Book & Manuscripts Library, University of Pennsylvania)

SAGO

Put a table spoonful of Sago into a pint of water, stir it and boil gently till it is as thick as you wish, about 1 1/2 hour, then add wine, sugar and nutmeg to your taste and the juice of a lemon.

(Source: Recipe Book: Manuscript, 1841–1862; Ms. Codex 884. Rare Book & Manuscripts Library, University of Pennsylvania)

TAPIOCA

Put 2 table spoonsful of tapioca into a qt of cold water let it boil gently till it becomes transparent; add a glass of wine and about double the quantity of milk if you choose it and sweeten it to your taste.

(Source: Recipe Book: Manuscript, 1841–1862; Ms. Codex 884. Rare Book & Manuscripts Library, University of Pennsylvania)

WATER GRUEL

Take a pint of water and a tablespoonful of oatmeal or Indian meal, stir it together and let it boil up to 10 minutes, let it not boil over; add wine and sugar to your taste.

(Source: Recipe Book: Manuscript, 1841–1862; Ms. Codex 884. Rare Book & Manuscripts Library, University of Pennsylvania)

Notes

PREFACE

1. Dunne and Mackie, "Philadelphia Story," 72; Hines, Marshall, and Weaver, *The Larder Invaded*.

CHAPTER ONE: WHO WAS MRS. GOODFELLOW?

1. Dunne and Mackie, "Philadelphia Story," 72.
2. Records of Gloria Dei (Old Swedes) Church, Philadelphia. Correspondence with Peg Berich, History Committee, Gloria Dei (Old Swedes) Church, Philadelphia, May 2010.
3. Weaver interview, January 21, 2009.
4. Stafford, *Philadelphia Directory for 1801*, 97.
5. Robinson, *Philadelphia Directory for 1802*; Robinson, *Philadelphia Directory for 1803*; Robinson, *Philadelphia Directory for 1804*.
6. Jackson, *Literary Landmarks*, 211–212.
7. Philadelphia, 1789–1880 Naturalization Records.
8. Telephone conversation with Abigail Coane Leibell, March 2009.
9. *Accounts of the Treasurer of the United States of Payments and Receipts of Public Monies; War Department Accounts Report Books*, 1797, 25.
10. Robinson, *Philadelphia Directory for 1805*.
11. Ancestry.com message board; http://boards.ancestry.com/surnames.coane/10/mb.ashx.
12. Records of Gloria Dei (Old Swedes) Church, Philadelphia. Correspondence with Peg Berich, History Committee, Gloria Dei (Old Swedes) Church, Philadelphia May 2010.
13. Dallett, files on Elizabeth Goodfellow.
14. Dallett, files on Elizabeth Goodfellow; Hardie, *The Philadelphia Directory and Register*.
15. Records of Gloria Dei (Old Swedes) Church, Philadelphia. Correspondence with Peg Berich, History Committee, Gloria Dei (Old Swedes) Church, Philadelphia May 2010.
16. *Aurora General Advertiser*, no. 4631, November 4, 1805, 3.
17. Robinson, *Philadelphia Directory for 1809*.
18. www.standrewsociety.org; An Historical Catalogue of the St. Andrew's Historical Society, 1907

19. Thomas, *A Century of Universalism in Philadelphia and New York*, 161.

20. Schlereth, "A Tale of Two Deists," 7.

21. Ibid., 1.

22. *United States Gazette*, July 4, 1818.

23. Eckhardt, *Pennsylvania Clocks and Clockmakers*, 74–77.

24. Philadelphia Register of Wills for the Estate of William Goodfellow, A172–18.

25. *Poulson's American Daily Advertiser*, July 3, 1818, 983.

26. Keshatus, *Historic Philadelphia*, 7.

27. David, *English Bread and Yeast Cookery*, 10.

28. Weaver, *A Quaker Woman's Cookbook*, xxii.

29. Stevens, *Pennsylvania*, 77.

30. Weigley, *Philadelphia*, 218. Johnson, *Pattern for Liberty*, 26.

31. Staib, *City Tavern Baking and Dessert Cookbook*, 11.

32. Weigley, *Philadelphia: A 300–Year History*, 6–10, 221–222.

33. Ibid., 220.

34. Kirtley, *Athens of America*.

35. Weigley, *Philadelphia: A 300–Year History*, 220.

36. Kirtley, *Athens of America*.

37. Weigley, *Philadelphia: A 300–Year History*, 214–215.

38. Oberholtzer, *Philadelphia*, 434.

39. Dock Street Views—Campbell Collection, HSP. Newspaper clipping—*Dock Street: Development and Associations of the Old Thoroughfare*, by Jo Jackson, April 3, 1891.

40. Stafford, *The Philadelphia Directory for 1801*.

41. Cotter, Roberts, and Parrington, *The Buried Past*, 36.

42. Warner, *The Private City*, 6.

43. *Poulson's Daily Advertiser*, November 3, 1803, 4.

44. Gum arabic is a natural gum made of hardened sap taken from two species of the acacia tree. Mrs. Goodfellow would have used it in a powdered form to make wine and cake icing.

45. *Poulson's American Daily Advertiser*, December 2, 1818, 1; December 21, 1813, 2.

46. *Poulson's American Daily Advertiser*, August 12, 1817, 1.

47. *Poulson's American Daily Advertiser*, March 9, 1819, 3.

48. Betsy Ross Homepage http://www.ushistory.org/betsy/.

49. Wulf, *Not All Wives*, 98–99.

50. Ancestry.com. 1810 United States Federal Census. Philadelphia

Dock Ward, Philadelphia, Pennsylvania; Roll 55, p. 516; Family History
Number: 0193681; Image: 00211.
51. Cowan, *More Work for Mother*, 28–29.
52. Ancestry.com. 1820 United States Federal Census. Philadelphia
Dock Ward, Philadelphia, Pennsylvania, Page 26; NARA Roll:
M33_108; Image: 37.
53. Cotter, Roberts, and Parrington, *The Buried Past*, 235.
54. Robinson, *Philadelphia Directory*, 1828, 1829, 1835, 1845.
55. Robinson, *Philadelphia Directory*, 1830.
56. E. Goodfellow & Son receipt, September 1837—from the archives
of the Atwater Kent Museum of Philadelphia, file 53.32.41.
57. Ancestry.com. *1850 United States Federal Census.*
58. McElroy, *McElroy's Philadelphia City Directory.*
59. *Encyclopedia of Pennsylvania Biography*, 510.
60. From Dallett, files on Elizabeth Goodfellow, *Daily Chronicle*,
Philadelphia, June 16, 1831.
61. Ancestry.com. *1850 United States Federal Census.*
62. Death Notices, *Philadelphia Inquirer*, May 29, 1883, 4.
63. Davis, *The Bouviers*, 20–22.
64. Ibid., 54.
65. Dallett files on Elizabeth Goodfellow, taken from Stephen Girard
Papers, Reel 209, Bills and Receipts– Wedding.
66. *Society Small Collections "C,"* Daniel W. Coxe, "E. Goodfellow &
Son's Receipt for Pastry and Cakes"; "Mrs. Goodfellow Receipt for
Pastry," Historical Society of Pennsylvania. Edward Shippen Burd,
Papers 1799–1848, "Goodfellow & Coane's Receipt for pastry and
cakes," January 24, 1842, Historical Society of Pennsylvania.
67. Golovin, "William Wood Thackara," 322.
68. E-mail correspondence with Pat O'Donnell, Archivist at the Friends
Historical Library of Swarthmore College, January 18, 2010.
69. E-mail correspondence with Ann Upton, Quaker Bibliographer &
Special Collections Librarian, Haverford College, January 19, 2010.
70. E-mail correspondence with Pat O'Donnell, Archivist at the Friends
Historical Library of Swarthmore College, January 18, 2010.
71. Dallett, files on Elizabeth Goodfellow.
72. Stevens, *Pennsylvania*, 81.
73. Reed, *The Philadelphia Cookbook of Town and Country*, x.
74. Williams, *Food in the United States*, 119.
75. "The Middle Atlantic States."

76. Weaver, *A Quaker Woman's Cookbook*, xli.
77. Weaver, *Thirty-Five Receipts from "The Larder Invaded,"* 45.
78. Giger, *Colonial Receipt Book*, 121, 131.
79. Nash, *First City*, 61.
80. Snodgrass, *The Encyclopedia of Kitchen History*, 291.
81. Hechtinger, *The Seasonal Hearth*, 115.
82. Bacon, *Mothers of Feminism*, 61.
83. Comfort, *The Quakers*, 27.
84. Kashatus, *William Penn's Holy Experiment in Education*, 6.
85. Ibid., 8–9.
86. Taylor, *The Writer's Guide to Everyday Life in Colonial America*, 236.
87. Bacon, *Mothers of Feminism*, 164–165.
88. Nash, *First City*, 61.
89. Weaver interview, January 21, 2009.
90. Weaver interview, January 21, 2009.
91. Snodgrass, *Encyclopedia of Kitchen History*, 495–496.
92. Jackson, *Literary Landmarks*, 211–212.
93. Weaver interview, January 21, 2009.
94. Leslie's mother's maiden name was Lydia Baker, the same maiden name as Mrs. Goodfellow's. Even though Baker is a rather common name, this could be where the connection comes in.
95. Weaver, "Goodfellow, Elizabeth," 139–140.
96. Weaver interview, January 21, 2009.
97. Healy and Bugat, *The Art of the Cake*.
98. Leslie, *The Lady's Receipt-Book*, 193–194.
99. Leslie, *Directions for Cookery in Its Various Branches*, 29.
100. Fussell, *Masters of American Cookery*, 379.
101. "Queries and Answers," 447–448.
102. Weaver, *Thirty-Five Receipts from "The Larder Invaded,"* 32.
103. "Queries and Answers," 447–448.
104. Simmons, *American Cookery*, xiii–xv.
105. Weaver, *Thirty-Five Receipts from "The Larder Invaded,"* 32.
106. Fry, "The Paris Hippodrome," 6.
107. Arthur, *Orange Blossoms, Fresh and Faded*, 181.

Chapter Two: Ingredients

1. The Bank of Pennsylvania was built in 1798–1801 from Benjamin H. Latrobe's groundbreaking designs that began the Greek Revival movement in American architecture. The bank failed during the global finan-

cial panic of 1857, and was torn down ten years later, after having served as a federal prison during the Civil War. Teitelman, *Birch's Views of Philadelphia*, 27.

2. Keels, *Forgotten Philadelphia*, 49.

3. Jackson, *America's Most Historic Highway*, 2–3.

4. Garrett, *Memories of Philadelphia in the Nineteenth Century*, 5.

5. Thomas, *Foods of Our Forefathers*, 153–154; Montgomery, *Old Ben Franklin's Philadelphia*, 69–70.

6. Montgomery, *Old Ben Franklin's Philadelphia*, 67.

7. Thomas, *Foods of Our Forefathers*, 154.

8. Hooker, *Food and Drink in America*, 99.

9. Jackson, *America's Most Historic Highway*, 12.

10. Garrett, *Memories of Philadelphia in the Nineteenth Century*, 5–6.

11. Jackson, *America's Most Historic Highway*, 14; Thomas, *Foods of Our Forefathers*, 154–155.

12. Trollope, *Domestic Manners of the Americans*, 223.

13. Montgomery, *Old Ben Franklin's Philadelphia*, 67.

14. Cummings, *An American and His Food*, 25.

15. Hooker, *Food and Drink in America*, 99.

16. Cope, *Philadelphia Merchant*, 105.

17. Royall, *Sketches of History*, 207.

18. Flint, *Letters from America*, 34.

19. Janson, *The Stranger in America*, 187.

20. Weld, *Travels Through the United States*, 184.

21. Janson, *The Stranger in America*, 187.

22. Cummings, *An American and His Food*, 38–39.

23. Volo and Volo, *The Antebellum Period*, 166.

24. Patent, *Baking in America*, 405.

25. Hooker, *Food and Drink in America*, 102.

26. Leslie, *The House Book*, 244–245.

27. Smith, *Oxford Companion to Food and Drink*, 570.

28. Depew, *1795–1895: One Hundred Years of American Commerce*, 625.

29. Woloson, *Refined Tastes*, 21.

30. Depew, *1795–1895: One Hundred Years of American Commerce*, 625.

31. Smith, *Oxford Companion to Food and Drink*, 570.

32. Woloson, *Refined Tastes*, 23.

33. Smith, *Oxford Companion to Food and Drink*, 438.

34. Belden, *The Festive Tradition*, 166.

35. Weaver interview, January 21, 2009.

36. Richardson, *Sweets*, 194.

37. Chapman, *The Candy-Making Industry in Philadelphia*, 3.

38. Belden, *The Festive Tradition*, 74; Woloson, *Refined Tastes*, 155–156.

39. Staib, *City Tavern Baking and Dessert Cookbook*, 11.

40. Cadwalader Collection: Gen. John Cadwalader, Bills & Receipts, Dec. 8, 1744, Library Company of Philadelphia.

41. Woloson *Refined Tastes*, 33.

42. Hines, Marshall, and Weaver, *The Larder Invaded*, 25.

43. Depew, *1795–1895: One Hundred Years of American Commerce*, 625.

44. A survey of food-related occupations within Philadelphia in 1790 taken from census reports and tax lists found the following breakdown among those utilizing sugar to make a living: 114 bakers, 26 biscuit bakers, 11 sugar refiners, 9 chocolate makers, 7 sugar bakers, 5 pastry cooks, 4 loaf bakers, cake bakers, and 1 confectioner. By 1816 there were 20 known confectioners in Philadelphia, and in 1820 the ratio in the city was one confectioner for every 6,854 people, a figure which rose to one per every 867 residents in 1860. And about 200 confectioners were operating in Philadelphia by 1867, including larger manufacturers, which had become possible by this time with the introduction of steam power. Schweitzer, "The Economy of Philadelphia and Its Hinterland," 125; Chapman, "The Candy-Making Industry in Philadelphia," 4; Woloson, *Refined Tastes*, 7; Freedley, *Philadelphia and Its Manufactures*, 231.

45. Williams, *Food in the United States, 1820s–1890*, 77.

46. Jones, *American Food*, 79.

47. Funderburg, *Chocolate, Strawberry, and Vanilla*, 12–13.

48. Hooker, *Food and Drink in America*, 123.

49. Society Small Collections "C," Daniel W. Coxe, "E. Goodfellow & Son's Receipt for Pastry and Cakes," "Mrs. Goodfellow Receipt for pastry," Historical Society of Pennsylvania; Edward Shippen Burd, Papers 1799–1848, "Goodfellow & Coane's Receipt for pastry and cakes, Jan. 24, 1842, Historical Society of Pennsylvania.

50. Belden, *The Festive Tradition*, 3, 94.

51. Garrett, *Memories of Philadelphia in the Nineteenth Century*, 5.

52. Belden, *The Festive Tradition*, 4.

Chapter Three: Dining Out

1. Allen, *The Business of Food*, 193.

2. Davidson, *The Oxford Companion to Food*, 661.

3. McIntosh, *American Food Habits in Historical Perspective*, 85.

4. Weaver interview, January 2009; Burt, *Philadelphia*, 303.

5. Weaver interview, January 21, 2009.

6. Burt, *Philadelphia*, 303–304.

7. Weigley, *Philadelphia*, 221.

8. Weaver interview, January 21, 2009.

9. Jones, *American Food*, 36.

10. Coyle, *Cook's Books*, 18.

11. Pillsbury, *From Boarding House to Bistro*, 24.

12. Scharf and Westcott, *History of Philadelphia*, 2: 981; Pillsbury, *From Boarding House to Bistro*, 22–24.

13. *Pennsylvania Trail of History Cookbook*, 18.

14. Pillsbury, *From Boarding House to Bistro*, 3.

15. Staib, *City Tavern Cookbook*, 11.

16. *Pennsylvania Trail of History Cookbook*, 18; Staib, *City Tavern Cookbook*, 11.

17. Scharf and Westcott, *History of Philadelphia*, 2: 981.

18. *Watson's Annals, The Penn Family*, 1857, vol. 1.

19. Pillsbury, *From Boarding House to Bistro*, 4.

20. Staib, *City Tavern Cookbook*, 11.

21. Scharf and Westcott, *History of Philadelphia*, 2: 982.

22. Pillsbury, *From Boarding House to Bistro*, 20–22.

23. Ibid., 22.

24. Milnor, *A History of the Schuylkill Fishing Company*, 5–6.

25. Felten, "What America's Oldest Club May Quaff," W8.

26. Wecter, *The Saga Of American Society*, 257–258; Issenberg, Miller, and Patel, "Members Only."

27. Warner, *The Private City*, 20–21.

28. Staib, *City Tavern Cookbook*, 5–7; Warner, *The Private City*, 20–21.

29. Staib, *City Tavern Cookbook*, 5–7.

30. Ibid., 5.

31. Watson, *Annals of Philadelphia and Pennsylvania*, 464.

32. George, "Philadelphia: A Pictorial Celebration," 33.

33. Weaver, *Thirty-Five Receipts from "The Larder Invaded,"* 35.

34. Scharf and Westcott, *History of Philadelphia*, 2: 938.

35. Schloesser, *The Greedy Book*, 117–118.

36. Willcox, *A History of the Philadelphia Savings Fund Society*, 58.

37. Weaver, *Thirty-Five Receipts from "The Larder Invaded,"* 35.

38. Leslie, *Directions for Cookery*, 66–67.

39. Weaver interview, January 21, 2009.

40. Patterson, *"The Old Patterson Mansion,"* 80–84.

41. Ellen Markoe Emlen recipe book, Markoe and Emlen Family Correspondence, 1811–1876, at HSP (Phi) 2071.

42. Scharf and Westcott, *History of Philadelphia, 2:* 991; McCall, *Old Philadelphia Houses on Society Hill,* 23.

43. This grand late eighteenth-century building was one of the most distinguished Philadelphia residences before its two fires. Michel Bouvier purchased the property in 1848 and in its place constructed three brownstones that still exist today in Philadelphia's exclusive Society Hill section. He made the middle house—260 South Third Street—his own residence for four years. Dallett, "Michel Bouvier," 198–200. In August 2011, this restored property was listed for sale at a price of $3.2 million.

44. Weaver interview, January 21, 2009.

45. Funderburg, *Chocolate, Strawberry, and Vanilla,* 12–13.

46. Weaver, "Was There a Philadelphia Style?" 88.

47. Funderburg, *Chocolate, Strawberry, and Vanilla,* 76.

48. *The Philadelphia Shopping Guide and Housekeeper's Companion for 1859.*

49. Funderburg, *Chocolate, Strawberry, and Vanilla,* 76.

50. Hines, Marshall, and Weaver, *The Larder Invaded,* 28–29.

51. *Poulson's American Daily Advertiser,* November 13, 1817, 3.

52. *Poulson's American Daily Advertiser,* October 21, 1818, 1.

53. Epicurus, "Maxims to Feed By," 545.

54. *Poulson's American Daily Advertiser,* December 23, 1817, 3.

55. Thomas, *Foods of Our Forefathers,* 155.

56. Ibid., 152, 155.

57. Reed, *The Philadelphia Cookbook of Town and Country,* 91.

58. Weaver, *Thirty-Five Receipts from "The Larder Invaded,"* 47.

Chapter Four: Mrs. Goodfellow's Cooking School

1. *Receipts of Pastry and Cookery,* ix–xi, 109–110.

2. Ibid., ix–xi.

3. Interview with Janet Theophano, March 2009.

4. Ruffald, *The Experienced English Housekeeper,* 156–157.

5. Davidson, *Oxford Companion to Food,* 213.

6. Weaver interview, January 21, 2009.

7. Dunne and Mackie, "Cookery Books," 56.

8. Weaver interview, January 21, 2009.

9. Jackson, *With the British Army in Philadelphia,* 152.

10. *Aurora General Advertiser*, June 28, 1796, 1.

11. *Recipe Book*, Philadelphia, early nineteenth century. U.S. Department of the Interior, National Park Service, Independence National Historic Park. Catalogue No. 3696, Accession No. 1370.

12. Staib, *City Tavern Baking and Dessert Cookbook*, 22.

13. Belden, *The Festive Tradition*, 103.

14. Williams, *Food in the United States*, 42.

15. Belden, *The Festive Tradition*, 103.

16. Trollope, *Domestic Manners of the Americans*, 226.

17. Recipe book: manuscript, 1841–1862; Ms. Codex 884. Rare Book & Manuscripts Library, University of Pennsylvania, Van Pelt Library.

18. Marjorie P.M. Brown Collection, 1763–1871 (Phi) 2015 at Historical Society of Pennsylvania.

19. Ellen Markoe Emlen recipe book, Markoe and Emlen Family Correspondence, 1811–1876 (Phi) 2071, at Historical Society of Pennsylvania.

20. McBride, *Harvest of American Cooking*, 55–56.

21. *Colonial Receipt Book*, 10.

22. Weaver interview, January 21, 2009.

23. Griswold, "Eliza Leslie."

24. Weaver interview, January 21, 2009.

25. Weaver, *A Quaker Woman's Cookbook*, xvii.

26. Widdifield, *Widdifield's New Cook Book*.

27. Ibid.

28. Recipe book: manuscript, 1841–1862; Ms. Codex 884. Rare Book and Manuscript Library, University of Pennsylvania, Van Pelt Library.

29. *Colonial Receipt Book*, 10.

30. Smith, *Famous Old Receipts*, 84.

31. Levick, *Recollections of Her Early Days*, 20–24.

32. Ibid., 24.

33. Weaver interview, January 21, 2009.

34. Weaver interview, January 21, 2009.

35. Dunne and Mackie, "Cookery Books," 57.

36. Ibid.

37. Deventer, "The Cookbook in America."

38. Ibid.

39. Fisher, *The American Cookbook*, 15.

40. Longone, "From the Kitchen," 57.

41. McWilliams, *A Revolution in Eating*, 228; Briggs, *The English Art of Cookery*.

42. Marjorie P.M. Brown Collection, 1763–1871 (Phi) 2015 at Historical Society of Pennsylvania.

43. Crag, *The Tangram*, 27.

44. Ibid, 27.

45. Leslie, *Directions for Cookery, in Its Various Branches*, 7.

46. Hartshorn salt (ammonium carbonate), also known simply as hartshorn, or baker's ammonia, was used as a leavening agent, in the baking of cookies and other edible treats. It was used mainly in the seventeenth and eighteenth centuries as a forerunner of baking powder. Davidson, *Oxford Companion to Food*, 372.

47. Leslie, *Miss Leslie's New Cookery Book*, 526.

48. McCutcheon, *The Writer's Guide to Everyday Life in the 1800s*, 98.

49. Franklin Fire Insurance Company Survey, Book 28–4787 (from HSP).

50. Leslie, *Miss Leslie's New Cookery Book*, 474.

51. Smith, *Famous Old Receipts*, 84.

52. *Colonial Receipt Book*, 10.

53. Crag, *The Tangram*, 28.

54. Weaver interview, January 21, 2009.

55. Weaver interview, January 21, 2009.

56. Crag, *Tangram*, 29.

57. Ibid., 29–30.

58. Ibid., 30.

CHAPTER FIVE: DIRECTIONS FOR COOKERY

1. Dunne and Mackie, "Philadelphia Story," 72.

2. Johnston, *History of Cecil County, Maryland*, 520; Haven, "Personal Reminiscences of Miss Eliza Leslie," 347.

3. *Autobiographical Recollections by the Late Charles Robert Leslie*, 1. County land records indicate that Robert Leslie's name could have originally been spelled Lasley.

4. Johnston, *History of Cecil County, Maryland*, 520.

5. Haven, "Personal Reminiscences of Miss Eliza Leslie," 347.

6. Prime, *The Arts & Crafts in Philadelphia, Maryland and South Carolina*, 253.

7. Ibid., 253–256.

8. McCauley, "Eliza Leslie," 161.

9. Haven, "Personal Reminiscences of Miss Eliza Leslie," 347.

10. *Autobiographical Recollections by the Late Charles Robert Leslie*, 19–20.

11. McCauley, "Eliza Leslie," 257.
12. Haven, "Personal Reminiscences of Miss Eliza Leslie," 347.
13. Ibid., 348–49.
14. *Autobiographical Recollections by the Late Charles Robert Leslie*, 2–3.
15. McCauley, "Eliza Leslie," 161–162.
16. Scharf and Westcott, *History of Philadelphia*.
17. Haven, "Personal Reminiscences of Miss Eliza Leslie," 347–348.
18. *Autobiographical Recollections by the Late Charles Robert Leslie*, 21.
19. Haven, "Personal Reminiscences of Miss Eliza Leslie."
20. Smith and Smith, *A Buckeye Titan*, 195.
21. Haven, "Personal Reminiscences of Miss Eliza Leslie."
22. Longone, "From the Kitchen," 47.
23. Hess and Hess, *The Taste of America*, 96.
24. Beshero-Bondar "Eliza Leslie," 167.
25. Jamison and Jamison, *American Home Cooking*, 197.
26. Haven, "Personal Reminiscences of Miss Eliza Leslie."
27. Weaver, Preface to *Eliza Leslie's Seventy-Five Receipts*, 1.
28. Smith and Smith, *A Buckeye Titan*, 195–198.
29. Ibid., 198.
30. Leslie, *Miss Leslie's New Cookery Book*, 520.
31. Weaver interview, January 21, 2009.
32. Leslie, *Miss Leslie's New Receipts for Cooking*.
33. Weaver interview, January 21, 2009.
34. Leslie, *Miss Leslie's New Cookery Book*, 1
35. Weaver interview, January 21, 2009.
36. Smith, "Charles and Eliza Leslie," 526–527.
37. Smith and Smith, *A Buckeye Titan*, 195.
38. Weaver interview, January 21, 2009.
39. Jamison and Jamison, *American Home Cooking*, 197.
40. Dunne and Mackie, "Philadelphia Story," 73
41. Hess and Hess, *The Taste of America*, 96–97.
42. Longone, "From the Kitchen," 50.
43. Williams, *Food in the United States*, 60.
44. Leslie, *Directions for Cookery*, 322, 329, 335, 447.
45. Leslie, *Leslie's Complete Cookery*, 8.
46. Leslie, *Miss Leslie's New Receipts for Cooking*, 3, 365.
47. Walker, *The Little House Cookbook*, 12, 53.
48. Temple, *"The Taste Is in My Mouth a Little,"* 32.
49. Fleming, *The Lincolns*, 41.

50. Dunne and Mackie, "Philadelphia Story," 73.
51. Leslie, *Seventy-Five Receipts for Pastry, Cakes, and Sweetmeats*, iii.
52. Ibid.
53. Weaver, "Goodfellow, Elizabeth," 139–140.
54. Plante, *The American Kitchen 1700 to the Present*, 25.
55. Leslie, *Domestic French Cookery*, iii–iv.
56. Ibid.
57. Dunne and Mackie, "Philadelphia Story," 73; Longone, "From the Kitchen," 47.
58. Weaver interview, January 21, 2009.
59. Fussell, *Masters of American Cookery*, 56.
60. Robins, "Changing Taste in Food in Pennsylvania," 9–11.
61. Pierre Blot entry on Feeding America website: http://digital.lib.msu.edu/projects/cookbooks/html/authors/author_blot.html.
62. Recipe book: manuscript, 1841–1862; Ms. Codex 884. Rare Book and Manuscript Library, Manuscripts, University of Pennsylvania, Van Pelt Library.
63. "Ragout," in Davidson, *Oxford Companion to Food*, 651.
64. Smith, *Oxford Companion to American Food and Drink*, 551.
65. "Queries and Answers Column, Query No. 4870," 468.
66. Leslie, *Domestic French Cookery*, 44, 74, 75.
67. *The Lady's Receipt-Book*, 97.
68. Leslie, *Directions for Cookery*, 209–210.
69. Longone, "From the Kitchen," 52.
70. Weaver, *Thirty-five Receipts from "The Larder Invaded,"* 32.
71. Longone, "From the Kitchen," 52.
72. Leslie, *New Receipts for Cooking*, 440.
73. Ibid., 439–440.
74. Leslie, *Miss Leslie's New Cookery Book*, 331.
75. Ibid., 325–330.
76. Davidson, *Oxford Companion to Food*, 433.
77. Hess and Hess, *The Taste of America*, 99.
78. Crump, *Hearthside Cooking*, 4.
79. Randolph, *The Virginia House-wife*, 60, 80–81.
80. Leslie, *Miss Leslie's New Cookery Book*, 332–333.
81. Smith, *The Oxford Encyclopedia of Food and Drink in America*, 441.
82. Leslie, *New Receipts for Cooking*, 3.
83. Ibid., 406.

84. Leslie, *Miss Leslie's Behavior Book*, 132–133.

85. Ibid., 136.

86. Leslie, *Miss Leslie's Complete Cookery*, 7–8.

87. Beshero-Bondar, "Eliza Leslie," 167.

88. Scharf and Westcott, *History of Philadelphia*, 2: 1162.

89. Hale, *Woman's Record*, 722.

CHAPTER SIX: LEMON MERINGUE PIE

1. Weaver interview, January 21, 2009.

2. Food Timeline—www.foodtimeline.org.

3. Longbotham, *Luscious Lemon Desserts*, 6.

4. Yockelson, *Baking by Flavor*, 400.

5. Healy and Bugat, *The Art of the Cake*, 173; Davidson, *The Oxford Companion to Food*, 499–500.

6. Leslie, *Seventy-Five Receipts*, 34–36.

7. Ibid., 49–50.

8. Ibid., 58.

9. Leslie, *Directions for Cookery, in Its Various Branches*, 454.

10. Coleman, *Cook Book*, 61; Hale, *The Ladies' New Book of Cookery*, 316.

11. Putnam, *Mrs. Putnam's Receipt Book*, 145.

12. *Milwaukee Journal*, November 19, 1913.

13. Fussell, *I Hear America Cooking*, 232.

14. Neal, *Biscuits, Spoonbread, and Sweet Potato Pie*, 275.

15. Weaver, *America Eats*, 69–70.

16. Kummer, *1,001 Foods to Die For*, 751.

17. *Cookery As It Should Be*, 13, 206.

18. Leslie, *Miss Leslie's New Cookery Book*, 425.

19. Handwritten recipe in *Cookery As It Should Be*.

20. Patent, *Baking in America*, 4–5.

21. *Colonial Receipt Book*, 178.

22. Patent, *Baking in America*, 123.

23. Leslie, *Miss Leslie's New Cookery Book*, 526.

24. Patent, *Baking in America*, 123.

25. Nutmeg was a popular spice in Goodfellow's time that is not used as much today. This is unfortunate, as nutmeg adds a unique, almost woodsy component to baked goods, especially when freshly grated.

26. Patterson, *Recipe Book*.

27. Leslie, *Directions for Cookery, in its Various Branches*, 343.

28. Leslie, *Miss Leslie's New Cookery Book*, 526.

29. Leslie, *Seventy-Five Receipts*, 50–51, 102.
30. Ibid., 61.
31. Rundell, *A New System of Domestic Cookery*, 237.
32. Farmer, *Original 1896 Boston Cooking-School Cook Book*, 431.
33. Mercuri, "Cookies," in *The Oxford Companion to American Food and Drink*, ed. Smith, 156.
34. Patent, *Baking in America*, 390.
35. Baggett, *The All-American Cookie Book*, 40.
36. http://www.ifood.tv/network/rose_water.
37. *The Colonial Receipt Book*, 145.
38. Leslie, *History of Philadelphia*.
39. Sax, *Classic Home Desserts*, 274; Weaver, *A Quaker Woman's Cookbook*, 339.
40. Colimore, *The Philadelphia Inquirer's Guide to Historic Philadelphia*, 116.
41. Franklin Fire Insurance Company Survey Book 28:4787 (Historical Society of Pennsylvania).
42. Franklin Fire Insurance Company Survey Book 57:7907 (Historical Society of Pennsylvania).
43. *The Encyclopedia of Pennsylvania Biography*, 510.
44. West, *In the Matter of the Straightening of Girard Avenue Through the Grounds of Girard College*, 67–68.

Chapter Seven: Modern Cooking Schools

1. Shackleton, *The Book of Philadelphia*, 272–273.
2. Weaver interview, January 19, 2009.
3. Smith, "Cooking Schools," in *The Oxford Companion to American Food and Drink*, ed. Smith, 162.
4. Longone, "Professor Blot and the First French Cooking School in New York, Part 1," 65–66.
5. "Cooking as a Fine Art. Success of Prof. Blot's Academy Assured," *New York Times*, April 7, 1865.
6. Longone, "Professor Blot and the First French Cooking School in New York, Part 1," 66.
7. Ibid.
8. Longone, "Professor Blot and the First French Cooking School in New York, Part 2," 53–59.
9. Arndt, *Culinary Biographies*, 55–56.
10. Cowan, *More Work for Mother*, 44.

11. Arndt, *Culinary Biographies*, 56.

12. Newman, "Home Economics"; *Encyclopedia of Food and Culture*, ed. Katz, Katz, and Weaver, 206.

13. Eisenmann, *Historical Dictionary of Women's Education in the United States*, 275.

14. Smith, "Cooking Schools," in *The Oxford Companion to American Food and Drink*, ed. Smith, 163.

15. Cowan, "Ellen Swallow Richards," 148.

16. Scheone, *A Thousand Years Over a Hot Stove*, 246.

17. Ibid.

18. Arndt, *Culinary Biographies*, 118.

19. Bevier and Usher, *The Home Economics Movement*, 44–45.

20. Ibid., 45–46.

21. An Amateur Cook, "The Cooks Cooking School" *Christian Union* (1870–1893); March 21, 1877, 15, 12, p. 251.

22. Bevier and Usher, *The Home Economics Movement*, 45–46.

23. *The City of Philadelphia As It Appears in the Year 1894*, 129.

24. "The New Century Cooking-School," *Arthur's Home Magazine* (1880–1897); Oct. 1880; 48, 10, 620.

25. Weigley, "The Philadelphia Chef," 239–240.

26. "Culinary Art—How to Make Puff Paste and Soupe a la Reine," *Philadelphia Inquirer*, Dec. 15, 1880, 3.

27. Ibid.

28. Ibid.

29. Bevier and Usher, *The Home Economics Movement*, 50–51.

30. Ibid.

31. Ibid.

32. Arndt, *Culinary Biographies*, 315.

33. Weigley, "The Philadelphia Chef," 232–235.

34. Weigley, "The Philadelphia Chef," 229–233.

35. Kimball, *Fannie's Last Supper*, 23.

36. Bevier and Usher, *The Home Economics Movement*, 49.

37. Ibid.

38. Rachman, "Biography of Mary Johnson Lincoln" on Feeding America website.

39. Kimball, *Fannie's Last Supper*, 24.

40. Bevier and Usher, *The Home Economics Movement*, 49–50.

41. Arndt, *Culinary Biographies*, 282–283.

42. Ibid., 283.

43. Jamison and Jamison, *American Home Cooking*, 407.

44. Shapiro, *Perfection Salad*, 54–55.

45. Ibid., 54–55, 58–59.

46. Lincoln, "Cookery," 140; Oldham, ed., *The Congress of Women*.

47. Rachman, "Biography of Mary Johnson Lincoln" on Feeding America website.

48. Ibid.

49. Ibid.

50. Kimball, *Fannie's Last Supper*, 24–25.

51. Shapiro, *Perfection Salad*, 58–59.

52. Farmer, *Original 1896 Boston Cooking-School Cook Book*, 531–535.

53. Shapiro, *Perfection Salad*, 104.

54. Ibid.; Kimball, *Fannie's Last Supper*, 25–26.

55. Willan, *Great Cooks and Their Recipes*, 185.

56. Ibid.

57. Kimball, *Fannie's Last Supper*, 53.

58. Ibid., 57.

59. Willan, *Great Cooks and Their Recipes*, 186; Kimball, *Fannie's Last Supper*, 28.

60. Bevier and Usher, *The Home Economics Movement*, 50.

61. Ashby and Ohrn, *Herstory*, 145.

62. Willan, *Great Cooks and Their Recipes*, 186–188.

63. Ashby and Ohrn, *Herstory*, 145.

64. Shapiro, *Perfection Salad*, 107.

65. DuSablon, *America's Collectible Cookbooks*, 63.

66. Kimball, *Fannie's Last Supper*, 46.

67. Shapiro, *Perfection Salad*, 68, 101.

68. DuSablon, *America's Collectible Cookbooks*, 63.

69. Kimball, *Fannie's Last Supper*, 27.

70. Allen and Albala, eds., *The Business of Food*, 101–102; Smith, "Cooking Schools," in *The Oxford Companion to American Food and Drink*, ed. Smith, 163.

71. Smith, "Cooking Schools," 163.

72. Allen and Albala, *The Business of Food*, 102; "About James Beard," James Beard Foundation Website, http://jamesbeard.org/index.php?q=about_james_beard.

73. Allen and Albala, *The Business of Food*, 102.

74. Ibid.; Smith, "Cooking Schools," 164.

75. Beard, *James Beard's American Cookery*, x.

76. Fussell, *Masters of American Cookery*, 85.
77. Jamison and Jamison, *American Home Cooking*, 4.
78. Bittman, Foreword to *Beard on Food*, ix.
79. Mendoza, "Queen of Mexican Cuisine Pens New Cookbook."
80. Bittman, Foreword to *Beard on Food*, ix.

Bibliography

UNPUBLISHED SOURCES

Bellah, Henrietta ("Hetty") Ann. Manuscript Recipe Book written for Martha Canby Morris, 1860, National Park Service, U.S. Department of the Interior, Independence National Historic Park Library.

Brown, Marjorie P.M. Collection, 1763–1871 (Phi) 2015. Historical Society of Pennsylvania.

Burd, Edward Shippen. Papers 1799–1848. "Goodfellow & Coane's Receipt for pastry and cakes, Jan. 24, 1842." Historical Society of Pennsylvania, Philadelphia.

Burd, Margaret Coxe. Receipt Books, 1801–1852. (Phi)Am.912339, Historical Society of Pennsylvania.

Campbell Collection v.23 a, p. 242–245. Dock Street Views. Newspaper clipping—"Dock Street: Development and Associations of the Old Thoroughfare," by Jo Jackson, April 3, 1891. Historical Society of Pennsylvania.

Dallett, Francis James. Files on Elizabeth Goodfellow. Sent to author by Matthew Dallett, September 16, 2009.

———. Stephen Girard Papers, 1793–1857. Reel 209, Bills and Receipts-Wedding. American Philosophical Society, Philadelphia.

Franklin Fire Insurance Company of Philadelphia, for insurance against loss by fire records 1820–1890. [Philadelphia, Pa.]: Franklin Fire Insurance Company. Book 28-4787 and Book 57:7907. Historical Society of Pennsylvania.

E. Goodfellow & Son receipt, September 1837. Archives of the Atwater Kent Museum of Philadelphia, file 53.32.41.

Haines, Hannah Marshall. Receipt Book for Cooking 1811–1824. American Philosophical Society Library, Philadelphia.

Handwritten recipe in *Cookery as it Should Be*. Philadelphia: W.P. Hazard, 1855, Rare Book & Manuscripts Library, University of Pennsylvania.

Kane, Eliza. Recipe Book (New York, ca. 1847–1852). William L. Clements Library, University of Michigan.

Markoe and Emlen Family Correspondence, 1811–1876. Ellen Markoe Emlen recipe book. Historical Society of Pennsylvania.

McCauley, Helen A. "Eliza Leslie." Genealogy file GEN RO29. Historical Society of Pennsylvania.

Morris Family Papers, 1741–1989 (bulk dates: 1830–1950). Prepared by Northeast Museum Services. National Park Service, U.S. Department of the Interior, Independence National Historic Park Library.

Patterson, Mrs. Fred, Recipe book, [ca. 1870–ca. 1879], Doc. 391, Winterthur Library, Wilmington, DE.

Recipe Book: Manuscript, 1841–1862; Ms. Codex 884. Rare Book & Manuscripts Library, University of Pennsylvania.

Recipe Book, Philadelphia, early nineteenth century. Catalogue No. 3696, Accession No. 1370. National Park Service, U.S. Department of the Interior, Independence National Historic Park Library.

Recipe Books, ca. 1829–1884 (unknown, possibly Quaker), Doc. 1381, Winterthur Library, Wilmington, DE.

Society Small Collections "C." Daniel W. Coxe, "E. Goodfellow & Son's Receipt for Pastry and Cakes"; "Mrs. Goodfellow Receipt for pastry." Historical Society of Pennsylvania, Philadelphia.

Van Deventer, Willis. "The Cookbook in America: A History." Talk given to the Culinary Historians of Washington, D.C., October 3, 2004.

Published Sources

"About James Beard." James Beard Foundation Website, http://jamesbeard.org/index.php?q=about_james_beard.

Allen, Gary, and Ken Albala, editors. *The Business of Food: Encyclopedia of the Food and Drink Industries.* Westport, Conn.: Greenwood Press, 2007.

Arndt, Alice. *Culinary Biographies: A Dictionary of the World's Great Historic Chefs, Cookbook Authors and Collectors, Farmers, Gourmets, Home Economists, Nutritionists, Restaurateurs,*

Philosophers, Physicians, Scientists, Writers, and Others Who Influenced the Way We Eat Today. Houston, Tex.: YES Press, 2006.

Ashby, Ruth, and Deborah Gore Ohrn, eds. *Herstory: Women Who Changed the World.* Introduction by Gloria Steinem. New York: Viking, 1995.

Bacon, Margaret Hope. *Mothers of Feminism: The Story of Quaker Women in America.* San Francisco: Harper & Row, 1986.

Baggett, Nancy. *The All-American Cookie Book.* Boston: Houghton Mifflin, 2001.

Beard, James. *Beard on Food: The Best Recipes and Kitchen Wisdom from the Dean of American Cooking.* New York: Bloomsbury, 2007.

————. *James Beard's American Cookery.* Boston: Little, Brown, 1972.

Belden, Louise Conway. *The Festive Tradition: Table Decoration and Desserts in America, 1650–1900.* New York: W. W. Norton, 1983.

Beshero-Bondar, Elisa E. "Eliza Leslie." In *Nineteenth-Century American Fiction Writers*, ed. Kent P. Ljunguist. Worcester, Mass.: Worcester Polytechnic Institute, 1999.

Bevier, Isabel, and Susannah Usher. *The Home Economics Movement.* Boston: Whitcomb and Barrows, 1906.

"Blot, Pierre." Biography. *Feeding America: The Historic Cookbook Project.* http://digital.lib.msu.edu/projects/cookbooks/html/authors/auth or_blot.html.

Briggs, Richard. *The English Art of Cookery, According to the Present Practice: Being A Complete Guide to All Housekeepers, on a Plan Entirely New; Consisting of Thirty-Eight Chapters.* London: G. G. J. and J. Robinson, 1788.

Bureau of the Census. *1810 United States Federal Census.* Philadelphia Dock Ward, Philadelphia, Pennsylvania; Roll 55, p. 516; Family History Number: 0193681; Image: 00211.

————. *1820 United States Federal Census.* Philadelphia Dock Ward, Philadelphia, Pennsylvania, Page 26; NARA Roll M33_108; Image 37.

————. *Seventh Census of the United States, 1850.* Washington,

D.C.: National Archives and Records Administration, 1850. M432, 1,009 rolls.

Burt, Maxwell Struthers. *Philadelphia, Holy Experiment.* Garden City, N.Y.: Doubleday, Doran, 1945.

"Cakes, Puddings, etc." (Mrs. Goodfellow's lemon pudding recipe). *Godey's Lady's Book*, 88, January 1874.

Chapman, Ellwood B. *The Candy-Making Industry in Philadelphia.* Philadelphia: Philadelphia Chamber of Commerce Educational Committee, 1917.

Cohen, S. E. *The Philadelphia Shopping Guide and Housekeeper's Companion for 1859.* Philadelphia: S. E. Cohen, 1859.

Coleman, Debbie. *Cook Book.* n.p., 1855.

Colimore, Edward. *The Philadelphia Inquirer's Guide to Historic Philadelphia.* Philadelphia: Camino Books, 2004.

Comfort, William Wistar. *The Quakers: A Brief Account of Their Influence on Pennsylvania.* Edited by Frederick B. Tolles. Rev. and reissued with additions by Edwin B. Bronner. University Park: Pennsylvania Historical Association, 1986.

"Cooking as a Fine Art. Success of Prof. Blot's Academy Assured." *New York Times*, April 7, 1865.

Cope, Thomas P. *Philadelphia Merchant: The Diary of Thomas P. Cope, 1800–1851.* Edited and with an introduction and appendices by Eliza Cope Harrison. South Bend, Ind.: Gateway Editions, 1978.

Cotter, John L., Daniel G. Roberts, and Michael Parrington. *The Buried Past: An Archaeological History of Philadelphia.* Philadelphia: University of Pennsylvania Press, 1992.

Cowan, Ruth Schwartz. *More Work for Mother: The Ironies of Household Technologies from the Hearth to the Microwave.* New York: Basic Books, 1983.

———. "Ellen Swallow Richards: Technology and Women." In *Technology in America: A History of Individuals and Ideas*, ed. Carroll W. Pursell, Jr. Cambridge, Mass.: MIT Press, 1981.

Coyle, L. Patrick. *Cook's Books.* New York: Facts on File Publications, 1985.

Crag, Christopher. *The Trangram, or Fashionable Trifler.* Philadelphia: George E. Balke, 1809.

Crump, Nancy Carter. *Hearthside Cooking: Early American*

Southern Cuisine Updated for Today's Hearth & Cookstove. Chapel Hill: University of North Carolina Press, 2008.

"Culinary Art – How to Make Puff Paste and Soupe à la Reine." *Philadelphia Inquirer*, 103, Dec. 15, 1880, 3.

Cummings, Richard Osborn. *An American and His Food*. Chicago: University of Chicago Press, 1940 and 1941.

Dallett, Francis James. "Michel Bouvier, Franco-American Cabinetmaker." *Antiques Magazine*, February 1962.

David, Elizabeth. *English Bread and Yeast Cookery*. New York: Viking Press, 1980.

Davidson, Alan. *The Oxford Companion to Food*. 2nd edition, New York: Oxford University Press, 2007.

Davis, John H. *The Bouviers: Portrait of an American Family*. New York: Farrar, Straus and Giroux, 1969.

Dean, Joyce. "Enjoy Artichoke Flowers and Eat Them, Too." *Redlands Daily Facts*, July 18, 2011. http://www.redlandsdaily-facts.com/greenthumb/ci_18503058.

Depew, Chauncey Mitchell, and D. O. Haynes, eds. *1795–1895. One Hundred Years of American Commerce. . . : A History of American Commerce by One Hundred Americans, with a Chronological Table of the Important Events of American Commerce and Invention Within the Past One Hundred Years*. New York: D. O. Haynes, 1895.

Desilver, Robert, compiler and publisher. *Desilver's Philadelphia Directory and Stranger's Guide for 1828*. Philadelphia: R. Desilver.

———. *Desilver's Philadelphia Directory and Stranger's Guide for 1829*. Philadelphia: R. Desilver.

———. *Desilver's Philadelphia Directory and Stranger's Guide for 1830*. Philadelphia: R. Desilver.

———. *Desilver's Philadelphia Directory and Stranger's Guide for 1835*. Philadelphia: R. Desilver.

Donehoo, George P. *Pennsylvania, A History*. New York: Lewis Historical Publishing Co., 1926.

Dunne, Patrick, and Charles L. Mackie. "Cookery Books." *Historic Preservation*, 42, no. 3, May–June 1990.

———. "Philadelphia Story." *Historic Preservation*, July–August 1994.

DuSablon, Mary Anna. *America's Collectible Cookbooks: The History, the Politics, the Recipes.* Athens: Ohio University Press, 1994.

"Early Settlers in Cecil. The Leslie-Baker Family." *Cecil Whig,* February 25, 1899.

Eckhardt, George H. *Pennsylvania Clocks and Clockmakers: An Epic of Early American Science, Industry, and Craftsmanship.* New York: Bonanza Books, 1955.

Editors of Stackpole Books and the Pennsylvania Historical and Museum Commission. *Pennsylvania Trail of History Cookbook.* Foreword by William Woys Weaver. Mechanicsburg, Pa.: Stackpole Books, 2004.

Eisenmann, Linda. *Historical Dictionary of Women's Education in the United States.* Westport, Conn.: Greenwood Publishing Group, 1998.

Epicurus. "Maxims to Feed By." *Philadelphia Monthly Magazine,* 1, no. 8, June 1829.

Farmer, Fannie Merritt. *Original 1896 Boston Cooking-School Cook Book.* Boston: Little, Brown, 1896.

Felten, Eric. "What America's Oldest Club May Quaff." *Wall Street Journal,* March 21, 2009.

Fisher, Carol. *The American Cookbook: A History.* Jefferson, N.C.: McFarland, 2006.

Fleming, Candace. *The Lincolns: A Scrapbook Look at Abraham and Mary.* New York: Schwartz & Wade Books, 2008.

Flint, James. *Letters from America: Containing Observations on the Climate and Agriculture of the Western States, the Manners of the People, the Prospects of Emigrants.* Edinburgh: W. & C. Tait, and London: Longman, Hurst, Rees, Orme and Brown, 1922.

Freedley, Edwin Troxell. *Philadelphia and Its Manufactures: A Hand-Book of the Great Manufactories and Representative Mercantile Houses of Philadelphia in 1867.* Philadelphia: E. Young, 1867.

Fry, William H. "The Paris Hippodrome." *Sartain's Union Magazine of Literature and Art,* 9, no. 6, Dec 1851.

Funderburg, Anne Cooper. *Chocolate, Strawberry, and Vanilla: A History of American Ice Cream.* Bowling Green, Ohio: Bowling Green State University Popular Press, 1995.

Fussell, Betty Harper. *Masters of American Cookery: M. F. K. Fisher, James Andrew Beard, Raymond Craig Claiborne, Julia McWilliams Child.* New York: Times Books, 1983.

————. *I Hear America Cooking.* New York: Elisabeth Sifton Books, Viking, 1986.

Garrett, Martha H. *Memories of Philadelphia in the Nineteenth Century.* [Philadelphia?: s.n.], 1910.

George, Alice L., and Elan Penn. *Philadelphia: A Pictorial Celebration.* New York: Sterling, 2006.

Giger, Mrs. Frederick Sidney, comp. and ed. *Colonial Receipt Book: Celebrated Old Receipts Used a Century Ago by Mrs. Goodfellow's Cooking School: also, Famous Old Creole and Moravian Receipts, Together with Some of the Best Formulas of Our Well Known Modern Chefs.* Philadelphia: J. C. Winston, 1907.

Golovin, Anne Castrodale. "William Wood Thackara, Volunteer in the War of 1812." *Pennsylvania Magazine of History and Biography,* 91, no. 3, July 1967.

Griswold, Rufus Wilmot. "Eliza Leslie." *The Prose Writers of America.* 4th edition. Philadelphia: A. Hart, 1852.

Hale, Sarah Josepha Buell. *Woman's Record, or, Sketches of All Distinguished Women: From the creation to A.D. 1854: arranged in four eras: with selections from female writers of every age.* New York: Harper & Bros., 1855.

————. *The Ladies' New Book of Cookery.* New York: H. Long & Brother, 1852.

Hardie, James. *The Philadelphia Directory and Register: Containing the names, occupations and places of abode of the citizens, arranged in alphabetical order, a register of the executive, legislative, and judicial magistrates of the United States and the state of Pennsylvania . . . and the magistrates of the city: also, an account of the different societies, charitable and literary institutions, with the names of their present officers. : To which is added, an accurate table of the duties on goods, wares, and merchandise.* Philadelphia: Printed for the author, by T. Dobson, 1793.

Haven, Alice B. "Personal Reminiscences of Miss Eliza Leslie." *Godey's Lady's Book,* 56, April 1858.

Healy, Bruce, and Paul Bugat. *The Art of the Cake: Modern French Baking and Decorating.* New York: William Morrow, 1999.

Hechtlinger, Adelaide. *The Seasonal Hearth: The Woman at Home in Early America.* Woodstock, N.Y.: Overlook Press, 1977.

Hess, John L., and Karen Hess. *The Taste of America.* Urbana: University of Illinois Press, 2000.

Hines, Mary Anne, Gordon M. Marshall, and William Woys Weaver. *The Larder Invaded: Reflections on Three Centuries of Philadelphia Food and Drink.* Philadelphia: Library Company of Philadelphia, Historical Society of Pennsylvania, 1987.

Hooker, Richard James. *Food and Drink in America: A History.* Indianapolis: Bobbs-Merrill, 1981.

Hughes, Meredith Sayles. *Green Power: Leaf and Flower Vegetables.* Minneapolis: Lerner Publications, 2001.

Issenberg, Sasha, Blake Miller, and Roxanne Patel. "Members Only." *Philadelphia Magazine,* May 2005.

Jackson, John W. *With the British Army in Philadelphia, 1777–1778.* San Rafael, Calif.: Presidio Press, 1979.

Jackson, Joseph. *Literary Landmarks of Philadelphia.* Philadelphia: David McKay Co., 1939.

———. *America's Most Historic Highway, Market Street, Philadelphia.* Philadelphia, New York: J. Wanamaker, 1926.

Jamison, Cheryl Alters, and Bill Jamison. *American Home Cooking: Over 300 Spirited Recipes Celebrating Our Rich Tradition of Home Cooking.* New York: Broadway Books, 1999.

Janson, Charles William. *The Stranger in America: Containing Observations Made During a Long Residence in That Country, on the Genius, Manners and Customs of the People of the United States.* London: J. Cundee, 1807.

Johnson, Gerald W. *Pattern for Liberty: The Story of Old Philadelphia.* New York: McGraw-Hill, 1952.

Johnston, George. *History of Cecil County, Maryland, and the Early Settlements Around the Head of Chesapeake Bay and on the Delaware River with sketches of some of the old families of Cecil County.* Elkton [Md.]: Author, 1881.

Jones, Evan. *American Food: The Gastronomic Story.* New York: E. P. Dutton, 1975.

Jordan, John W., Thomas Lynch Montgomery, Ernest Spofford, and Frederic Antes Godcharies. *Encyclopedia of Pennsylvania Biography, Illustrated.* New York: Lewis Historical Publishing Co., 1914.

Kashatus, William C. III, ed. *William Penn's Holy Experiment in Education: Past, Present, and Future.* Philadelphia: Committee on Education, Philadelphia Yearly Meeting, 1992.

Katz, Solomon H., Jonathan Katz, and William Woys Weaver, eds. *Encyclopedia of Food and Culture.* Farmington Hills, Mich.: Gale/Cengage Learning, 2002.

Katz, Solomon H., and William Woys Weaver, eds. *Encyclopedia of Food and Culture,* New York: Scribner, 2003.

Keels, Thomas H. *Forgotten Philadelphia: Lost Architecture of the Quaker City.* Philadelphia: Temple University Press, 2007.

Kidder, Edward. *Receipts of Pastry and Cookery: For the Use of His Scholars by Edward Kidder,* ed. David E. Schoonover. Iowa City: University of Iowa Press, 1993.

Kimball, Christopher. *Fannie's Last Supper: Re-Creating One Amazing Meal from Fannie Farmer's 1896 Cookbook.* New York: Hyperion, 2010.

Kirtley, Alexandra Alevizatos. "Athens of America." *The Encyclopedia of Greater Philadelphia.* Published in partnership with the Historical Society of Pennsylvania, with support from the Pennsylvania Humanities Council, 2011. http://philadelphiaencyclopedia.org/archive/athens-of-america/.

Konvitz, Josef W. "Gastronomy and Urbanization." *A Conference on Current Research in Culinary History: Sources, Topics, and Methods, Proceedings.* Conference sponsored by the Schlesinger Library of Radcliffe College and the Culinary Historians of Boston. Radcliffe College, June 14–16, 1985.

Kummer, Corby. *1,001 Foods to Die For.* Kansas City, Mo.: Madison Books, Andrews McMeel Publishing, 2007.

Leslie, Charles Robert. *Autobiographical Recollections.* Edited by Tom Taylor. Boston: Ticknor and Fields, 1860.

Leslie, (Miss) Eliza. *Seventy-Five Receipts for Pastry, Cakes, and Sweetmeats.* Boston: Munroe and Francis, 1832.

———. *Directions for Cookery: In Its Various Branches.* Philadelphia: Carey and Hart, 1840.

———. *Domestic French Cookery: Chiefly Translated from Sulpice Barue?* Philadelphia: Carey & Hart, 1832.

———. *History of Philadelphia: A Game For Children.* Philadelphia: [s.n.], 1872.

Bibliography

———. *The House Book: or, A Manual of Domestic Economy.*
Philadelphia: Carey & Hart, 1840.

———. *The Lady's Receipt-Book: A Useful Companion for Large or
Small Families.* Philadelphia: Carey and Hart, 1847.

———. *Miss Leslie's Behavior Book.* Philadelphia: Peterson, 1839.

———. *Miss Leslie's Complete Cookery: Directions for Cookery, In Its
Various Branches.* Philadelphia: H. C. Baird, 1851.

———. *Miss Leslie's Lady's House-Book; A Manual of Domestic
Economy.* Philadelphia: A. Hart, 1850.

———. *Miss Leslie's New Cookery Book.* Philadelphia: T. B.
Peterson, 1857.

———. *Miss Leslie's New Receipts for Cooking.* Philadelphia, T.B.
Peterson, 1854.

Levick, Elizabeth W. *Recollections of Her Early Days.* Philadelphia,
1881.

Lincoln, Mrs. David A. "Cookery." *The Congress of Women: Held
in the Women's Building, World's Columbian Exposition, Chicago,
U.S.A., 1893,* ed. Mary Kavanaugh Oldham. Chicago: Monarch
Book Company, 1894.

"Lincoln's Lemon-Custard Pie; Mrs. Breedlove Tells, for the First
Time, the Famous Recipe." *Milwaukee Journal,* Nov. 19, 1913.

Longbotham, Lori. *Luscious Lemon Desserts.* San Francisco:
Chronicle Books, 2001.

Longone, Jan. "From the Kitchen." *American Magazine and
Historical Chronicle,* 4, no. 2, Autumn 1988–Winter 1989.

———. "Professor Blot and the First French Cooking School in
New York, Part 1." *Gastronomica,* Spring 2001.

———. "Professor Blot and the First French Cooking School in
New York, Part 2." *Gastronomica,* Summer 2001.

McBride, Mary Margaret. *Harvest of American Cooking; With
Recipes for 1,000 of America's Favorite Dishes.* New York: Putnam,
1957.

McCall, Elizabeth. *Old Philadelphia Houses on Society Hill,
1750–1840.* New York: Architectural Book Publishing, 1966.

McCutcheon, Marc. *The Writer's Guide to Everyday Life in the
1800s.* Cincinnati, Ohio: Writer's Digest Books, 1993.

McElroy, Archibald. *McElroy's Philadelphia Directory for 1845: containing the names of the inhabitants, their occupations, places of
business, and dwelling houses; also, a business directory, containing*

an alphabetical arrangement of the subscribers to this work, under their appropriate business heads; besides a list of the streets, lanes, alleys, the city offices, public institutions, banks, &c. Philadelphia: Edward C. & John Biddle, 1845.

———. *McElroy's Philadelphia Directory, for 1856: containing the names of the inhabitants of the consolidated city, their occupations, places of business, and dwelling houses: a business directory, a list of the streets, lanes, alleys, the city offices, public institutions, banks, &c. Also, the names of housekeepers, &c. in Camden, N.J.* Philadelphia: Edward C. & John Biddle, 1856.

McIntosh, Elaine N., Ph.D., R.D. *American Food Habits in Historical Perspective.* Westport, Conn.: Praeger, 1995.

McWilliams, James E. *A Revolution in Eating: How the Quest for Food Shaped America.* New York: Columbia University Press, 2005.

Mendoza, Martha. "Queen of Mexican Cuisine Pens New Cookbook." Associated Press, *Boston Globe,* July 6, 2010.

Milnor, William and the Schuylkill Fishing Company. *A History of the Schuylkill Fishing Company of the State in Schuylkill.* Philadelphia: The Members of the State in Schuylkill, 1889.

Montgomery, Elizabeth Rider. *Old Ben Franklin's Philadelphia.* Champaign, Ill.: Garrard Publishing, 1967.

"Mrs. Goodfellow's Cheese Cake recipe." *American Kitchen Magazine* 14 (October 1900–March 1901). Boston: Home Science Publishing Company.

Nash, Gary B. *First City: Philadelphia and the Forging of Historical Memory.* Philadelphia: University of Pennsylvania Press, 2002.

Neal, Bill. *Biscuits, Spoonbread, and Sweet Potato Pie.* New York: Alfred A. Knopf, 1996.

"The New Century Cooking-School." *Arthur's Home Magazine (1880–1897)* 48, no. 10, October 1880.

Nicholson, Elizabeth. *What I Know: or, Hints on the Daily Duties of a Housekeeper.* Philadelphia: W. P. Hazard, 1856.

Oberholtzer, Ellis Paxson. *Philadelphia: A History of the City and Its People, a Record of 225 Years.* Philadelphia: S.J. Clarke Publishing Company, 1912.

Olver, Lynne, editor and researcher. "About Lemon Cookery." *Food Timeline* – www.foodtimeline.org.

Patent, Greg. *Baking in America: Traditional and Contemporary Favorites from the Past 200 Years.* Boston: Houghton Mifflin, 2002.

Patterson, Mrs. Lindsay. "The Old Patterson Mansion, the Master and His Guests." *Pennsylvania Magazine of History and Biography*, 39, 1915.

Peden, Henry C. Jr. *Revolutionary Patriots of Cecil County, Maryland.* Westminster, Md.: Family Line Publications, 1991.

Pennsylvania Horticultural Society. *Report of the Committee Appointed by the Horticultural Society of Pennsylvania for Visiting the Nurseries and Gardens in the Vicinity of Philadelphia.* Philadelphia: Wm. F. Geddes, 1831.

Philadelphia Register of Wills for the Estate of William Goodfellow. A172-18, July 14, 1818.

Philadelphia, 1789–1880 Naturalization Records [database on-line]. Provo, Utah: Generations Network, 2003. Original data: Filby, P. William, ed. *Philadelphia Naturalization Records*. Detroit: Gale Research Co., 1982.

Pillsbury, Richard. *From Boarding House to Bistro: The American Restaurant Then and Now.* Boston: Unwin Hyman, 1990.

Plante, Ellen M. *The American Kitchen 1700 to the Present.* New York: Facts on File, 2009.

Prime, Alfred Coxe and Walpole Society (U.S.), comp. *The Arts and Crafts in Philadelphia, Maryland and South Carolina Gleanings from Newspapers.* Topsfield, Mass.: Walpole Society, 1929.

Putnam, Mrs. E. *Mrs. Putnam's Receipt Book: and Young Housekeeper's Assistant.* New York: Sheldon and Co., 1867.

"Queries and Answers Column, Query No. 4870." *American Cookery Magazine* 35, no. 6, January 1931.

Rachman, Anne-Marie. Biography of Mary Johnson Bailey Lincoln. *Feeding America: The Historic Cookbook Project.* http://digital.lib.msu.edu/projects/cookbooks/html/authors/author_lincoln.html.

Raffald, Elizabeth. *The Experienced English Housekeeper: For the Use and Ease of Ladies, Housekeepers, Cooks, &c: written purely from practice, and dedicated to the Hon. Lady Elizabeth Warburton, whom the author lately served as housekeeper, consisting of near nine*

hundred original receipts, most of which never appeared in print.
Philadelphia: Printed for Thomas Dobson by John Bioren,
1801.

Reed, Mrs. Anna Wetherill. *The Philadelphia Cook Book of Town
and Country.* New York: M. Barrows, 1940.

Richardson, Tim. *Sweets: A History of Candy.* New York:
Bloomsbury, 2002.

Robins, Caroline. "Changing Taste in Food in Pennsylvania."
Radnor Historical Society Bulletin, Spring 1963, v. 2, no. 3.

Robinson, James, editor. *The Philadelphia Directory for 1802 containing the names, trades, and residence of the inhabitants of the city,
Southwark, Northern liberties.* Philadelphia: W. W. Woodward.

———. *The Philadelphia Directory for 1803 containing the names,
trades, and residence of the inhabitants of the city, Southwark,
Northern liberties.* Philadelphia: W. W. Woodward.

———. *The Philadelphia Directory for 1804 containing the names,
trades, and residence of the inhabitants of the city, Southwark,
Northern liberties.* Philadelphia: W. W. Woodward.

———. *The Philadelphia Directory for 1805 containing the names,
trades, and residence of the inhabitants of the city, Southwark,
Northern liberties.* Philadelphia: W. W. Woodward.

———. *The Philadelphia Directory for 1809 containing the names,
trades, and residence of the inhabitants of the city, Southwark,
Northern liberties.* Philadelphia: W. W. Woodward.

"Rose Water." *ifood.tv Encyclopedia.*
http://www.ifood.tv/network/rose_water.

Ross, Betsy. Homepage, ushistory.org. Copyright ©1996–2010 by
the Independence Hall Association.
http://www.ushistory.org/betsy/

Rundell, Maria Eliza Ketelby. *A New System of Domestic Cookery:
Formed upon principles of economy, and adapted to the use of private
families.* Boston: Oliver C. Greenleaf, 1807.

Rutledge, Sarah. *The Carolina Housewife: or, House and home.*
Charleston, S.C.: W.R. Babcock, 1847.

St. Andrew's Society of Philadelphia. *An Historical Catalogue of the
St. Andrew's Society of Philadelphia, with biographical sketches of
deceased members.* 1749–1913. Philadelphia: Printed for the
Society, 1907–13.

Sax, Richard. *Classic Home Desserts: A Treasury of Heirloom and Contemporary Recipes from Around the World.* Shelburne, Vt.: Chapters Pub., 1994.

Scharf, J. Thomas, and Thompson Westcott. *History of Philadelphia, 1609–1884.* Philadelphia: L. H. Everts & Co., 1884.

Schenone, Laura. *A Thousand Years over a Hot Stove: A History of American Women Told Through Food, Recipes, and Remembrances.* New York: W. W. Norton, 2004.

Schlereth, Eric. "A Tale of Two Deists: John Fitch, Elihu Palmer, and the Boundary of Tolerable Religious Expression in Early National Philadelphia." *Pennsylvania Magazine of History and Biography,* 132, no. 1, January 2008.

Schloesser, Frank. *The Greedy Book.* London: Gay & Bird, 1906.

Schweitzer, Mary McKinney. "The Economy of Philadelphia and Its Hinterland." In *Shaping a National Culture: The Philadelphia Experience, 1750–1800.* Edited by Catherine E. Hutchins. Winterthur, Del.: Henry Francis du Pont Winterthur Museum, 1994.

Shackleton, Robert. *The Book of Philadelphia.* Philadelphia: Penn Publishing Company, 1920.

Shapiro, Laura. *Perfection Salad: Women and Cooking at the Turn of the Century.* New York: Farrar, Straus and Giroux, 1986.

Simmons, Amelia. *American Cookery, or, the art of dressing viands, fish, poultry, and vegetables, and the best modes of making puff-pastes, pies, tarts, puddings, custards and preserves, and all kinds of cakes, from the imperial plumb to plain cake, adapted to this country, and all grades of life.* 2nd edition, with a new introduction by Karen Hess. Bedford, Mass.: Applewood Books, 1996.

Simmons, William. "Payment of Private Robert Coane and Private John Lockner, soldiers servants of Brigadier General Wilkinson." National Archives and Records Administration: War Department Account Reports Books, January 2, 1797.

Smith, Andrew F. *Oxford Companion to Food and Drink.* Oxford: Oxford University Press, 2007.

Smith, Jacqueline Harrison. *Famous Old Receipts Used a Hundred Years and More in the Kitchens of the North and the South.* Philadelphia: J. Winston, 1908.

Smith, Ophia D. "Charles and Eliza Leslie." *Pennsylvania Magazine of History and Biography*, October 1950.

Smith, William E., and Ophia D. Smith. *A Buckeye Titan.* Cincinnati: Historical and Philosophical Society of Ohio, 1953.

Snodgrass, Mary Ellen. *Encyclopedia of Kitchen History.* New York: Fitzroy Dearborn, 2004.

Stafford, Cornelius William, editor. *The Philadelphia Directory for 1801: containing the names, occupations, and places of abode of the citizens, arranged in alphabetical order : also a register of the Constitution of the United States, ministers, consuls, &c. from foreign powers to the United States, and from the United States to foreign powers: with an accurate table of the duties on goods, wares, and merchandise, with further information respecting the Custom House: to which is prefixed, an alphabetical list of the streets, lanes and alleys.* Philadelphia: William W. Woodward, 1802.

Staib, Walter. *City Tavern Baking and Dessert Cookbook: 200 Years of Authentic American Recipes.* Philadelphia: Running Press, 2003.

———. *City Tavern Cookbook: 200 Years of Classic Recipes from America's First Gourmet Restaurant.* Philadelphia: Running Press, 1999.

Stevens, Sylvester K. *Pennsylvania: Birthplace of a Nation.* New York: Random House, 1964.

Stradley, Linda. "History of Artichokes." *What's Cooking America* website, copyright 2004. http://whatscookingamerica.net/History/ArtichokeHistory.htm.

Taylor, Dale. *The Writer's Guide to Everyday Life in Colonial America.* Cincinnati, Ohio: Writer's Digest Books, 1997.

Taylor, Frank Hamilton, and Philadelphia Chamber of Commerce. *The City of Philadelphia As It Appears in the Year 1894; a compilation of facts supplied by distinguished citizens for the information of business men, travelers, and the world at large.* Philadelphia: G. S. Harris & Sons, 1894.

Teitelman, S. Robert. *Birch's Views of Philadelphia: A Reduced Facsimile of The City of Philadelphia—as it appeared in the year 1800: with photographs of the sites in 1960 & 2000 and commentaries.* Philadelphia: Free Library of Philadelphia, Antique Collectors' Club, 2000.

Temple, Wayne C., comp. and ed. *"The Taste Is in My Mouth a Little . . ." Lincoln's Victuals and Potables.* Mahomet, Ill.: Mayhaven Publishing, 2004.

Thomas, Abel Charles. *A Century of Universalism in Philadelphia and New York: With Sketches of its History in Reading, Hightstown, Brooklyn and Elsewhere.* Philadelphia: Collins, 1872.

Thomas, Gertrude Ida. *Foods of Our Forefathers.* Philadelphia: F. A. Davis Company, 1941.

Trollope, Frances Milton. *Domestic Manners of the Americans.* London: Richard Bentley, 1839.

Volo, James M., and Dorothy Denneen Volo. *The Antebellum Period.* Westport, Conn.: Greenwood Press, 2004.

Walker, Barbara M. *The Little House Cookbook: Frontier Foods from Laura Ingalls Wilder's Classic Stories.* New York: Harper & Row, 1979.

Warner, Sam Bass. *The Private City; Philadelphia in Three Periods of Its Growth.* Philadelphia: University of Pennsylvania Press, 1968.

Watson, John Fanning. *Annals of Philadelphia and Pennsylvania, in the Olden Time: Being a Collection of Memoirs, Anecdotes, and Incidents of the City and Its Inhabitants, and of the Earliest Settlements of the Inland Part of Pennsylvania, for the Days of the Founders.* Philadelphia: Whiting & Thomas, 1857.

———. *The Penn Family*: Vol. 1. Contributed for use in USGenWeb Archives by EVC. http://files.usgwarchives.org/pa/philadelphia/areahistory/watson0105.txt.

Weaver, William Woys. *America Eats: Forms of Edible Folk Art.* New York: Museum of American Folk Art: Perennial Library, 1989.

———. Preface to Facsimile Edition of *Eliza Leslie's Seventy-Five Receipts* (Boston, 1828), San Francisco: American Institute of Wine & Food, 1986.

———, ed. *A Quaker Woman's Cookbook: The Domestic Cookery of Elizabeth Ellicott Lea.* Mechanicsburg, Pa.: Stackpole Books, 2004.

———. *Thirty-Five Receipts from "The Larder Invaded."* Philadelphia: Library Company of Philadelphia; Historical Society of Pennsylvania, 1986.

———. "Was There a Philadelphia Style?" *A Conference on Current Research in Culinary History: Sources, Topics, and Methods, Proceedings. A conference sponsored by the Schlesinger Library of Radcliffe College and the Culinary Historians of Boston.* Radcliffe College, June 14–16, 1985.

Wecter, Dixon. *The Saga of American Society: A Record of Social Aspiration, 1607–1937.* New York: Charles Scribner's Sons, 1937.

Weigley, Emma Seifrit. "The Philadelphia Chef: Mastering the Art of Philadelphia Cookery." *Pennsylvania Magazine of History of Biography*, 96, no. 2, April 1972.

Weigley, Russell F., ed., and Nicholas B. Wainwright and Edwin Wolf, 2nd assoc. eds. *Philadelphia: A 300-Year History.* New York: W. W. Norton, 1982.

Weld, Isaac. *Travels Through the United States of North America, and the Province of Upper & Lower Canada.* London: T. Tegg, 1801.

West, R. A., reporter. *In the Matter of the Straightening of Girard Avenue Through the Grounds of Girard College: testimony of witnesses, and proceedings before the jury appointed by the Court of Common Pleas of the city of Philadelphia.* Court of Common Pleas (Philadelphia County), Philadelphia. Board of Directors of City Trusts. Philadelphia: G.V. Town & Son, 1875.

White, Miles Jr. *Henry Baker and Some of his Descendants.* United States: s.n., 1901.

Widdifield, Hannah. *Widdifield's New Cook Book, or, Practical receipts for the housewife: comprising all the popular and approved methods for cooking and preparing all kinds of poultry, omelets, jellies* . . . Philadelphia: T. B. Peterson, 1856.

Willan, Anne. *Great Cooks and Their Recipes: From Taillevent to Escoffier.* London: Pavilion, 2000.

Willcox, James M. *A History of the Philadelphia Savings Fund Society: 1816–1916.* Philadelphia: Press of J. B. Lippincott Company, 1916.

Williams, Susan. *Food in the United States, 1820s–1890.* Westport, Conn.: Greenwood Press, 2006.

Woloson, Wendy A. *Refined Tastes: Sugar, Confectionery, and Consumers in Nineteenth-Century America.* Baltimore: Johns Hopkins University Press, 2002.

Wulf, Karin. *Not All Wives: Women of Colonial Philadelphia.*
  Philadelphia: University of Pennsylvania Press, 2005.
Yockelson, Lisa. *Baking by Flavor.* New York: J. Wiley, 2002.

Index

Adelphia Club, 70
African American cuisine, 145–146
alcohol, 46, 186
Allen, William W., 23
Almond Puddings, 222
American Cookery Books, 1742-1860
　(Lowenstein), 127
American Cookery (Simmons), 38,
　171
American cuisine, 38, 58, 132–133,
　179
American Frugal Housewife, The, 136
American Home Cooking (Jamison),
　205
American Home Economics
　Association, 182
American Philosophical Society, 105,
　124
*Annals of Philadelphia and
　Pennsylvania* (Watson), 68
apees, 172–173
Apple Pudding, 222–223
apprenticeships, 30–31
Art of Cookery, The (Glasse), 107
Arthur, Timothy Shay, 39
artichokes, 3, 84, 85, 88, 92, 104,
　117, 154, 217
Asian cuisine, 144
Astolfi, Lawrence, 79
Audot, Louis-Eustache, 138
Augustin, Peter, 64–65

Bailey, Abby, 129
Bailey, Chester, 76
Baker, Ann, 7
Baker, William, 7
Baking in America (Patent), 205
baking powder, 166–167

Bank of Philadelphia, 43–44
Barley Water, 232
Barrington Rusk, 214
Barton, Benjamin Smith, 124
Barué, Suplice, 137, 138
Beard, James, 202, 204–205
Beard on Food (Beard), 206
Beck, Simone, 202
Beecher, Catharine, 180
Belden, Louise Conway, 62
Bennett, Robert, 58
Bertholle, Louisette, 202
Beshero-Bondar, Elisa E., 127–128
Bibliographie Gastronomique
　(Vicaire), 138
Bienville, Jean-Baptiste Le Moyne
　de, 97
Bingham, William, 76
Birch, Thomas, 14, 44
Bitting, Katherine, 138
Bittman, Mark, 206
Blot, Pierre, 139–140, 177–179, 183,
　202
Blue Anchor, 67
boardinghouses, 68–69
Bonaparte, Joseph, 23
Bossee, Peter, 77
Boston Cooking School, 189–196,
　198
Boston Cooking-School Cookbook, The
　(Farmer), 189, 192, 196–197
Boston School Kitchen Text-Book
　(Lincoln), 193
Bouvier, Eustache, 23
Bouvier, John, 24
Bouvier, Michael, 23
Bouvier, Sarah Pearson, 8, 23–24
Bradford, William, 71

brandy, 38
breads
    Barrington Rusk, 214
    Goodfellow's Buns, 214
    Potato Biscuit, 214
    Quick Waffles, 217
    serving of, 121
    Spanish Buns, 215–216
    Waffles, 216, 217
Breedlove, Nancy, 163
brick ovens, 112
Briggs, Richard, 108
Brillat-Savarin, Antoine, 63
Brown, Helen Evans, 204
Budd's Long Row, 67
Burd, Edward Shippen, 24
butcher, 47–48, 54, 85
butter, 3, 89–90, 96

cakes
    Cheese Cake, 230
    Indian Pound Cake, 230
    Mrs. Goodfellow's Queen Cake,
        230–231
    Queen Cake, 231
    Queen cakes, 5, 37, 161,
        169–170, 171, 207–208, 231
candy. see confectioners
Carey, Henry C., 126, 142
Carolina Housewife, The (Rutledge),
    133
Carter, Susannah, 38
cast-iron cookstoves, 111–112
centerpieces, 120
Chauveau, A. J., 60
cheesecakes, 5–6, 230
chess pie, 163
chicken fricassee, 88–89, 117–118,
    153–154, 218
Child, Julia, 202
Child, Lydia Maria, 136
Citron Puddings, 223
City Tavern, 43, 44, 71–72
cleaning, 2, 85

Coane, Elizabeth Goodfellow, 23
Coane, Robert (husband), 8–9,
    25–26, 98
Coane, Robert (son), 8, 20, 21–23,
    26, 41–42, 173, 176
Cocoanut Puddings, 224
coffee-houses, 66
Coleman, Debbie, 162
Colonial Receipt Book, 27, 104, 113,
    167, 172
Colony in Schuylkill, The, 69
Complete Confectioner, The
    (Parkinson), 79
Conestoga wagons, 50–51
confectioners/confectionery, 56–58,
    59
conversation, instructions regarding,
    155–156
Cook Book (Coleman), 162
cookbooks
    anonymous, 34–35
    format of recipes in, 111, 137
    Goodfellow's recipes in, 98,
        100–101, 104, 113
    Kidder and, 94–96
    Leslie and, 33–34, 122
    Raffald and, 33
    as textbooks, 106–108
    Widdifield and, 103
    see also individual titles
Cookery as It Should Be, 34–35, 165
cookies
    Cookies (recipe), 220
    Gingerbread, 220
    Gingerbread, Spiced, 221
    history of, 170–172
    Jumbles, 221
    Spice Nuts, 221–222
cooking school, Goodfellow's
    description of, 84–85
    first lesson at, 85–93
    serving meal at, 152–155
    students of, 94, 100, 101–102,
        108–109

cooking schools, overview of, 96–97, 102–103, 182–184
  see also individual schools
Coolidge, Calvin, 164
Cope, Thomas P., 53
Cordon Bleu cooking school, 202
cornmeal, 38, 142–143
Corson, Juliet, 183–184
Cox, Gideon, 134
Cox, James, 17, 18
Coxe, David W., 24
Crag, Christopher, 109–110, 113, 114–115
crème meringue, 162
Crowen, Mrs. T. J., 204
crumb-cloth, 119
Cuisinière de la Campagne et de la Ville, La (Audot), 138
Culinary Institute of America, 201
Cundith, Kathy, 10
cup cakes, 169
curries, 145
Custard, Lemon, 224
  see also puddings

Dearborn, Carrie, 194–195
desserts
  Floating Island, 232
  Swiss Cream, 232
  see also cakes; Custard, Lemon; puddings
Directions for Cookery (Leslie), 37, 74, 133, 135–136, 141, 161
Dock Street, description of, 16–17, 42
docks, description of, 12–13
Domestic Cookery (Lea), 27, 100
Domestic French Cookery (Leslie), 65, 137, 139, 141
Domestic Manners of the Americans (Trollope), 99–100
domestic science, 180–182, 190
Dunne, Patrick, 7, 136

education, Quakers and, 29–30
eggs, 36–37, 90, 152, 169
embroidery lessons, 105
Emlen, Ellen Markoe, 75–76, 101
Emlen Cresson family, 101
Engle, Sarah. *see* Patterson, Sarah Engle
entertaining, 61–62
Evans, Oliver, 124
Every Lady's Book (Crowen), 204
Experienced English Housekeeper, The (Raffald), 33, 95–96

Famous Old Receipts, 104, 112–113
Fannie Farmer Cookbook, The (Farmer), 198
Fannie's Last Supper (Kimball), 199
Farmer, Fannie Merritt, 170, 189, 191, 195–200, 204
farmers' markets, 48, 205
Festive Tradition, The (Belden), 62
fireplace, 2, 87, 88, 111, 209–210
fireworks, 77
Fish House Club, 70
Fish Market, 52
Flint, James, 54
Floating Island, 231
Food and Cookery for the Sick and Convalescent (Farmer), 198
Francatelli, Charles Elme, 139
Franklin, Benjamin, 124
Franklin House Hotel, 73, 74
Free Training School for Women, 183
French Cook, The (Ude), 139
French cuisine, 63–65, 137–142, 179
frozen desserts, 62
Frugal Housewife, The, 38
fruit, sugared, 99
  see also individual fruits
Fussell, Betty, 205

Garrett, Martha J., 62
Gastronomic Bibliography, 138

Gazley, Martha, 96–97
Gingerbread, 220
Gingerbread, Spiced, 221
Girard, Stephen, 23, 24, 25
Glasse, Hannah, 8, 106–107, 144, 145
Gleim, Betty, 149
Goodfellow, Elizabeth
  background of, 7–9
  cooking education of, 28, 32
  description of, 1–2, 105–106, 109–110
  fellow merchants and, 17–18
  literary mentions of, 39–40
  at market, 45–48
  morning preparations of, 1–7
  nighttime and, 207–210
  signature of, 13
  success of, 81
Goodfellow, William, 10–11, 19, 26, 208, 210
Goodfellow's Buns, 214
Goodfellow's Jumbles, 221
Goodfellow's Spanish Bunns/Buns, 215
Greedy Book, The (Schloesser), 73
Greenough, Mrs. Ebenezer, 167
Griswold, Rufus Wilmot, 102
Guest, George, 67

Hale, Sarah Josepha, 148, 162
Hand-book of Practical Cookery (Blot), 140
Harper, H. W., 73
Haven, Alice B. (Neal), 125, 127
Head, Joseph, 76–77, 114
hearth. *see* fireplace
Henrion, Sebastion, 59–60
Henry, Alexander, 23
Hess, John, 127, 133
Hess, Karen, 107, 127, 133
High (Market) Street, 12, 14, 50
High Street Market, 47

hitching posts, 45
home economics, 179–182, 190
Hooper, Sarah E., 190
hotels, 72
House Book, The (Leslie), 136
Howell, Margaret Emlen, 100, 109
Howell, Nancy, 109

ice cream, 56, 62, 77–79
iceboxes, 55–56
Indian cuisine, 144–145
Indian Meal Book, The (Leslie), 142–143
Indian Pound Cake, 38–39, 230
ingredients
  importance of quality, 49, 85, 111, 134, 204, 205–206
  imported, 12–13, 49, 96, 143
  leavening, 35–36
  at market, 45–48
  native, 38
  preparation of, 2–3
  Quakers and, 26–27
  spoilage and, 54–56
Israel, Susan, 101–102, 113
Issac Newton's, 78
Italian cuisine, 79

James Beard Cooking School, 202
James Beard's American Cookery (Beard), 204
Jamison, Bill and Cheryl Alters, 205
Janson, Charles, 55
Jefferson, Thomas, 49, 64, 107, 124
Jersey Market, 45, 46, 52
Joy of Cooking, The (Rombauer), 204
jumbles, 4, 5, 170–172, 221

Kennedy, Diana, 205–206
Kennedy, Mrs. William Henry, 28
ketchup, 144
Kidder, Edward, 94–95
Kimball, Christopher, 190, 199
Kisses, 5, 152, 155, 161

Kitchener, William, 144
Krimmel, John Lewis, 65, 82

Ladies' New Book of Cookery, The
  (Hale), 162
Lady's Receipt-Book, The (Leslie), 36,
  141, 162
land-grant universities, 180–181
Langolis, Madame, 97
Lea, Elizabeth Ellicott, 27, 100
leavenings, 35–36, 133, 165–169
Leibell, Abigail Coane, 8
Lemon Custard, 224
lemon meringue pie, 158–159,
  163–164
Lemon Pudding, 225
lemon puddings, 4, 84, 85, 89, 98,
  116, 152, 157–158, 225
lemons
  as flavoring, 37–38, 158–159
  import of, 163
  Lemon Custard, 224
  Lemon Pudding, 225
  Mrs. Goodfellow's Lemon
    Pudding, 225
  Two Lemon Puddings, 225
Leslie, Ann, 125, 126
Leslie, Charles, 123, 126
Leslie, Eliza
  African American cuisine and,
    145–146
  American cuisine and, 132–133
  on apees, 172
  audience of, 134–136
  background of, 33–34, 123–126
  Beard and, 204
  on behavior, 146–147
  boardinghouse and, 69
  books by, 93–94
  clarity of, 136–137
  on confections, 96
  cookbooks and, 106, 126–129,
    131–132, 133–136
  fiction of, 128

French cuisine and, 65, 137–139,
  141–142
on Goodfellow, 110–111, 130
imported ingredients and,
  143–144
Indian cuisine and, 145
on leavenings, 35–36, 165–166
measurements and, 213
meringue and, 159–162
note taking and, 112, 121–122
recipe clarity and, 196
on refrigeration, 56
reputation of, 148–149
terrapins and, 74–75
travels of, 129
on yeast, 168
Leslie, Lydia Baker, 69, 123, 125
Leslie, Martha, 126
Leslie, Robert, 123–125
Leslie, Thomas Jefferson, 126,
  128–129
Levick, Elizabeth W., 104–106
Lincoln, Abraham, 135–136, 163
Lincoln, Mary Johnson Bailey,
  191–193, 194, 197, 199
Lincoln, Mary Todd, 135–136
liquor, 186
Little House Cookbook, The (Walker),
  135
living/working arrangements, 17
London Coffee House, 71
Longone, Jan, 108, 138, 143
Lowenstein, Eleanor, 127
Lucas, Dione, 202

Mackie, Charles L., 7, 136
Madeira wine, 49
mangoes, preserved, 219
Mansion House Hotel, 76–77, 114
Margarette, Mary, 23
markets
  comparisons of, 53–54
  description of, 45–48, 51–54
  development of, 49–50

Goodfellow at, 41–42
preparations for, 50–51
proximity to, 12
rules for, 50–51
Markoe, Mrs. John, 70
Marshall, Elizabeth, 96
Massachusetts Institute of
Technology, 181–182
Mastering the Art of French Cooking
(Child), 202
Masters of American Cookery (Fussell),
205
matchmaking, 85, 115, 156–157
Maynard, Ida, 194
Mease, James, 124
measurements, guide for, 213
meats
chicken, 88–89, 117–118,
153–154, 218
Mince Meat, 226
ragouts and, 141
stewed veal, 218–219
terrapins, 73–75, 219
White Fricassee Chickens, 218
see also butcher
*Memories of Philadelphia in the
Nineteenth Century* (Garrett), 62
Merchant's Coffee House and Place
of Exchange, 72
meringue, 152, 158–162
Michaux, André, 15
Millers, John William, 58
Mince Meat, 226
mise en place, 87
Miss Farmer's School of Cookery,
198
Miss Leslie's Behavior Book (Leslie),
146–147
Miss Leslie's Complete Cookery
(Leslie), 134
Miss Leslie's New Cookery Book
(Leslie), 111, 130, 131
Miss Parloa's Kitchen Companion
(Parloa), 191

*Miss Parloa's New Cook Book and
Marketing Guide* (Parloa), 191
Modern Cook, The (Francatelli), 139
Moffit, Robert, 22
Monroe, James, 172
Moore, Thomas, 55
Moravian Seminary, 97
Morrill Act, 180
*Mrs. Goodfellow's Cookery as It Should
Be*, 35, 106, 165
Mrs. Goodfellow's Lemon Pudding,
225
Mrs. Goodfellow's Queen Cake,
230–231
Mrs. Lincoln's Boston Cook Book
(Lincoln), 191, 197
Mrs. Putnam's Receipt Book, 162

napkins, 119–120
Neal, Bill, 163
New Art of Cookery (Briggs), 108
New Century Club, 184–185
New Century Cooking School,
184–187
New Haven Restaurant Institute,
201
New Receipts for Cooking (Leslie),
143, 146
New System of Domestic Cookery, A
(Rundell), 107–108, 169–170
New York Cooking Academy, 140,
177–179
New York Cooking School, 183
Newport, Mary, 97
*Nineteenth-Century American Fiction
Writers* (Beshero-Bondar), 127–128

omelette soufflé, 141–142
Onions, Ragou of, 140, 218
Orange Puddings, 226
oranges, as flavoring, 38
*Original Boston Cooking-School Cook
Book* (Farmer), 170
ovens, 3, 5, 6, 92, 112

oysters, 65, 66

Page, Ann, 172
Painter, Mrs. Thomas, 28
Parkinson, George and Eleanor, 79
Parkinson, James, 79
Parkinson's, 78–79
Parloa, Maria, 190–192
pastry (paste)
    definition of, 59
    importance of making, 99–100
    lesson on, 91–92, 93
    preparation of, 3–4
    recipes for, 227–229
    Rorer and, 187
Patent, Greg, 205
Patterson, Jonathan, Jr., 24
Patterson, Mrs. Fred, 167
Patterson, Robert, 75
Patterson, Sarah Engle, 75
Patterson, Therese Bouvier, 24
Peale, Charles Willson, 124, 150
Peale, Raphaelle, 150, 171
pearlash, 35, 133, 165–166
Pearson (husband), 8, 25
peel, 6, 31, 116
Penn, William, 15, 29–30, 49–50, 67
pepper pot, 80
Perfection Salad (Shapiro), 199
Philadelphia
    architecture of, 42–44
    description of, 12–16, 42–43
    famous foods from, 27
    as port, 49
Philadelphia Club, 70
Philadelphia Cooking School, 184
Philadelphia School, 188
Physick, Philip Syng, 100, 124
pickles, 219–220
pies, savory, 94–95
Pigs Feet Souced, 219
Platt, June, 204
poetry club, 115
Potato Biscuit, 214

Potato Puddings, 226
potatoes
    Potato Biscuit, 214
    potato pudding, 27–28
    Two Potato Puddings, 226
    White Potato Pie, 27–28, 227
preserves, 219–220
Price, Isaac, 124–125
Prichett family, 101
professional associations, 32
puddings
    Almond Pudding, 222
    Apple Pudding, 222–223
    Citron Puddings, 223
    Cocoanut Pudding, 224
    Lemon Pudding, 225
    Mrs. Goodfellow's Lemon
      Pudding, 225
    Orange Puddings, 226
    Potato Puddings, 226
puff pastry. *see* pastry (paste)

Quakers, 25–27, 29–30, 84
Quarterly Meeting Pie, 27
Queen cakes, 5, 37, 161, 169–170,
    171, 207–208, 231
Quick Waffles, 217

Raffald, Elizabeth Whitaker, 8,
    32–33, 95–96
Raffald, John, 32
Ragou of Onions, 140, 218
ragouts, 140–141
Randolph, Mary, 133, 144–145
Read, William, 17–18
Receipts of Pastry and Cookery
    (Kidder), 94–95
recipes
    breads, 214–217
    cakes, 230–231
    clarity of, 196
    cookies, 220–222
    egg and cream desserts, 231–232
    format of, 111, 137

meats, 218–219
pastry, 227–229
pies, 227
preserves and pickles, 219–220
puddings, 222–227
for the sick, 232–233
vegetables, 217–218
see also cookbooks
recreational cooking, 201–203
refrigeration, 55–56, 60
see also ice cream
Renshaw, William, 76
restaurants
development of, 63, 65
training for, 200–201
rice puddings, 162
Richards, Ellen Swallow, 181–182
Rombauer, Irma, 204
Rorer, Sarah Tyson, 185–189, 193, 204
rosewater, 38
Ross, Betsy, 19
Royall, Anne, 54
Rubicam, Elizabeth and Daniel, 72, 73–75, 102
Rubicam Pudding, 75–76
Rundell, Maria Eliza Ketelby, 8, 106–108, 169–170
Rush, Benjamin, 124
Rutledge, Sarah, 133

Sago, 232
saleratus, 35, 133, 165–166
salmis, 140–141
Sanderson, James M., 73, 74, 139
scales, 2, 89
Scharf, J. Thomas, 148
Scheone, Laura, 182
Schloesser, Frank, 73
Schuylkill Fishing Company, 69
servants, 19–20
serving meals, methods for, 152–154
Seventy-five Receipts for Pastry, Cakes and Sweetmeats (Leslie), 33–34,

106, 126–127, 128–129, 132, 137, 161, 169, 213
Shapiro, Laura, 199
shop locations
changes in, 20–21
Dock Street, 17–18
Washington Square, 173–176
Short Elbow Alley, 68
Simmons, Amelia, 38, 171
slavery, 60, 64–65, 72–73
Smith, Abraham, 58
Smith, Andrew F., 140
Smith, Parker, 22
social events, 61–62, 118–121
soufflé, omelette, 141–142
Southern cuisine, 145–146
Spanish buns, 4–5, 167–168, 208–209
Spanish Buns, 215–216
Spice Nuts, 221–222
spices, 38
sponge cakes, 37
St. Andrew's Society of Philadelphia, 10–11
State in Schuylkill, 70
Stinger, Mary McLeod, 23
Stowe, Harriet Beecher, 180
street vendors, 80
Stuart, Mary Patterson, 24
Sturgis, Elizabeth, 97
sugar
fruit and, 99
history of, 56–58
popularity of, 95–96
price of, 58–59
slavery and, 60
weighing of, 89
sugar cone, 2
sugar nippers, 2
sugar work, 59, 120
Sully, Thomas, 129
Surgeons Hall, 14
Sweeney, Johanna, 190, 191–192
sweetmeats, definition of, 59

Swiss Cream, 232

table linens, 118–120
table manners, 146–147
table setting, 118–121
Tapioca, 232–233
taverns, 66–68
    see also City Tavern
tea parties, 62
terminology, definitions for, 59
terrapins, 73–75, 219
Thackara, William Wood, 24–25
Theophano, Janet, 95
Thomas Butler Mansion, 70
Thousand Years Over a Hot Stove, A
    (Scheone), 182
Trollope, Frances, 52–53, 99–100
tuition assistance, 185
turtles, 72–73
    see also terrapins

Ude, Louis Eustache, 139
Universal Recipe Book, The (Harper),
    73
Universal Society, 11
utensils, 120

Vauxhall Gardens, 77
veal, stewed, 218–219
Vernou, Louise, 24
vinegar pie, 164
Virginia House-wife, The (Randolph),
    133, 144–145

Waffles, 216, 217
waiters, 154
Walker, Barbara M., 135
War of 1812, 24–25
Warburton, Sir Peter and Lady
    Elizabeth, 32, 33
Washington, George, 107, 124
Washington Hotel, 72
Washington Square, 173–176
watches, 11–12

Water Gruel, 233
Waterhouse, Benjamin, 105
Watson, John Fanning, 68
Weaver, William Woys, 34, 35, 75,
    102, 113–114, 130, 139, 158
Weld, Issac, 55
West Indies, 12–13
Westcott, Thompson, 148
What to Eat and How to Cook It
    (Blot), 139–140, 177
wheat, 13
White Fricassee Chickens, 218
    see also chicken fricassee
White Potato Pie, 27–28, 227
Widdifield, Hannah, 102–103
Widdifield's New Cook Book
    (Widdifield), 103
Willan, Anne, 200
Willing, Elizabeth Hannah, 59
wine, Madeira, 49
Wistar, Caspar, 124
Woman's Record, 148–149
women, employment and, 19, 31–32
Women's Education Association,
    189–190, 193
Wood, Sarah, 10

yeast, 168
*Young Ladies' Guide in the Art of
    Cookery, The* (Marshall), 96

Acknowledgments

In order to properly tell the story of Mrs. Goodfellow and her cooking school, I needed to explore a variety of resources. As someone who loves to do research, I thoroughly enjoyed this "treasure hunt," especially as I encountered such enthusiasm about the book along the way.

It was an honor to meet with the incredibly knowledgeable food historian William Woys Weaver, with whom I share a passion for early American foodways and food history. He graciously invited me into his beautiful historic home and allowed me to interview him—I can't thank him enough. Jan Longone and Janet Theophano also shared their expertise and patiently allowed me to pepper them with questions. My discussions with these three helped me improve the book and sparked ideas for further investigation. In addition, reading the extensive studies and analyses they have written over the years was fascinating. I learned a great deal from each of these historians and I thank them.

I would also like to extend my gratitude to Glenn R. Mack, President of Le Cordon Bleu College of Culinary Arts in Atlanta, for his continued interest, helpful advice, and information.

A portion of my research centered on the genealogy of the Goodfellow and Leslie families. My sincere appreciation goes to the late Jim Dallett for all his work in this area, and to Matthew Dallett (Jim's son) for sharing the file of his father's findings. In addition, I am indebted to Bouvier descendants Sharon Brandt and Kees van den Berg, and to Kathy Cundith and Abigail Coane Leibell of the Coane family, for disclosing and confirming information about their respective ancestors.

Tracking down background information about Eliza Leslie was not always easy, and the following people kindly fielded my phone calls and e-mails: Charles Virts, Curator of the Champaign County (Ohio) Historical Museum; Etta Madden, English Professor at Missouri State University; Valerie Elliott and Rebecca Evans of the Smith Library of Regional History; Kimberly Tully, Special Collections Librarian at Miami University (Ohio); and Lisa Long of the Ohio Historical Society. Tony Demchak, Ph.D. candidate at Kansas State University saved me a trip to Kansas by transcribing and sending me notes about a noncirculating thesis on Eliza Leslie located in the library there.

Pat O'Donnell, Archivist at the Friends Historical Library of Swarthmore College; Ann Upton, Quaker Bibliographer & Special Collections Librarian at Haverford College; and Diana Franzusoff Peterson of the Magill Library of Haverford College provided assistance with Quaker inquiries and clarifications.

William Rubel and Mercy Ingram answered my questions about hearth cookery, and Mercy even skillfully demonstrated the types of equipment and methods that Mrs. Goodfellow would have used.

Consulting with architecture and public works experts helped me to create an accurate picture of Philadelphia in the early 1800s. Architectural historian Jeff Cohen of Bryn Mawr College was indispensable in offering information about nineteenth-century Philadelphia maps, streets, and buildings. Drew Brown and Adam Levine of the City of Philadelphia Water Department provided detailed responses about the city's water supply during that time frame. Bruce Laverty of the Athenaeum of Philadelphia helped me sort through old Philadelphia maps, directories, and building descriptions.

The numerous libraries and historical societies I visited were extremely accommodating and attentive to my needs. In particular, I would like to thank all the staff at the Historical Society of Pennsylvania, especially Sarah Heim and Steve Smith, who retrieved a seemingly endless number of materials for me. Connie King and Linda August of The Library

Company of Philadelphia provided valuable guidance and suggestions. The Rare Book and Manuscript Library at the University of Pennsylvania proved a great resource for manuscript cookbooks and back copies of *American Kitchen* magazine, and librarians Caitlin Anderson, Lynne Farrington, and Lauren Rile Smith were very responsive to my questions and requests regarding the materials located there.

The Winterthur Library also has a sizable collection of manuscript cookbooks and other Philadelphia-area documents, which Emily Guthrie and Jeanne Solensky helped me sort through. The Independence National Historic Park Library yielded some unexpected finds, including a few handwritten recipe books, which I was able to view with enthusiastic assistance from Karen Stevens. The librarians at the Yardley-Makefield branch of the Bucks County Public Libraries were also very helpful, particularly Barb Likens, who worked tirelessly to obtain all the interlibrary loans I requested.

I would also like to thank the staff of the Spruance Library of the Mercer Museum in Doylestown, Pennsylvania, the Historical Society of Cecil County (Maryland), the Maryland Historical Society, the University of Delaware Special Collections Department, the American Philosophical Society, and the Free Library of Philadelphia for handling my questions and helping me track down various materials.

This project would never have come to completion without all the support I received from friends and family. My husband and children patiently endured my highs and lows as my research revealed some surprising discoveries—and some dead ends. Luckily I was able to regain my family's favor when I tried my hand at baking some of Mrs. Goodfellow's specialties and enlisted them to sample and comment on the experimental treats. I would also like to thank my fellow members of the Yardley United Methodist Church who willingly tasted several Goodfellow concoctions that I served during coffee hour on various occasions.

I am grateful to my friend Carol Lambard, who was instrumental in getting the book started by recommending Bruce H. Franklin as a publisher. In turn, I am very appreciative of Bruce for giving me this opportunity and having faith that I could piece together an interesting story. Both Bruce and his wife Laura listened to my ideas, made suggestions, and gave me constructive suggestions along the way.

I would also like to thank Kristen Greaves, Elisa Malinoff, Lori Raso, Amy Gazaleh, and Terri Hawkes for child care assistance so I could make the many necessary research trips into Philadelphia, and Theresa Derderian for generously reading the manuscript and offering meaningful observations.

Many thanks to my parents, Arthur and Mary Libourel, who have always encouraged me in all my endeavors and taught me the strong work ethic that helped get me through this project. Most important, I probably would never have had this idea in the first place if it were not for the life-long cooking inspiration I have received from the talented women in my family. I continue to acquire cooking skills from my mother, Mary Libourel, who is simply a wonder in the kitchen. She makes hosting holiday meals and cookouts for our ever-growing family several times a year look effortless. She and my grandmother, Catherine Ellsworth, were both exceptionally adept at putting wholesome food on the table for large families. I'd also like to mention the influence of my aunts: Nancy Prince, Joan Mansell, and Sally Brough—three great cooks whom I have enjoyed observing over the years. These five ladies—all graduates of home economics programs—helped shape my interest in cooking. I thank you all.